109 WALKS

IN BRITISH COLUMBIA'S LOWER MAINLAND

ALICE PURDEY, JOHN HALLIDAY
AND MARY & DAVID MACAREE

109 ... WALKS

IN BRITISH COLUMBIA'S LOWER MAINLAND

GREYSTONE BOOKS

Vancouver/Berkeley

Greystone Books Ltd.
www.greystonebooks.com

Cataloguing data available from Library and Archives Canada
ISBN 978-1-77100-000-0 (pbk.)
ISBN 978-1-77100-001-7 (epub)

Editing by Lucy Kenward (seventh edition)
Copy editing by Shirarose Wilensky (seventh edition)
Cover and interior design by Jessica Sullivan
Cover photograph by iStockphoto.com

All interior photographs by Alice Purdey and John Halliday except
pages 141, 215 (Paul Adam) and page 193 (Stephen Mullock)
Maps by Mary Macaree and Gray Mouse Graphics
Printed and bound in Canada by Friesens
Distributed in the U.S. by Publishers Group West

We gratefully acknowledge the financial support of the Canada Council
for the Arts, the British Columbia Arts Council, the Province of British
Columbia through the Book Publishing Tax Credit and the Government of
Canada through the Canada Book Fund for our publishing activities.

Greystone Books is committed to reducing the consumption of old-growth
forests in the books it publishes. This book is one step towards that goal.

CONTENTS

. . . . .

KEY TO MAP SYMBOLS

≡≡≡≡	highway	Ⓟ	parking	★	point of interest
▬▬▬	paved road			♠	old-growth tree
=========	unpaved road	☀	navigational light	▲	campground
+++++++	railroad			开	picnic area
------------	described trail	▯	tower, water tower, lookout		
▬ ▬ ▬	trail is parallel to road			][	bridge, boardwalk, trestle
••••••••••••	walk on road	✴	viewpoint		
--------------	other trail	⌂	school	✻ ✻	marsh
‖ ‖ ‖ ‖	stairway	⛪	church		
••••••••••••••	route				river or stream
▬ ▪ ▪ ▬ ▪	park boundary or other boundary	⌂	building, cabin or shelter	⫫	waterfall
⋀ ⋀ ⋀	power line	▭	reservoir		
⨯ ⨯ ⨯ ⨯ ⨯	fence	▭	sports field		direction of river flow
•—•—•—•	ski lift	Ⓣ	toilets		
•—•	gate				body of water

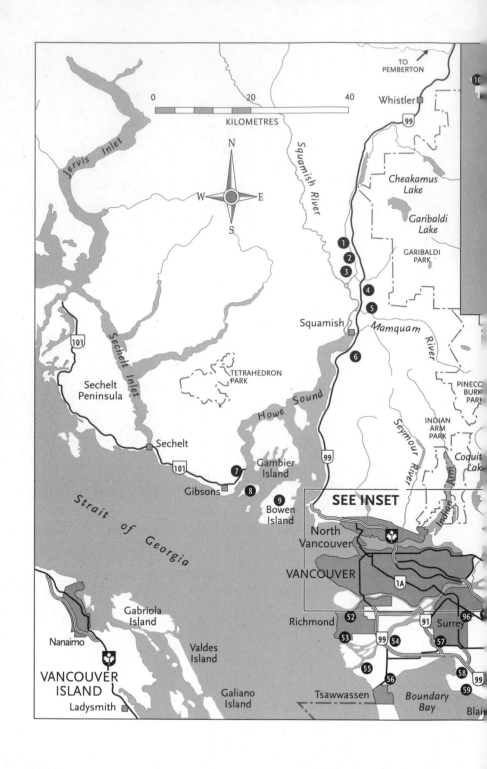

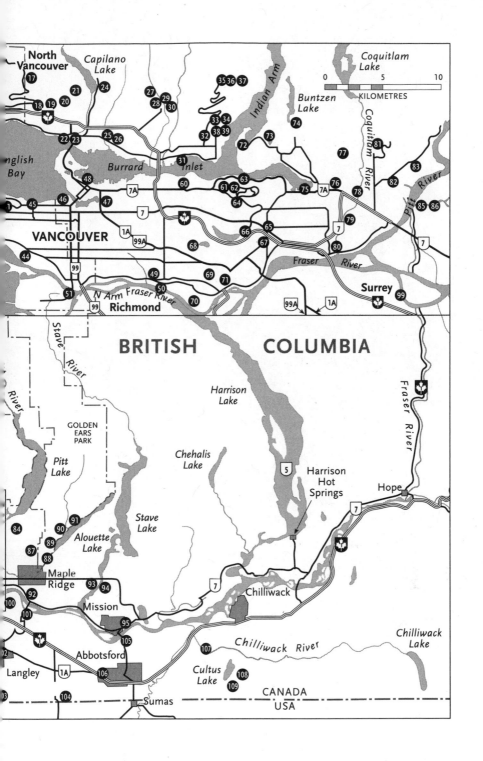

INTRODUCTION

WELCOME! We invite you to explore, on foot, the outstanding urban paths and wild trails of the Lower Mainland. The abundant natural beauty and the joy of walking will surely revitalize your joie de vivre. This seventh edition of *109 Walks* continues the pattern set by the original authors, Mary and David Macaree, by describing walks that are generally less than 4 hours long, with, for the most part, modest elevation gains if any, over easy to moderate, or lightly challenging terrain.

We have added fourteen new walks, removed as many and refocussed thirteen of the old-timers in this edition. To reflect the relentless population shift to the suburbs, the walks north of Squamish have been replaced with new walks to the south of the Fraser River and to the east of the Port Mann Bridge. All walks in the book have been rewalked, and the changes are incorporated into this edition, both in the descriptions and on the maps. Time and change stand still for no one, and alterations to trail conditions continue to occur, including disruptions and improvements wrought by municipal works and natural devastation. Perhaps the most common change is the growth of trees that obscure once fine views!

WHAT IS A WALK?

Throughout the revision of this book, we had many discussions about the difference between a walk and a hike. Is it smoothness of path? Elevation gain? Length of time taken? Given the nature of the terrain in the Lower Mainland, the terms are often used interchangeably. However, to distinguish these trails from those described in the sister book, *103 Hikes in Southwestern British Columbia*, the characteristics for inclusion are: generally 4 hours or less, elevation gain of 400 m (1300 ft) or less and clearly established routes. We have made a few exceptions, however, most notably the hike to the top of Shannon Falls, which is rated as Extra Challenging. Generally speaking, the walks are categorized by difficulty as follows:

EASY: little or no elevation gain, mainly even surface, less than 3 hours
MODERATE: some elevation gain, uneven trail, up to 4 hours
CHALLENGING: significant elevation gain, rough trail (gravel, roots), longer than 4 hours

How long a walk will take depends on the state of the trail and its ups and downs, as well as your walking pace. We provide liberal time estimates and include elevation gains of more than 150 m (500 ft). The gains are not cumulative but a simple measure of the difference between your starting and high points.

TERRAIN

Metro Vancouver sits atop once-forested rolling hills, creeks now buried in drains and estuaries now altered beyond recognition. However, visionary city planners have preserved for us urban oases of nature both large and small. And they continue to do so with the ongoing construction of picturesque intra- and interurban greenways and pathways that are shared by walkers and cyclists.

The walks in this book offer a wide range of terrain. In or near the urban settlement, there are walks through protected forest and ravines surrounded by busy city activities. Farther afield, there are gentle trails adjacent to rivers, dyked marshes and ocean shores, and trails through farmlands abandoned or active. Many are on multi-use paths. Dykes and greenways are shared with bicycles and horses; mountainside trails may be shared with mountain bikers. Beyond the urban boundaries, mainly north of Burrard Inlet and up Howe Sound, there are trails on mountainsides, in valleys and through wild forests.

As well, part of the pleasure of walking is combining it with other pursuits: watching birds, observing plant life and geological features, watching the variety of activity on rivers and waterways, and thinking about the local history.

USING THIS BOOK

New for this edition, we have arranged the book in sections that run from north to south and west to east. Each walk is organized into quick facts, access directions, trail map and walk description. The quick facts give you at-a-glance information about the walk, such as round-trip time, length of walk and difficulty. The access directions provide basic travel instructions to the trailhead by transit, where available, and by vehicle. For the first time, we have included key intersection coordinates for people who use car GPS units (but if you don't, paper maps still work!) and trailhead latitude-longitude coordinates for hand-held units. The trail map illustrates the route in relation to local natural and human-built features. Familiarize yourself with the Key to Map Symbols on page ix to better understand the symbols used on the maps. The walk description presents a guided tour of the trail by describing important junctions and landmarks and by pointing out natural and historical items of interest. And a photo accompanying most of them provides a visual clue to the nature of the walk. Some walks can accommodate all-terrain strollers, and we've indicated these with the following symbol 🛒. We have not identified walks accessible by wheelchair; these are designated as such in park brochures, on websites or on a sign at the trailhead. Distances and elevations are given in both metric and imperial units, except for distances of less than one kilometre; these are given in metres only, as one yard is roughly equivalent to one metre.

SAFETY

Personal safety may be of concern on the non-urban walks where there are fewer people. Accidents—a twisted ankle, a serious medical problem—can happen unexpectedly. Would anyone know if you did not return home? Leave a note with someone as to your destination and expected time of return. It's always a good idea to carry a small first-aid packet, some water, snacks, a jacket and hat, a whistle and a lightweight flashlight.

Of course, on urban walks, it is mainly the changeable weather that you need to prepare for. Even if it doesn't look like rain, a rain jacket could save the day. Or, preferably, you may be reaching for your sunscreen and sunglasses. And, of course, sturdy footwear is essential. Toes stubbed or feet cut by unseen hazards can ruin an outing.

Be aware that you cannot rely entirely on your cellphone in case of trouble on the more remote walks, as batteries may fail and reception may be patchy or nil. Be prepared for the unforeseen. People do occasionally get lost, so a map and compass (know how to use them!) would provide a good back-up.

OUTDOOR ETIQUETTE

Unpaved trails are subject to damage with the passage of many feet. Mud holes can develop in soggy areas, and these grow ever larger when walkers try to go around them. Shortcutting on mountain slopes leads to erosion and rapid deterioration of the footbed. Please be aware of these issues and do your part to maintain the integrity of a trail. Another way to help is to carry an extra bag in which to pack out your garbage and that carelessly left behind by others.

What if you get the urge "to go"? The locations of toilets are noted on the maps where these exist, but if they don't? In the forest, please be considerate of others and bury your waste and carry out your toilet paper to avoid unsightliness.

DOGS

The human's best friend loves to go on walks with you, but, please, respect other trail users and wildlife. Use common sense and keep your dog under control at all times and out of wetlands and like habitat, the home to tiny living creatures. And, of course, scoop the poop and take it away with you. Many of the regional parks included in this book have designated off-leash areas within their boundaries.

REGIONAL PARKS

Metro Vancouver's twenty-two regional parks serve to promote the well-being of users through outdoor activities in the natural environment. Walks in seventeen of these parks are included in this book. Smoking is now prohibited in all Metro Vancouver regional parks and greenways, except for designated areas. This law took effect in 2012, to reduce the amount of litter associated with smoking, to protect birds and other wildlife from cigarette butts and to reduce the risk of fire.

PUBLIC TRANSPORTATION AND VEHICLE ACCESS

Walks accessible by public transportation are so noted in the quick facts section. To plan your own transit route to a walk, you may call TransLink's information line at 604-953-3333 or visit www.translink.ca. Free printed schedules are available in public libraries and other select locations.

Vehicle access is not described in detail, since there are often many approaches to a trailhead. If you are unfamiliar with an area, you'll need to consult a map for directions, or use the car GPS-entry street coordinates provided. These will take you to the nearest intersection or address from which you can follow directions in the walk access description.

Major, ongoing construction on the roads and highways may result in detours or delays. Please check road reports at www.drivebc.ca.

REFERENCES

A list of hiking clubs and online references may be found at the end of this book. Most municipal websites have downloadable trail maps. It is a good idea to check for the latest trail information, such as temporary closures, on a related website before setting out, especially during spring runoff or after heavy rains.

BROHM LAKE

Brohm Lake and Powerline Trails: 7.2 km (4.5 mi)   **Allow:** 3 hours

Brohm Lake circuit: 4 km (2.5 mi)   **Allow:** 1.5 hours

Surface: rough   **Elevation gain:** 105 m (345 ft)   **High point:** 390 m (1280 ft)

Rating: moderate to challenging   **Season:** May to November

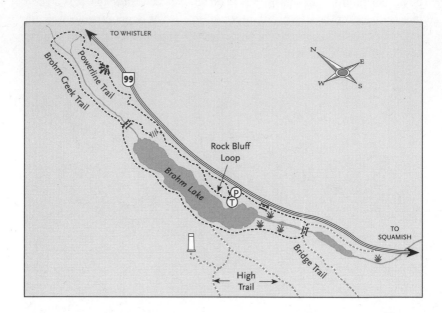

ACCESS

Vehicle: On Highway 99 (Sea to Sky Highway), drive 4.5 km (2.8 mi) north of Alice Lake Road (north of Brackendale) to a parking lot partially hidden by trees on the west side of the highway.

Car GPS entry: Sea to Sky Highway & Alice Lake Road

Trailhead: 49° 49.324′ N, 123° 8.014′ W

HIKERS, SWIMMERS AND fisherfolk are all attracted to beautiful Brohm Lake on a nice day, so plan to arrive early, as parking is limited. Roadside parking, where allowed, is strictly enforced by authorities. The popular lake loop carries you up and down from water's edge to bluffy overlooks, along soft-footed track and over longish stairways.

Ease into your walk by going south on a gentle trail paralleling the highway, crossing the bridge over the reedy narrows and turning north (right) at the fork where the Bridge Trail goes left. Now you begin your upsy-downsy way along the lake, passing occasional interpretive signs in the trees, blackened remains from a 1953 forest fire, 200-plus-year-old survivors of logging during the 1930s to 1960s and the occasional approach to water's edge. Stay on the Brohm Lake Trail past the fork leading to the High Trail before arriving at a junction with the now defunct Thompson Trail. Continue another 100 m to another junction where left becomes the Brohm Creek then Powerline Trail. To complete your loop of the lake, go right across a connector trail, up and down several sets of stairs that may be slippery when wet, over moss- and fern-covered cliffs with peek-a-boo views of the lake and mountains, and past huge boulders (erratics) left by retreating glaciers, before arriving at your vehicle. (Another trail, which forks left around the Rock Bluff Loop, drops more quickly to the parking lot.)

Alternatively, instead of taking the connector trail, continue onto the Brohm Creek Trail, which follows a peaceful, mossy old logging road near the creek for 1 km (0.6 mi) or so before swinging right across the creek and towards the adjacent highway. Peer into the wooded slopes to see what looks like a giant game of pick-up sticks. These fallen logs are thinnings, cut to reduce competition for nutrients and sunlight in a forest being managed for future logging. At the creek crossing, the trail becomes known as the Powerline Trail, following, as it does, B.C. Hydro's 500,000-volt transmission right-of-way, which carries electricity south from the Peace River. B.C. Hydro ensures that the power lines are clear of trees, but the trail itself may be shrubby and requires a sharp eye as it climbs up and down in steep, well-built sections. Once you gain the rocky knolls for a rest, you are rewarded with views of the spectacular Tantalus Range dominating the horizon. Continue south on the trail to return to your start, keeping left at the fork with the previously mentioned connector trail.

BROHM LAKE INTERPRETIVE FOREST

Return: 7.6 km (4.7 mi)   **Allow:** 3 hours

Surface: packed, rough   **Elevation gain:** 170 m (558 ft)   **High point:** 420 m (1378 ft)

Rating: easy to moderate   **Season:** May to October

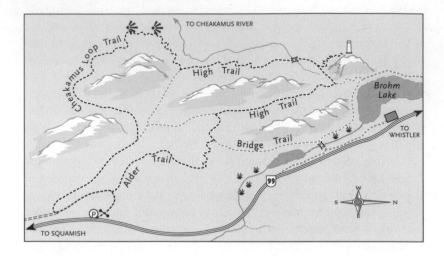

ACCESS

Vehicle: On Highway 99 (Sea to Sky Highway), just over 2 km (1.2 mi) north of Alice Lake Road (north of Brackendale), watch on the left for a small parking area with an information kiosk. You cannot turn left into the lot, so continue 2.2 km (1.4 mi) to the Brohm Lake parking lot, partially hidden by trees. Turn around here and drive back south to the desired parking area.

Car GPS entry: Sea to Sky Highway & Alice Lake Road

Trailhead: 49° 48.385′ N, 123° 7.384′ W

LOOP TRAILS IN the wooded area south of Brohm Lake offer a variety of options for both walkers and mountain bikers, all of which wind—mostly gently—through lush forest. One side trip climbs to an old fire lookout; another trail features two viewpoints of the Cheakamus River below and snowy mountains above. For more information about the area, see www.for. gov.bc.ca/dsq/interpForests/interpretive.htm.

From the parking area, pass the information board and gate and proceed for a couple of minutes on an old roadbed (the original Highway 99) to the

The Cheakamus River from the Cheakamus Loop Trail.

Alder Trail, where you turn right. The trail ascends easily, sidehills above a ravine, passes through mixed forest with lush undergrowth, then passes through a tangle of cut tree thinnings before meeting Bridge Trail, so-called because going right takes you to the bridge at the Brohm Lake narrows. (This trail provides alternate access from the Brohm Lake parking lot and here connects with Walk 1.) Your route, however, goes left briefly on Bridge Trail to the junction with High Trail, where it veers right to continue past a small pond, over a boardwalk and through a rocky stretch to a fork where right again leads to Brohm Lake. The route swings abruptly to the left and crosses more bridging before another option presents itself: a steep, rugged trail that requires occasional hands-on, assisted by even steeper steps, to a one-time fire lookout and a little shelter with views of the majestic Tantalus Range.

Back on High Trail, you work round a knoll and emerge on a south-facing slope before beginning a steady zigzag descent into the valley, where the trail merges with an old forest road. Now, another decision: take the direct route to the parking lot, or follow the longer Cheakamus Loop Trail. (The former eventually rejoins and turns left on old Highway 99 in a hollow below the present thoroughfare.) Turning right onto the Loop Trail, you ascend to near a precipitous cliff edge where trees somewhat compromise views of mountains towering over the sinuous Cheakamus River far below. A few paces farther along is another viewpoint, this one with a table. Where the trail levels, watch for remnants of partially buried wire cable, evidence of long-ago logging activity. The trail next merges into an old logging road that winds its way to the main forest road; here a right, then a final left leads back to your vehicle.

LEVETTE LAKE LOOP

Copperbush-Skyline Loop: 7.2 km (4.5 mi) **Allow:** 4 hours

Including Levette Lake diversion: 10.5 km (6.5 mi) **Allow:** 5 hours

Surface: rough trails and roads **Elevation gain:** 280 m (920 ft)

Rating: challenging **High point:** 430 m (1410 ft) **Season:** May to November

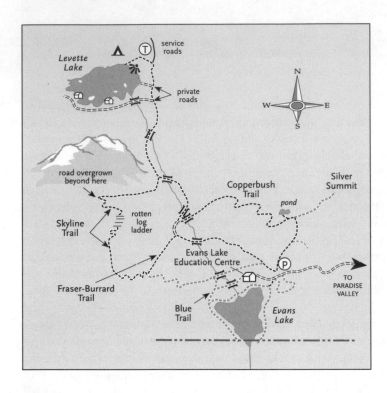

ACCESS

Vehicle: Driving north from Squamish and Brackendale on Highway 99 (Sea to Sky Highway), turn left onto the Squamish Valley Road (opposite the Alice Lake Provincial Park turnoff), cross the Cheakamus River Bridge and immediately turn right onto the Paradise Valley Road. After 2.1 km (1.3 mi), turn left onto Evans Lake Road. This road rises steeply for 1.3 km (0.8 mi) to a fork. Stay right and park in the tiny lot near the gate.

Car GPS entry: Squamish Valley Road & Paradise Valley Road

Trailhead: 49° 48.905' N, 123° 10.123' W

THE LEVETTE LAKE LOOP is a trail system featuring bluffy ridges on either side of a road, viewpoints overlooking both the Cheakamus and Squamish River Valleys, and the option of swimming in pretty Levette Lake. (Of course, you could trudge up the uninspiring road directly to Levette Lake [6 km/3.7 mi return].)

Check the information board near the gate, then start your excursion by heading into the woods on the nearby Copperbush Trail. This begins by rising steeply before easing and setting the tone for the circuit ahead: ups and downs, mossy and rocky bluffs that you thread between or hike up and over, swampy places that may be dry or wet according to the season and forest understorey that varies between open and heavy. Within 15 minutes you may divert to Silver Summit, a 4-minute, hands-on scramble that leads to a knoll, but your route bears left, soon arriving at attractive little Copperbush Pond with its wooden platform, a one-time cabin site. After about an hour on this energetic trail, you exit onto the road, turn right and cross two bridges. At the second, note the beginning of the Skyline Trail angling back sharply behind a large boulder. This you will follow later, after your visit to Levette Lake, about 1.3 km (0.8 mi) up the road. Stay with the road, ignoring branches to the left leading to private properties, until you reach a signed trail to the lake, where, other than an outhouse, there are no conveniences. This is a nice, though "unimproved," spot for a break.

Refreshed, return to the start of the Skyline Trail by the bridge. Within about 15 minutes, the rocky, old road ends and a narrow trail rises sharply left. This winds up and down ridges with views of the rugged Tantalus Range. On one descent, you'll have to watch your footing while descending where a one-time log ladder has mostly rotted away. Continue until the trail widens and you reach a junction with an information board; go straight ahead to join the (unsigned) Fraser-Burrard Trail. (The right fork leads to the private Evans Lake Forest Education Centre.) After another half-hour on the trail, making a right turn onto the forestry road returns you to your vehicle.

FOUR LAKES TRAIL

Return: 7 km (4.3 mi) or less   **Allow:** 2.5 hours

Surface: trail   **Rating:** easy   **Season:** April to November

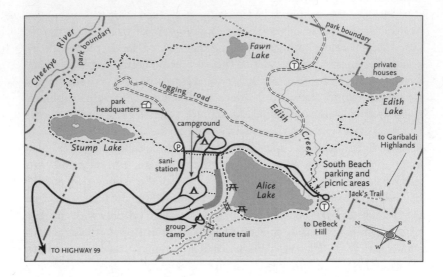

ACCESS

Vehicle: Drive Highway 99 (Sea to Sky Highway) north through Brackendale and watch for the Alice Lake Provincial Park turnoff. At the park entrance, keep left and drive uphill to a small parking area just beyond the sani-station, instead of heading for the lake.

Car GPS entry: Sea to Sky Highway & Alice Lake Road

Trailhead: 49° 47.017′ N, 123° 7.209′ W

ALICE LAKE PROVINCIAL PARK, a popular destination for families and campers, has a network of hiking trails. The longer Four Lakes Trail, as its name implies, links four lakes via a circuit through the forest, and two of these lakes, Stump and Alice, are encircled by their own trails, making shorter walks. Both Alice and Fawn Lakes are particularly nice for swimming.

On foot, backtrack a few paces from your vehicle to the information kiosk and the trailhead to Stump Lake. Your walk begins in thick bush, but

An old-growth cedar stump, the remains of a giant.

this thins out when you reach the fork where the arms of the Stump Lake circuit separate and you must choose your direction. The right branch gives glimpses over DeBeck Hill (Walk 5) and towards the Tantalus Range; the left, of Mount Garibaldi and Alice Ridge. Gaps in the trees along the undulating trail provide peek-a-boo views of the lake and its sphagnum moss islets. The trails meet at the north end of the lake, where you turn left into lush understorey.

Now you become aware of the increasing sound of rushing water; this is the Cheekye River to your left, flowing down from Mount Garibaldi. Plants such as skunk cabbage (swamp lantern) grow along this moisture-rich stretch. Next, you climb eastwards into a different environment, passing an escape route back to Alice Lake on the right, then rising to the trail's high point as you near Fawn Lake. Surrounded by young forest, Fawn Lake is a little off the trail to the right; where the spur road goes off to it, the foot trail you have been on becomes a firm road that takes you directly to Edith Lake.

On the way, you come to a major intersection, your route crossing the main approach to Alice (Cheekye) Ridge, an approach that predated creation of the park. (Surprisingly, there is a pit toilet here.) Stay right at a fork just before the lake to go along the lake's west side until you come to a signposted junction. The route straight ahead leads to Thunderbird Ridge in Garibaldi Highlands, but you go right and uphill before descending to the South Beach of Alice Lake. From here, you may follow either shore to complete your outing. The east side is shorter and perhaps prettier, having views of DeBeck Hill across the water. However, if you choose the longer west and north sides, you may add a little nature walk on the Swamp Lantern Interpretive Trail at the lake's northwest corner.

Finally, at the lake's northeast corner, you walk up through the campsites to the park headquarters road and your vehicle.

DEBECK HILL

Return: 4 km (2.5 mi) **Allow:** 2 hours

Surface: road **Elevation gain:** 270 m (885 ft) **High point:** 460 m (1510 ft)

Rating: easy **Season:** April to November

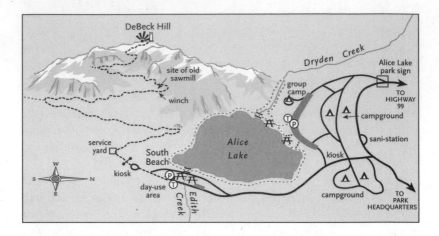

ACCESS

Vehicle: Drive Highway 99 (Sea to Sky Highway) north through Brackendale and watch for the Alice Lake Provincial Park turnoff. At the park entrance, go right at the fork to the South Beach parking area.

Car GPS entry: Sea to Sky Highway & Alice Lake Road

Trailhead: 49° 46.523′ N, 123° 7.195′ W

IN THE 1950S, Dennis DeBeck constructed the road up DeBeck Hill to access timber for his sawmill. Communication towers now adorn the summit, but hints of past activity along the way, the gentle grade and views to the west make this a worthwhile destination.

Your trail begins at a road gate and kiosk at the south end of the South Beach parking area and soon passes a service yard. As you walk, watch for bits of old hauling cable and stumps from the logging days, which ended in the mid-1960s, now being hidden by regrowth of mixed deciduous and coniferous trees. After some 20 minutes, you come to an elbow bend in the

An abandoned donkey engine.

road, then find yourself travelling below some impressive bluffs on your left. It is on this stretch that you come to a defunct donkey engine, still protected from the weather under its little roof. (Donkey engines, used for various tasks in logging, were powered by steam generated in a boiler and had one or more winches to manage steel log-hauling cables. They generally sat on log skids to facilitate their relocation.) A short distance beyond, a level area is the only indication of the former sawmill site. Now the summit is only about 15 minutes away. Brace yourself to enter "tower town," where your first thought might be: Where are the views?

Good views of the Tantalus Range on the west side of the Squamish River Valley may be enjoyed from a rocky bluff behind the communication dish. Here, also, are signed trailheads for mountain bikers. Unfortunately, views to the east have been obscured by that inevitable forest growth. After a rest, you retrace your steps to return.

Should you wish to take a longer walk or should the road access to South Beach be closed, as is usual in the off-season, you may start from the main day-use area and add a walk around the lake to your outing, allowing an extra hour for the added distance. Another option might be to pair this excursion with an easy walk to Stump Lake (about 250 m from the trailhead on Alice Lake Road) or to Edith Lake, which starts out rather steeply then becomes easier over the 900 m from its trailhead (Walk 4).

SHANNON FALLS

Olesen Creek Bridge return: 2.5 km (1.6 mi)
High Bluff return: 8.2 km (5.1 mi)
Surface: steep trail, stairs
Rating: easy to extra challenging
Season: April to November

Allow: 1 hour
Allow: 4.5 hours
Elevation gain: 445 m (1460 ft)
High point: 485 m (1590 ft)

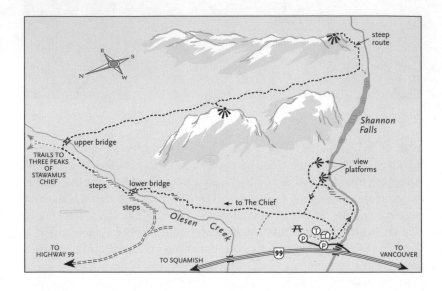

ACCESS

Vehicle: Travel north on Highway 99 (Sea to Sky Highway). Seven km (4.3 mi) past the Britannia Beach mining museum, turn east at a traffic light into Shannon Falls Provincial Park. This junction is 800 m south of the Stawamus Chief Provincial Park, which offers an alternative parking and access point for this walk.

Car GPS entry: Sea to Sky Highway & Darrell Bay Road
Trailhead: 49° 40.297′ N, 123° 9.524′ W

SHANNON FALLS PROVIDES an eye-catching attraction at any time of year, and more so when in full spate during spring runoff. It is no wonder that this area holds significant spiritual value for the Squamish First Nation. Quite a different spiritual value was placed on the falls by Carling O'Keefe,

Howe Sound.

which brewed its beer with the water until the company donated the land to B.C. Parks in 1982. Two platforms at the base of the falls offer terrific views, and a steep, rugged trail leads to expansive views from granite knolls above the falls.

At the parking lot (it fills quickly on sunny days), check the trails map at an information kiosk, then walk past picnic tables and the concession stand to the viewing platforms at the base of the falls. Next, backtrack and look for the Chief trail; this begins wide then narrows and gradually rises through forest and over boulders for just over 1 km (0.6 mi) to the lower Olesen Creek bridge. Here, in the middle of an endless-looking staircase, you join the crowds on the very popular trail up the Chief. Or, sufficiently satisfied with the view from here across Howe Sound, you may return.

To continue, ascend the steep steps and trail for about 20 minutes to a signed junction where you branch right to Shannon Falls. Recross Olesen Creek on its upper bridge, then travel for some 20 minutes on varying terrain, sometimes level, sometimes steep, to another Howe Sound viewpoint on a rocky knoll. After the viewpoint the trail passes through a mini "canyon" slot between granite bluffs and weaves up and down through mossy forest en route to Shannon Creek at the top of the falls.

Your final destination lies another 15 to 20 minutes farther along. After briefly following Shannon Creek, you begin a steep ascent through the forest and over rocky outcrops, assisted at times by a handline. Your reward is an expansive view of Howe Sound, Squamish and the surrounding mountains, and lots of room for sitting or wandering a bit—but remember your return point from the slabs!

To return, retrace your steps, using extra care on the steep portions, and follow the trail markers back to the Olesen Creek bridge, which, if you parked at Shannon Falls, you must cross to return to your vehicle.

LANGDALE FALLS/SIDEWINDER LOOP

Return: 12.4 km (7.7 mi)   **Allow:** 5 hours

Surface: paved, rough   **Elevation gain:** 540 m (1770 ft)   **High point:** 560 m (1835 ft)

Rating: moderate to challenging   **Season:** April to October

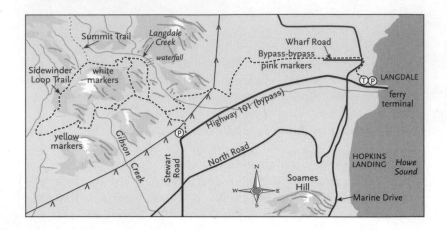

ACCESS

Transit: Route #250 or #257 Horseshoe Bay

Vehicle: Drive to Horseshoe Bay on Highway 1/99 (Upper Levels Highway) and follow signs to the village. Find paid parking near the ferry terminal. (Note: parking may be crowded seasonally and on long weekends.)

Car GPS entry: Keith Road & Bay Street (ferry terminal)

Trailhead at the Langdale terminal: 49° 26.061′ N, 123° 28.540′ W

THIS WALK, WHICH can be done entirely on foot from Horseshoe Bay, highlights a 40-minute ferry ride to Langdale, a high waterfall and a pleasant, mountainside forest walk. Although the area is popular with mountain bikers, there is room for everyone. Check the ferry schedule at www.bcferries.com. Your ticket is a round-trip fare.

After disembarking, follow the sidewalk north, ascend the stairs, walk right on the road for 200 m, turn left onto Wharf Road and follow this to its end, where you enter the woods. It will be important to follow the differently coloured, and plentiful, markers on trees to stay on the route. This

An original-style footbridge.

is not a walk for the colour illiterate! Begin with the pink markers, which lead about 1.4 km (0.9 mi) along an old, gently ascending logging road with occasional artifacts; this can be quite wet after a rainfall. Follow markers, right, past a quarry then left along the power line clearing. Within 5 minutes you re-enter the woods, this time to traverse a slope with the rushing sound of Langdale Creek below. A couple of bridge crossings on fragile structures require care and attention. Another 5 minutes lead to a major four-way junction, which you cross directly, now to follow yellow markers. (Left leads to a parking lot.)

Within 10 to 15 minutes, a sign on a tree points the way to Langdale Falls, indicated by both red and blue markers. The trail now becomes fairly steep to the Langdale Falls viewpoint and beyond. From the falls, follow mauve-with-white-stripe markers, paralleling above the creek until you reach a road, where you go left. A few paces along, go right at a junction to join the loop trail, identified by white markers. (Left goes to the previously mentioned parking lot.) Soon thereafter, a mossy bench, at about your halfway point, invites you to rest. Continue following white markers as you pass the summit trail junction, traverse the blowdown and cross Gibson Creek. From the creek, it is about 20 minutes to a sharp switchback left, then another 40 minutes, recrossing Gibson Creek en route, to Sidewinder Loop Trail's signed southern junction.

Should you prefer to avoid the steep falls trail and do only the loop (travelling clockwise features more downhill), then proceed to this junction, which is 5 minutes beyond the falls junction, at the beginning of your hike. Descending now with yellow markers, you soon meet the falls junction, then the sign and the pink markers that direct you back to the ferry.

KEATS ISLAND

Return: 10 km (6.2 mi)   **Allow:** 4 hours

Surface: trail, road   **Elevation gain:** 175 m (575 ft)   **High point:** 190 m (625 ft)

Rating: easy to moderate, except some easy scrambling required on Lookout Trail

Season: all year

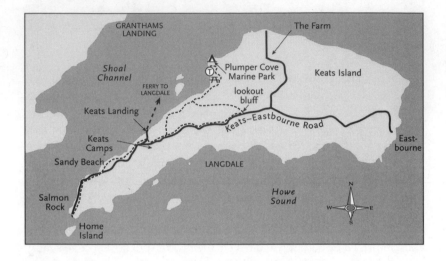

ACCESS

Transit: Route #250 or #257 Horseshoe Bay

Vehicle: Drive to Horseshoe Bay on Highway 1/99 (Upper Levels Highway) and follow signs to the village. Find paid parking near the ferry terminal. (Note: parking may be crowded seasonally and on long weekends.)

Car GPS entry: Keith Road & Bay Street (ferry terminal)

Trailhead at Keats Landing: 49° 23.639′ N, 123° 29.007′ W

KEATS ISLAND IS a little gem that lies unobtrusively between Bowen Island and the Sunshine Coast, its "remoteness" protected by ferry and water taxi rides with disconnected schedules. Note that you must coordinate both your morning and afternoon ferry and water taxi schedules between Horseshoe Bay and Langdale. Note also that you must bring your own drinking water and food, as there are no stores. Planning your logistics is worth the effort, however, for this adventurous outing. (See www.bc ferries.com and www.keatsisland.net.)

On foot in Horseshoe Bay, board the Langdale ferry. When you disembark, turn immediately right and descend a ramp to the water taxi dock for your onward journey to Keats Landing (additional fare required).

From Keats Landing, you may choose any or all of three destinations: Plumper Cove Marine Park, the lookout and Salmon Rock. To get to Plumper Cove, follow the road that curves through the Keats Camps property. You quickly arrive at a small building on the left bearing a B.C. Hydro sign where, just beyond, you enter the woods on the trail to the marine park. Watch for signs at all junctions and follow the yellow markers. In about 20 minutes, note where a right fork heads steeply up a road leading towards the lookout. For now, stay left on the narrower trail that descends to Plumper Cove, an attractive destination with picnic tables and tent sites.

Back at the Plumper Cove–lookout junction, should you wish to ascend, you must stretch your definition of "walk." Although the road begins steeply, it soon levels to a pleasant stroll following green markers, then narrows to a trail. The final rise to the lookout requires some scrambling for about 40 m, where the upper part of the path becomes narrow and steep-sided but solid. At a fork on the final rise, left is easier. After enjoying the view, you may descend the way you came or, for an easy alternative, ascend a few paces higher to a smooth rock patch. Find a trail towards the right that descends comfortably to an overgrown road, where you keep right to emerge on a high point of the cross-island Keats Road, 20 minutes from the B.C. Hydro building. You could reach the lookout from this direction, though the trailhead is not clearly marked.

Back at Keats Camps, to get to Salmon Rock at the southwest end of the island, follow a road to the left of the central building, walk past the boat storage, then continue through open forest for 30 minutes, noting the fork to Sandy Beach. After exploring the rocky point with its great views, return via the Sandy Beach trail, which, just after the path to the water, serves as access to a string of cottages and returns you directly to the wharf.

KILLARNEY LAKE

Return: 8 km (5 mi)   **Allow:** 2.5 hours

Surface: roads, unimproved trail   **Rating:** easy   **Season:** most of the year

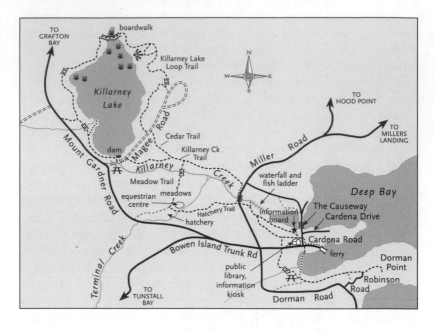

ACCESS

Transit: Route #250 or #257 Horseshoe Bay

Vehicle: Drive to Horseshoe Bay on Highway 1/99 (Upper Levels Highway) and follow signs to the village. There is paid parking near the ferry terminal. (Note: parking may be crowded seasonally and on long weekends.)

Car GPS entry: Keith Road & Bay Street (ferry terminal)

Trailhead (Cardena Road): 49° 22.786′ N, 123° 20.008′ W

THIS EXCURSION BEGINS with a delightful 20-minute ferry ride from Horseshoe Bay to Bowen Island in Howe Sound, with panoramic sights of mountains, forest and water. On disembarking at Snug Cove, walk one block north on Bowen Island Trunk Road and turn right on Cardena Road, the first intersection above the ferry terminal. Pamphlets for Crippen

Regional Park (Killarney Lake) are available at an information kiosk beside the public library.

Begin your walk about 100 m along Cardena Road, at a Metro Vancouver park sign. Divert briefly through a memorial garden for a fine view over Deep Bay to the mountains above Howe Sound. Continuing, you pass above a tidy little stream, complete with fish ladders and a viewing platform, and arrive at Miller Road, which you cross onto Hatchery Trail. This leads you through mixed forest to a wide meadow and an intersection, with the hatchery to the left. Go right, however, past the equestrian centre and cross the meadows to meet a major trail, where you proceed left for a short distance to another fork, this time going right on Cedar Trail to eventually come out on a country lane, Magee Road. On this, walk a few metres to the left before turning right onto Killarney Lake Loop Trail to begin your circuit of the lake.

The ground drops away to the left, giving glimpses of the lake through the trees and of the Mount Gardner massif behind. Then, finally, after a detour to a viewpoint, you reach marshy ground at the north end of the lake, a good place for bird watching. Boardwalks traverse this and another marsh on the west side as you stay on the Killarney Lake Loop, ignoring branches to the right. At the lake's south end, your track lies close to Mount Gardner Road; however, you soon turn left towards a picnic area by the lake's dam. Back at Magee Road, go left and cross the outlet, then, after a few metres, go right on a track that starts up the roadside bank and eventually rejoins the Killarney Creek Trail back to Miller Road. Here, you turn right to find your outward trail on the left just after crossing the bridge over Killarney Creek.

If you have time before catching your ferry home, you might walk south across the picnic area near the ferry terminal and ascend the track on the wooded slope to Dorman Point, with more views of Howe Sound. The round trip is about 2 km (1.2 mi), but the steepness of the last part of the climb suggests that you should allow at least 45 minutes to return.

WHYTECLIFF

Return: 4 km (2.5 mi)   **Allow:** 1.5 hours

Surface: trail, paved   **Rating:** easy   **Season:** all year

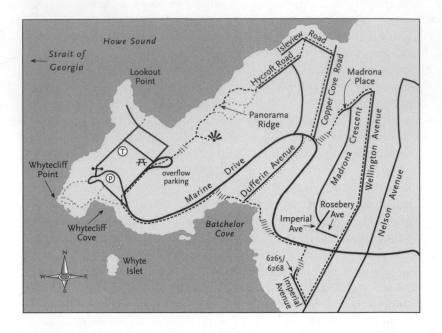

ACCESS

Transit: various to Marine Drive at Nelson; join the route at Wellington, one block west

Vehicle: Travelling west on Highway 1/99 (Upper Levels Highway), take Exit 2 (Marine Drive–Eagleridge), veer left to cross the overpass, then stay with Marine Drive to Whtyecliff Park.

Car GPS entry: Marine Drive & Dufferin Avenue

Trailhead: 49° 22.374′ N, 123° 17.378′ W

WHYTECLIFF PARK AND Batchelor Cove are two worthwhile destinations at the westernmost end of West Vancouver. This outing links the two via a route along a natural ridge and along streets through attractive residential areas where you may follow your own inclinations.

On foot in Whytecliff Park, head towards the far end of the overflow parking lot to find the start of a steepish trail to Panorama Ridge, built over

Whyte Islet.

a waterline and, interestingly, through a not insignificant rock cut. What were once, undoubtedly, impressive views are now obstructed by tall trees, except for a snapshot north to Mount Brunswick and Mount Harvey, with its nearby junior summit known as Harvey's Pup. Choosing left forks as you proceed brings you to the northern margin of the park. (If you wish to take only a short outing, turn back right, then left, rejoining your outward route for a return to the busier regions of the park. Now, you may drop down to the shore at Whyte Cove, then, if the tide is favourable, cross the causeway to Whyte Islet.)

For a longer circuit, mainly on streets, descend Hycroft Road at the park's northern extremity and go left at its bend on a track connecting with Isleview Road. Walk down Isleview to its junction with Copper Cove Road, where you turn right. As you walk, look for a few houses that appear to date from the early cottage days. Once at Marine Drive, you have a choice: a jog right then left onto Dufferin Avenue takes you to Batchelor Cove, a secluded little beach enclosed by rocky cliffs; alternatively, a jog left then quickly left again puts you onto an inconspicuous track with stairs up to Madrona Place. At Madrona Crescent, go left to Wellington Avenue.

Now it's an easy stride down Wellington, with an occasional backwards glance to the distant mountains, until you cross Rosebery Avenue and Marine Drive in quick succession, then, just when you think you are approaching a dead end, you go right on Imperial Avenue, another cul-de-sac! But look for the stone stairs between house numbers 6265 and 6268, which, despite first impressions, are public and lead to Marine Drive. Now, a few metres to your left, you escape the busy road down another set of steps, down to Batchelor Cove.

Finally, to make your retreat, follow the sand or the boardwalk and trail to the western end of the cove, where stairs ascend to Marine Drive and a picturesque 5-minute walk back to your vehicle.

SEAVIEW/LARSEN BAY

Return: 6.7 km (4.2 mi)   **Allow:** 2.5 hours

Surface: packed, paved, trail   **Rating:** easy   **Season:** all year

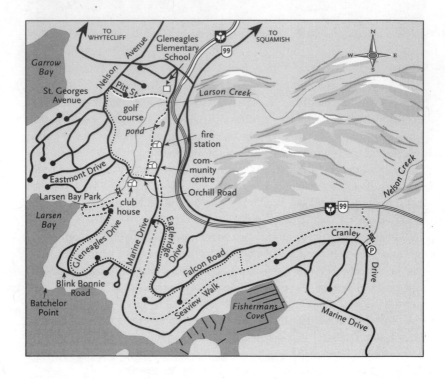

ACCESS

Transit: Route #250 Marine Drive to Cranley Drive or various stops to join the route midway

Vehicle: Travelling west on Highway 1/99 (Upper Levels Highway), take Exit 4 (Caulfeild Road) to Westport Road. Descend to Marine Drive, turn right, then, in the 5700 block, turn right again onto Cranley Drive. Park by the side of the road at Nelson Creek. If approaching from the north, access Marine Drive at Horseshoe Bay and follow it to Cranley Drive.

Car GPS entry: 5743 Cranley Drive, West Vancouver

Trailhead: 49° 21.611′ N, 123° 15.805′ W

THIS WALK FOLLOWS an abandoned railway right-of-way (Seaview Walk) and residential streets to its highlight, the secluded little Larsen Bay.

You begin on a path beside Nelson Creek, almost beneath the towering Nelson Creek Bridge. Ascend for about 10 minutes to a junction where to the right is the tunnel entrance for the railway that once occupied the roadbed on which you now proceed west. The marine views and the plants, notably arbutus and mosses, provide the main attractions along this stretch. Soon after the 1.5 km marker, a short track beside a small bluff leads to Falcon Road, where you turn left. Ignore cul-de-sacs on your left until you reach Eagleridge Drive, where you go left again, downhill to rejoin Seaview Walk just short of Marine Drive. (If you prefer to avoid the 20 minutes of street walking, you may stay on Seaview.)

Proceed right on Seaview to the crosswalk, cross to Orchill Road, then drop onto the path going right before the parking lot, past Gleneagles Community Centre and the fire station and over the deck of a building to a small pond and footbridge. Continue alongside the golf course to its end, where you turn left onto a narrow path at the edge of a school playground. (This is opposite the Lions Club parking lot below the highway at Horseshoe Bay.) Stay close to the fence until you exit onto St. Georges Avenue, near the junction with Nelson. Continue around the golf course until you come to a golfers' crossing, where you take the path that descends beside the fairway. Just beyond the tee box, a narrow track drops you into a different world, a little glen by a creek. Ignoring all trails on your left, keep descending until you emerge at Larsen Bay and its enjoyable little beach.

From this peaceful spot, you may return to St. Georges, which curves into Orchill Road and meets Marine Drive opposite the western end of Seaview Walk, on which you return to your transportation. Alternatively, ascend the steep service road, which begins near the benches, to Gleneagles Drive; follow it right as it winds through this pleasant residential area to meet Marine Drive beside a bus stop. Directly across is a steep track, which you ascend on an overgrown rocky slope for about 2 minutes until you reach Seaview Walk. Go right and you'll arrive back at your starting place in about 20 minutes.

WHYTE LAKE LOOP

Return: 6 km (3.7 mi)   **Allow:** 3 hours

Surface: rough   **Elevation gain:** 215 m (705 ft)   **High point:** 335 m (1100 ft)

Rating: moderate to challenging   **Season:** most of the year

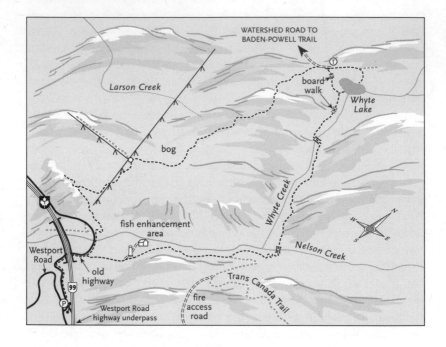

ACCESS

Vehicle: From Highway 1/99 (Upper Levels Highway) take Exit 4 (Caulfeild Road–Wood-green Drive), drive west on Westport Road and, immediately after passing under the highway, go right into a parking lot.

Car GPS entry: Trans-Canada Highway & Westport Road

Trailhead: 49° 21.645′ N, 123° 15.523′ W

THE TRAIL TO Whyte Lake, and beyond to Eagle Bluffs, is attractive and popular; somewhat less travelled is the western side of the loop, which is more strenuous and passes near a fine grove of arbutus trees.

From the parking area, pass an information kiosk and a yellow gate on the old highway, then pass under the current highway to reach the original 1956 Nelson Creek Bridge. Your trail exits on the near side of the bridge, but your route, beginning with the more demanding part of the circuit, plunges into the bush at the bridge's west end.

You immediately begin to climb, zigzagging upwards and trending generally westwards before coming to a fork, at which you may take a detour left for about 5 minutes, your destination being a lovely mossy area with a grove of young arbutus trees. Back at the fork, you head up over rocks, many bare of soil but with enough sustenance to encourage a few flowers in spring—delightful white camus and tiny yellow mimulus. After you cross the power line and ascend a short distance in the forest beside it, you again emerge into the open, where a helipad invites you to rest.

Next comes a very pleasant stretch, meandering and undulating past a boggy area with decaying bigleaf maple, mosses and ferns, and through mixed woods with remnants of a fire that swept from Hollyburn Mountain to Eagle Harbour in 1884. Within about 15 minutes, at a junction, bear left on the more heavily used trail and descend to meet the old watershed road to Whyte Lake. Going left here takes you down to connect with the Baden-Powell Trail, but staying right leads you in a few steps to another fork, with a sturdy boardwalk going off at right angles on what was an old logging road. Note here the attractive outhouse with Dutch doors. Also note that dogs must be leashed in the Whyte Lake watershed.

Follow the boardwalk to the south end of the lake, then follow a short side trail that leads to a floating platform with a bench where you can rest and enjoy the view and perhaps a quick dip.

The time will come when you must continue; your homebound route takes you down the left bank of the lake's outlet, Whyte Creek; through a stretch of magnificent old-growth forest; across Nelson Creek, which you stay alongside for a short distance; and uphill to join the Trans Canada Trail (TCT), which you descend to a service road, exiting at the 1956 bridge, thus completing the loop. (This walk connects to Walk 13 via the TCT, a convenient link should you wish to extend your ramblings in the area.)

TCT/NELSON CREEK LOOP

Return: 8.5 km (5.3 mi)   **Allow:** 3.5 hours

Surface: packed, rough   **Elevation gain:** 320 m (1050 ft)   **High point:** 450 m (1475 ft)

Rating: easy to moderate   **Season:** most of the year

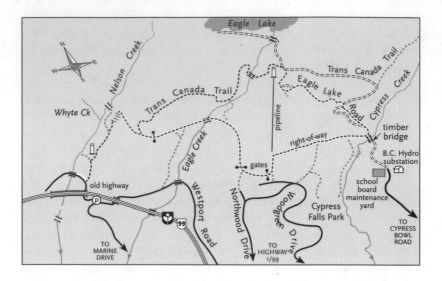

ACCESS

Vehicle: From Highway 1/99 (Upper Levels Highway), take Exit 4 (Caulfeild Road-Wood-green Drive), drive west on Westport Road and, immediately after passing under the highway, go right into a parking lot.

Car GPS entry: Trans-Canada Highway & Westport Road

Trailhead: 49° 21.645′ N, 123° 15.523′ W

THIS TRAIL FOLLOWS an upsy-downsy loop across the lower slopes of Black Mountain, with views over Burrard Inlet on a clear day. It is part of the Trans Canada Trail (TCT), begun in 1992, which is envisioned to stretch 24,000 km (15,000 mi) and link the Pacific, Atlantic and Arctic Oceans by 2017.

From the information kiosk, walk along the old road and under the highway to a signed trail heading uphill just before a 1956-built bridge over Nelson Creek. Ascend towards a water tower, to the right of which you embark on a delightful trail above the canyon of Nelson Creek. Stay right at a fork

Freighters in Burrard Inlet.

that goes to Whyte Lake (Walk 12). A sturdy set of stairs leads to the end of an abandoned road, which you follow briefly to a signed, significant trail leading left. This trail zigzags a little at first to gain elevation and often makes use of old forest roads amongst quite large second-growth trees. After about 15 minutes, you descend to a damp bottom near the small Eagle Creek. This you approach, then swing away left to arrive at a wooden bridge and a TCT sign pointing your way left at a junction. (Turning right offers you a shorter circuit.) Your track now rises, crosses the creek on a bridge, then emerges shortly thereafter on the grassy right-of-way of a water line, just below another water tower. It might surprise you to see a fire hydrant nearby; this and others are kept operational.

Next, you go right twice, skirting protected watershed lands and following the old Eagle Lake Road to meet the new, on which you go right again to a significant fork. Follow an old road to your right, signed to Cypress Bowl. Staying right again, at a power line watch for a beaten path heading into the woods on your right. This leads to a mossy, rocky knoll with a good view of the entrance to Burrard Inlet and Metro Vancouver beyond, the perfect place for a break. Next, continue downhill to meet an actively used road. This leads to a timber bridge high over Cypress Falls, but you head right just before this, to follow a wide right-of-way to another T-junction, where this time you drop left at another pipeline and hydrant. Just above a residential area, go right through a gated fence with a sign disclaiming liability, erected by British Properties.

Now, homeward bound and some 10 minutes after passing through a second fence, note a road forking back on one angle then a trail angling in from another—your exit point had you bailed out earlier. Continue westwards across Eagle Creek, encounter a third gated fence, pass your earlier TCT junction and continue to your vehicle.

CYPRESS FALLS PARK

Return: 3 km (1.9 mi) or more   **Allow:** 1.5 hours or more

Surface: trail, road   **Rating:** easy to moderate   **Season:** all year

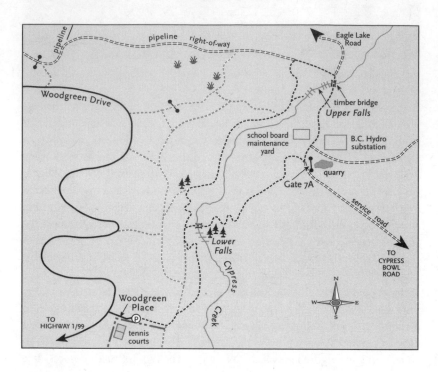

ACCESS

Transit: Route #253 flagstop on Woodgreen Drive at Woodgreen Place, then as below.

Vehicle: From Highway 1/99 (Upper Levels Highway), take Exit 4 (Caulfeild Road–Woodgreen Drive). Turn north onto Woodgreen Drive then right onto Woodgreen Place; a gravel road at its end angles to the left for parking.

Car GPS entry: Woodgreen Drive & Woodgreen Place

Trailhead: 49° 21.123′ N, 123° 14.463′ W

HARBOURING GROVES OF fine Douglas-fir and two sets of waterfalls, this low-elevation forest park makes a good destination at any time of year. It is popular with dog walkers.

The trail begins across a grassy area at the east end of the parking lot and forks immediately after entering the trees. Drop right to a path paralleling the main trail and note the bits of wood and wire poking through the surface, remains of a wood-stave water pipeline installed in the 1910s.

In about 10 to 15 minutes, you arrive first at a fenced view of the lower falls tumbling through a little canyon then, a little higher, at another fenced view at the top of the falls. Years ago, someone cut steps into the rounded rock and fashioned a bench from a large log, now tired and mossy. A footbridge crosses to the east side of the creek and a trail that you may choose to descend on your return.

Staying on the west side of the bridge for now, head uphill beside a once-functional set of stairs and watch for the impressive grove of towering Douglas-fir, some approaching 2 m (6 ft) in diameter and perhaps 300 years in age, that escaped both fire and logging. The trail continues and, in the wet season, crosses small watercourses that nourish Western red cedars. There are a couple of short side trails where you can access the creek. Within 30 minutes, your ears alert you to the nearness of the upper falls, which freefall about 10 m into a small pool. The edge of the viewpoint is unfenced and precipitous.

Now, you may either return by the same route or the aforementioned alternative. If you choose the latter, ascend until you exit onto a wide clearing with a power line. This is the pipeline route that carries water from Dick (Eagle) Lake to West Vancouver. (This junction also overlaps with Walk 13.) Turn right, then right again at the road, cross the vehicle bridge over Cypress Creek and proceed past the school board maintenance yard on the right and a B.C. Hydro substation on the left. Immediately thereafter, opposite Gate 7A at a quarry site, find a trail heading into the brush on your right. This leads to the footbridge at the lower falls and your return route.

There are other trails in the park that you may wish to explore if you just want a longer wander; some lead to the residential area on Woodgreen Drive, but none anywhere in the park are marked.

CAULFEILD TRAIL/KLOOTCHMAN PARK

Return: 7.2 km (4.5 mi)   **Allow:** 3 hours

Surface: roads, trails·   **Elevation gain:** 135 m (443 ft)   **High point:** 140 m (460 ft)

Rating: moderate to challenging   **Season:** all year

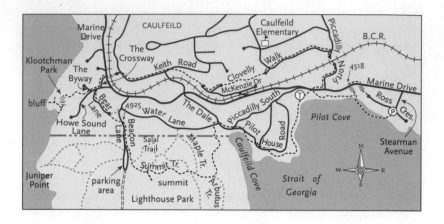

ACCESS

Transit: Route #250 to Cypress Park Shopping Centre, walk west 100 m to Stearman Avenue, then as below.

Vehicle: Make your way to Marine Drive and Stearman Avenue. Drive south on Stearman, turn right onto Ross Crescent then quickly left to park.

Car GPS entry: Marine Drive & Stearman Avenue

Trailhead: 49° 20.387′ N, 123° 14.573′ W

THIS EXCURSION HIGHLIGHTS an oceanside trail, water views, mature trees, the heights of Lighthouse Park and rocky shores. It complements Walk 16, overlapping on the Summit Trail.

If the tide is out, you may start your walk along the beach accessed from the parking lot, then clamber up a low rocky buttress 200 m west onto a trail not immediately obvious as it passes in front of a house. Alternatively, walk west along Ross Crescent to its end, climb steps to Marine Drive, then, a few paces along, descend again just before house number 4518 to join the cross-trail. Now your route undulates along the foreshore, out over rocky

The beach at Pilot Cove.

promontories and back amongst mature trees, until, moments beyond another access from Marine Drive, a track descends to a sandy beach. Finally, the trail emerges in a clearing, the site of an anchor embedded in a rock with a commemorative plaque to Francis Caulfeild, the visionary pioneer who designated the shoreline park. Exiting Caulfeild Trail, continue west on Pilot House Road and Piccadilly South, noting snug little Caulfeild Cove and, across The Green, the attractive church of St. Francis in the Woods, before you come to the junction with Water Lane and The Dale.

Now, you may stay with Water Lane to continue the route at Beacon Lane (see below) or climb steeply to the summit of Lighthouse Park. At The Dale, enter the woods on a narrow path that winds left and ever upwards, keeping right at a minor junction, then right again at a major junction where the trail begins to drop gently. At the next crossroads, stay straight ahead on Arbutus Trail, then quickly fork left on Summit Trail, which leads to the park's highest point. After a short detour left at a fire hydrant to the rounded hillock, continue towards Salal Trail, on which you descend left then right to the parking lot.

Leave the park on Beacon Lane and, beside house number 4925, find a short track connecting with Bear Lane. Proceed, go left on Howe Sound Lane and within moments find the entrance to Klootchman Park. A narrow path and more than 100 steps descend to the pleasant, rocky shores. Back at Howe Sound Lane, go left to The Crossway, which crosses the railway tracks to Keith Road. Turn right. Just past The Dale, go right into a cul-de-sac; Clovelly Walk begins at its end. Stay with Clovelly until you swing right to join Piccadilly North, descending over the tracks to Marine Drive. Turn right briefly to reach Caulfeild Trail, then left for the last lap of your outing.

LIGHTHOUSE PARK

Return: 6 km (3.7 mi)   **Allow:** 2 hours

Surface: trails, road   **Rating:** easy to moderate   **Season:** all year

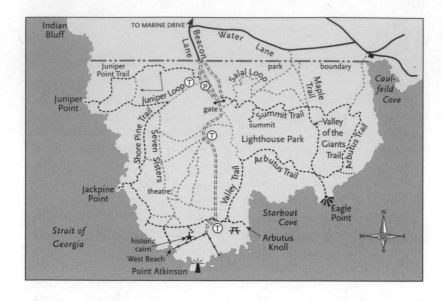

ACCESS

Transit: Route #250 to Marine Drive at Beacon Lane

Vehicle: Follow Marine Drive west through West Vancouver to Beacon Lane, which is 350 m beyond a firehall; turn left at the Lighthouse Park sign. Park at the road's end. Alternatively, from Highway 1/99 (Upper Levels Highway), take Exit 4 (Caulfeild Road–Woodgreen Drive) and go south. Turn left onto Headland Drive, make a quick right-left jog at Meadfeild Road, meet Keith Road and turn left onto The Dale, which leads to the firehall at Marine Drive.

Car GPS entry: Marine Drive & Beacon Lane

Trailhead: 49° 20.266′ N, 123° 15.810′ W

LIGHTHOUSE PARK, A preserve of old-growth forest, rocky shorelines and hidden coves, is an adventure destination for those who want a light stroll, a vigorous walk or a quiet oceanside view. The lighthouse itself sits prominently on rocky Point Atkinson, where it has been flashing its light

Point Atkinson lighthouse.

and sounding its foghorn since 1874, marking the spot where Burrard Inlet meets Howe Sound.

Pick up a trail pamphlet from one of the information kiosks, then walk towards the northwest end of the parking lot, to the trailhead of the northern Juniper Loop. This outing proceeds around the park's perimeter and leaves the intersecting trails for your own discovery.

Beginning on the northern Juniper Loop arm, you soon come to a wetland with an information board; keep right on Juniper Point Trail at the next junction and descend, crossing a boardwalk and stairs, to a rocky promontory. Instead of returning up the stairs, bear right, then right again, ascending to meet the southern arm of the Juniper Loop Trail. Watch for the stretched red cedar root in mid-air that resulted when its nurse log disintegrated long ago. Now go right onto Shore Pine Trail, which leads to another promontory with views of Howe Sound. Farther along, your next diversion lies a couple of minutes down a rocky track to West Beach, where you can get close to the water to look for little marine critters and have your first view of the lighthouse. A closer view of the 1912 tower is gained from a knoll near facilities used by the navy during World War II, now a nature house. You may now return up the road to your transportation or continue to the eastern side of the park.

Valley Trail climbs steadily, with diversions to views of Burrard Inlet at Arbutus Knoll and Starboat Cove. Continue ascending on Arbutus Trail, before immediately descending to two intersections in quick succession. Continue straight to Eagle Point lookout, which is rich with lilies in the spring. Now you must choose between the steep Arbutus Trail and the gentler Valley of the Giants Trail. They meet at the Summit Trail, from which any of the short tracks now before you lead back to the parking lot. Should you wish to extend your excursion, this is where you might join Walk 15.

HOLLYBURN MOUNTAIN

Return: 10 km (6.2 mi)   **Allow:** 4 hours

Surface: trail   **Elevation gain:** 425 m (1395 ft)   **High point:** 1325 m (4350 ft)

Rating: moderate to challenging   **Season:** July to November

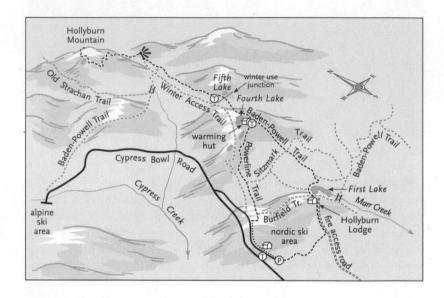

ACCESS

Vehicle: From Highway 1/99 (Upper Levels Highway), take Exit 8 to Cypress Bowl, drive 13 km (8 mi) to the cross-country/snow-play centre and park at the far end of the lot.

Car GPS entry: Trans-Canada Highway & Cypress Bowl Road

Trailhead: 49° 22.472′ N, 123° 11.581′ W

HOLLYBURN HAS BEEN a popular destination for mountain enthusiasts since early in the 20th century. This outing leads past historic Hollyburn Lodge, which harbours thousands of stories within its walls, and on to the summit itself at 1325 m (4350 ft).

At the far end of the parking lot, a trail heads into the trees and rises to meet the old fire access road to Hollyburn Lodge, which itself is reached about 20 minutes later. En route, you pass some of the private cabins

A tarn on the summit of Hollyburn Mountain.

remaining in use. The lodge, originally a logging mill's cookhouse on Hollyburn Ridge, has been in continuous use since it was reconstructed at First Lake and opened as Hollyburn Ski Camp in 1927. Take time to study the Pioneers' Table near the lake and imagine the enthusiasm of early skiers, who had to cross Burrard Inlet by ferry to Ambleside, then walk up the mountain, before construction of the Lions Gate Bridge in 1938 eased their journey. (For historical information, see www.hollyburnheritage.ca.)

Now, backtrack to the north side of the lodge and circle the lake on a narrow path leading to the Baden-Powell Trail, where you turn left onto a wide swath. Fifteen minutes later, at a junction with the power line, you reach the warming hut with its toilet a few paces right, semi-hidden in trees. Continue straight on, past the hut and past Fourth Lake, winding across the ski clearing and into the trees. Ten minutes later, you arrive at a major junction (with an outhouse), where you continue straight ahead, staying left at a narrow fork, the right side of which heads into a bog. Your next landmark is a major fork, where a signpost points the way to the peak. You pass a lovely little meadow with small ponds, your last respite before the final push to the top along an eroded track on which you may occasionally have to use your hands for balance. Next, you can enjoy a panoramic view as reward for your efforts, and the company of grey jays and ravens begging for a bite to eat.

To return, retrace your steps down the ridge, rejoining the Baden-Powell Trail and continuing as far as the power line, where, instead of returning past Hollyburn Lodge, you may descend on the trail down the power line with views of the Strait of Georgia and as far as the Olympic Peninsula and the mountains on Vancouver Island. All that remains is to walk the length of the parking lot to your vehicle. (You could also ascend on this power line route, which begins near the ticket office and is about 1.5 km/0.9 mi shorter, but you would miss seeing Hollyburn Lodge.)

LOWER HOLLYBURN

Return: 12 km (7.5 mi) **Allow:** 4.5 hours
Surface: rough trails **Elevation gain:** 500 m (1640 ft) **High point:** 945 m (3100 ft)
Rating: moderate to challenging **Season:** May to November

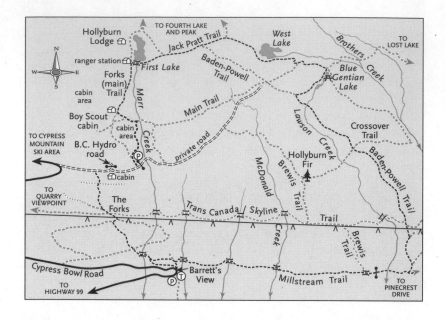

ACCESS

Vehicle: From Highway 1/99 (Upper Levels Highway), take Exit 8 and drive 6 km (3.7 mi) up Cypress Parkway to Barrett's View. Park here.

Car GPS entry: Trans-Canada Highway & Cypress Bowl Road

Trailhead: 49° 21.229′ N, 123° 10.630′ W

LOWER HOLLYBURN HAS a well-established trail system that can be walked when the upper hills (Walk 17) are still buried under snow. This excursion takes you in a large loop through peaceful forest and past attractive alpine lakes.

From your vehicle, walk east around the curve of the road to reach the (unsigned) Millstream Trail, which passes through a gated fence. Keep right as the trail rises, drops sharply to cross a stream, then rises again, repeating the process for a second creek before it settles to a gradual descent. Here and there, mountain-bike tracks cross your route. Within 30 minutes, you pass the Brewis Trail junction and stay with the main road, beyond another gated fence. Next comes Lawson Creek with its two bridges, then a significant junction where you turn uphill onto the Baden-Powell Trail. Now you rise steadily through the forest for about an hour, passing junctions to Shields Incline, Skyline/Trans Canada (which leads to Walks 19 and 20), Lost Lake and Crossover Trails until you arrive at the awaited junction to Blue Gentian Lake. Within 5 minutes, you enjoy a change of scenery where blue gentian flowers and other moisture-loving plants proliferate. Partway along the boardwalk is your onward route, but first you may want to rest at a table farther along.

From the boardwalk, you very soon turn left and uphill on the steep West Lake Trail, with West Lake Creek murmuring below. West Lake lies near a ski run, where blueberries are plentiful in season. Now follow the Jack Pratt ski trail, past a junction with the Baden-Powell Trail, to the outlet of First Lake, beyond which is the historic Hollyburn Lodge. Your route, however, turns immediately left at the bridge and ranger station to descend through the cabin area on the Forks (also called Main) Trail. Just past the Boy Scout cabin, turn left at a fork and descend to a parking area at the end of a gravel road. Follow the road downhill until, 45 seconds past a cabin opposite a spur road ascending right, you will find a trail on your left. This steep mountain-biking trail with obstacles requires care, and preferably walking poles, to negotiate. In about 15 minutes, you arrive at The Forks, a signposted four-way junction under the power line. (Although it's hard to believe today, a coffee shop and confectionery did business here in the 1930s.) Go left briefly, then right for another rapid descent. Within 20 minutes, the trail improves. Where the bike route goes uphill left, you go right on a rather disguised old road. Finally, watch for a junction where you go right, down through the last fence and along a bench above the highway, to exit near your start.

HOLLYBURN HERITAGE TRAILS

Return: 6.7 km (4.2 mi)   **Allow:** 3.5 hours

Surface: unimproved trail   **Elevation gain:** 315 m (1030 ft)   **High point:** 665 m (2180 ft)

Rating: easy to moderate   **Season:** May to November

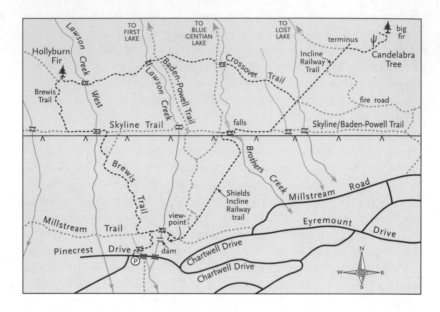

ACCESS

Vehicle: From Highway 1/99 (Upper Levels Highway), take Exit 11 and go north on 15th Street then up Cross Creek Road to Chartwell Drive, which climbs steeply to Pinecrest Drive. Turn left and park near the bridge.

Car GPS entry: Chartwell Drive & Pinecrest Drive

Trailhead: 49° 21.163′ N, 123° 9.631′ W

THIS FASCINATING WALK, a combination of two heritage circuits, winds through regenerated forest that was logged for local use and export during Vancouver's early years. Your route passes visible remnants of logging road-work and other landscape modifications that are explained in the informative Lawson Creek and Brothers Creek brochures, downloadable at www. westvancouver.ca (through Search). A small cairn and the blue-and-green heritage trail sign on the west side of the bridge spanning Lawson Creek on Pinecrest Drive mark your starting point.

The first stop of historical interest is Shields log dam and flume pond, with a shinglebolt mounted nearby. The pond was built in 1917 to store blocks of red cedar (shinglebolts) before flushing them down a flume (wooden channel) to a shingle mill 2 km (1.2 mi) below. Continuing uphill, turn right at a fence onto Millstream Trail, cross Lawson Creek, then turn uphill at a T-junction 5 minutes beyond. After another 5 minutes, bear right onto a narrower path, the Shields Incline Railway Trail. This leads to an overlook of Brothers Creek—and overlaps Walk 20, which explores the Brothers Creek area. Fifty metres farther uphill, look for an unnatural trench in the ground, dug by loggers to facilitate skidding logs down the mountain using steam-powered cable systems. At the Skyline Trail turn right, dropping steeply to cross Brothers Creek, then rising and continuing to a fork where you rejoin the Incline Trail. Pass the Crossover Trail and continue uphill to where the road turns sharply left. Pause here. If you want to see the Candelabra, a large Douglas-fir snag with a distinctive pitchfork-like shape, go straight ahead a few paces then right to descend for 5 minutes to its base. Now continue downhill through a graveyard of large snags to meet a 43 m- (140 ft-) tall Douglas-fir with a diameter of 2.7 m (8.8 ft), a living giant amongst the dead.

Next, retrace your steps to the Crossover Trail, where you turn right, ascending gradually towards a recrossing of Brothers Creek. At the Baden-Powell Trail junction, you may turn downhill to return to your start or continue onward, across Lawson Creek, to meet the Hollyburn Fir. This giant is nearly 1100 years old, 3 m (10 ft) in diameter and 44 m (145 ft) to its broken top. Now you head downhill on the Brewis Trail, sometimes a bit vague in the open understorey, to the power line and Skyline Trail, where you turn left, then quickly right to rejoin the Brewis Trail. After about 1 km (0.6 mi), at the Millstream Trail junction, go left, through the fence you passed earlier, downhill on the Shields Dam Trail and so back to your vehicle.

BROTHERS CREEK TRAILS

Return: 11 km (6.8 mi) or less

Surface: trails   **Elevation gain:** 450 m (1475 ft)

Rating: moderate to challenging

Allow: 4.5 hours or less

High point: 830 m (2725 ft)

Season: May to November

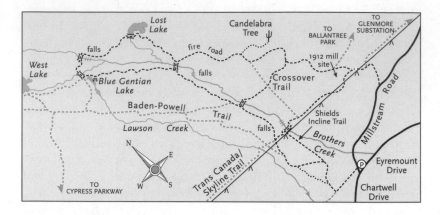

ACCESS

Transit: Route #254 to Eyremount Drive and Crestwell Road; walk two blocks west to Millstream Road then up to the gate.

Vehicle: From Highway 1/99 (Upper Levels Highway), take Exit 11 and turn north at 15th Street onto Cross Creek Road, turn left onto Chartwell Drive, then left on Millstream Road. Park here near a gated forest road reached immediately.

Car GPS entry: Chartwell Drive & Millstream Road

Trailhead: 49° 21.261′ N, 123° 9.199′ W

BLUE GENTIAN LAKE, with its boardwalks, water lilies and picnic table, provides a fine reward at your turnaround point after a variety of sights, including falls and canyons, enormous snags and logging artifacts.

Begin your outing by walking along the road-width Millstream Trail. Within 5 minutes, turn right towards the Baden-Powell/Skyline Trails, your path now a steady uphill. Continue past the junction with Shields Incline Trail, wonder at the history represented by ancient truck remains, then turn right at the next fork to Brothers Creek and Lost Lake. Within a few minutes, cross the power line right-of-way and continue straight ahead,

An artistic railing on the Brothers Creek bridge.

the creek well below on your right. A footbridge over Brothers Creek on the Crossover Trail leads to a shorter return route, for a round trip of 6 km (3.7 mi).

Staying left and continuing up the main trail, you enjoy a level stretch where the creek is a pleasant stream before you rise again to view a set of falls. The trail stays away from the bank and leads to another bridge, which you may cross if you now wish to return. (You would go right on the east bank and descend on a fire road to join the lower circuit trail for a round trip of 8.7 km/5.4 mi.) Otherwise, stay west of the creek for about 20 minutes to reach picturesque Blue Gentian Lake.

From the lake, stay right to go to Lost Lake, stepping across two creeks, just beyond which are views into the gorge of the upper falls. The track here is rough and eroded. From Lost Lake, use the trail down the east side of Brothers Creek to join and descend the fire road. Some portions of the route coincide with Heritage Trails (Walk 19). Lower still, the Crossover Trail enters from the right and departs later for Ballantree (Walk 21) by the site of a 1912 sawmill. Keep right, continue down to the power line, turn right on Skyline Trail, rise some 100 m, then drop sharply to Brothers Creek's lower falls. Cross the creek, rise equally fast out of its ravine, then turn left, down the Shields Incline Trail and so back to your transportation.

If, when you reach the power line on the fire road, you want no more climbing, you could go straight ahead, crossing Skyline (Baden-Powell) Trail out to Millstream Road and then back to your car.

BALLANTREE

Return: 2.7 km (1.7 mi) **Allow:** 1.5 hours
Surface: rough trail, road **Elevation gain:** 145 m (475 ft) **High point:** 465 m (1525 ft)
Rating: easy to moderate **Season:** April to November

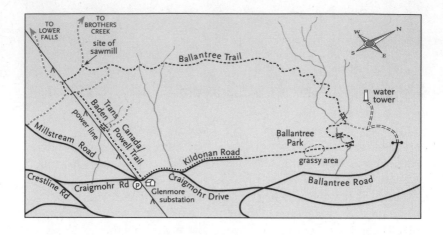

ACCESS

Transit: Route #254 on St. Andrew's Road at Greenwood Road. Walk north 50 m to the Baden-Powell Trail, and turn left to the trailhead on Craigmohr Road.

Vehicle: From Highway 1/99 (Upper Levels Highway), take Exit 13 (Taylor Way), turn north to a roundabout, go west on Southborough Drive, west onto Highland Drive, east on Hillside Road, east on Crestline Road, then left onto Craigmohr to its meeting with Millstream. Park immediately at the gravelled area with a trailhead sign.

Car GPS entry: Craigmohr Drive & Millstream Road

Trailhead: 49° 21.575′ N, 123° 8.041′ W

THIS TRAIL, WITH its ups and downs and eye-catching spots of interest, is good for a short, energetic outing. (For a longer walk, you might combine this with Walk 20.)

The trail begins with a rather lengthy set of steps to a power line, which it crosses, then parallels, rising steadily westwards, marked by red trail markers and occasional markers for the Trans Canada and Baden-Powell Trails. Within about 10 minutes, go left over a low bridge, then left again

Traversing second-growth forest.

at the next junction to cross the power line on a corduroy path that exits onto an old road. Early loggers frequently made corduroy roads, logs laid side by side perpendicular to the direction of travel, to facilitate log-hauling or to cross boggy areas. Go right at the sign, then right again within 100 m onto the Brothers Creek fire road. This quiet junction was once busy with sawmill activities; all that remains is the foundation for machinery and remnants of a stone wall. Your route now goes north and east through second-growth forest, where you'll see many burned snags and stumps, the latter perhaps with stone "eyes" placed in the springboard notches by playful walkers. For easier sawing above the base of a tree to be felled, hand-loggers would cut a ladder-like set of notches, insert short planks fitted with a metal cleat on the end for security, then stand on the planks (spring-boards), often with a partner on the other end of the saw.

Within another 10 minutes, you begin to carefully descend an eroded section of trail to a pair of old, short gateposts. Straight ahead takes you to a road leading to a water tower, but your route turns immediately right then left over a series of bridges, crossing and recrossing a small creek in quick succession. You are now within unannounced Ballantree Park. Stay right at a grassy clearing to pick up a trail that runs southwards in the woods on the west side of Ballantree Road. Watch for views to Grouse Mountain and over the city and inner harbour.

You'll soon exit onto the end of Kildonan Road; a short walk along this and Craigmohr Drive returns you to your starting point.

CAPILANO CANYON

Ambleside Park to dam return: 14.3 km (8.9 mi)

Loop, dam to dam: 3.6 km (2.2 mi)

Surface: packed, improved trail

High point: 160 m (525 ft)

Rating: easy to moderate

Allow: 5 hours

Allow: 1.5 hours

Elevation gain: 160 m (525 ft)

Season: all year

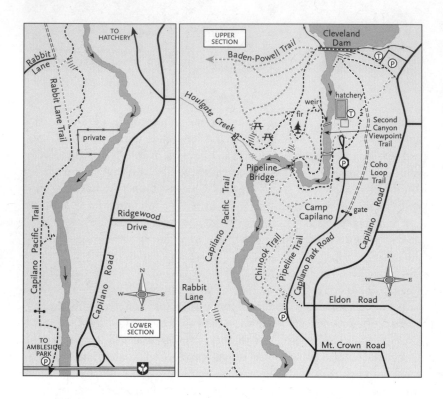

ACCESS

Transit: From Park Royal South, walk to the foot of Taylor Way; from Cleveland Dam, check transit on Nancy Greene Way at www.translink.ca.

Vehicle: From Marine Drive in West Vancouver, go south on 13th Street to Ambleside Park.

Car GPS entry: Marine Drive & 13th Street

Trailhead (Ambleside): 49° 19.354′ N, 123° 8.807′ W

For Cleveland Dam, turn west (signed) off Capilano Road at Nancy Greene Way.

Car GPS entry: Capilano Road & Nancy Greene Way (North Vancouver District)

Trailhead: 49° 21.592′ N, 123° 6.620′ W

THE SCENIC CAPILANO River valley with its deep canyons, lying between West and North Vancouver, provides an opportunity to walk from the oceanside Ambleside beaches upriver to the Cleveland Dam and Capilano Lake. Alternatively, you could customize your own route on trails near the dam, accessing this area from North Vancouver.

From Ambleside, head east along the seawall, pass the dogs' off-leash beach, swing north to follow the Capilano Pacific Trail on the river's west bank, then, after crossing Brothers Creek at its mouth, you approach the Woodcroft Residential complex. Now, go left and uphill to meet and turn right on Keith Road until you pass under Highway 1/99 (an alternative starting point) and through a gate onto an old logging railway grade. Just beyond the private Capilano Suspension Bridge grounds, turn right into the forest of majestic trees to pause at a platform with a treed canyon view. Some 10 minutes after crossing Houlgate Creek, at a clearing with a bench and junctions, stay with the Capilano Pacific Trail to the dam. The Cleveland Dam and Capilano Lake, constructed in 1954 as a reservoir for Vancouver, are proudly guarded by The Lions, prominent twin peaks to the northwest.

Now, to take in the highlights of the canyon from this popular picnic site, descend the road-width path near the toilets to a mid-height view of the dam's powerful cascade. Below this is the hatchery, where you join the Coho Loop Trail with its popular fishing spots. Stay left at the bridge with its viewing bays, check the Cable Pool viewing platform and continue on the trail that undulates well above the river, bending round a dogleg canyon then over the canyon on Pipeline Bridge. Keep close to the river on the Coho Trail until it (but not you) crosses the bridge you met earlier. Continue straight ahead, now on the Second Canyon Viewpoint Trail, to its misty destination. Next, retrace your steps to the first junction on your right, the Giant Fir Trail, which leads past a pair of very large Douglas-fir trees and then to Grandpa Capilano, a 61 m (200 ft) giant, which, for lack of its true top, would once have been even taller. Your trail now ascends to meet the Capilano Pacific Trail, where you turn left to return to Ambleside or right to return to the dam.

BOWSER TRAIL PLUS

Return: 7.9 km (4.9 mi)   **Allow:** 3 hours   **Surface:** paved, improved trail

Rating: easy to moderate (steps)   **Season:** all year

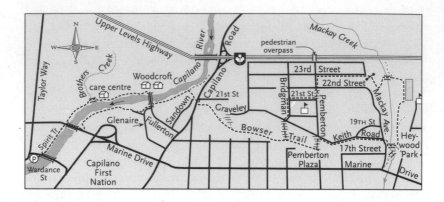

ACCESS

Transit: A variety of buses to Park Royal and other points along the route

Vehicle: Make your way to Park Royal South Mall in West Vancouver; go to the bottom of Taylor Way and park in the southeast corner. You may also find curbside parking along the route.

Car GPS entry: Taylor Way & Marine Drive (West Vancouver)

Trailhead: 49° 19.471′ N, 123° 8.063′ W

BOWSER TRAIL ITSELF, the namesake of this walk, is only a 15-minute stretch; but tagging on a stroll along the Capilano River to the west and a vigorous walk through Mackay Creek Park to the east makes for a very worthwhile outing.

Begin your walk on the Spirit Trail near the Capilano River. (This multiuse trail will eventually connect Deep Cove and Horseshoe Bay.) Heading east, pass under two roads, the second of which is Marine Drive. Here, you double back and up onto the sidewalk, cross the bridge, follow the first path left down to a lawn, then look for a trail into the woods on the riverbank. About 5 minutes later, head along the north side of playing fields and a parking lot, step over the barrier at Glenaire Drive, then go left at Fullerton

Flower beds beside the Capilano River.

Avenue to Woodcroft Bridge. Without crossing the bridge, find the track that drops to the riverbank behind shrubbery at its southeast corner. Just beyond the last house on this beautified path, a track leads right amongst young conifers to Capilano Road and a pedestrian crossing at West 21st Street. Bowser Trail lies a few paces south, a pleasant surprise close to Marine Drive. The official trail ends behind a shopping centre at Pemberton Avenue, but you may continue by ascending the many flights of wooden steps to tiny Ashdown Park, with its peek-a-boo view. Now go right on Keith Road, past West 19th Street, to reach Mackay Avenue and a track into Heywood Park across the road. Once in the park, descend to cross Mackay Creek, then turn immediately upstream on a rough track along the ravine. Keep to the left and creekside at a fork that terminates with a set of steps leading to a pair of sports fields.

At the north end of the fields, descend to a bridge over Mackay Creek, cross it, then climb out of the ravine; turn right onto a path at the edge of the trees and follow this to its end, emerging at a little playing field. Now on quiet residential streets, work your way west on West 23rd Street, south on Pemberton Avenue and up a few steps, west on West 21st Street, then south on Bridgman Avenue to cross Keith Road. Now you return to Bowser Trail by descending more than 200 steps.

Retrace your steps as far as Fullerton Avenue, but this time cross the bridge, turn downstream on the Woodcroft side and follow the Capilano River's west bank across the mouth of Brothers Creek and under Marine Drive to arrive back at the beginning.

BADEN-POWELL TRAIL (GROUSE MOUNTAIN)

Return: 4.7 km (2.9 mi)

Surface: rough trail, roadbed

High point: 500 m (1640 ft)

Rating: challenging

Allow: 2 hours

Elevation gain: 205 m (670 ft)

Season: April to November

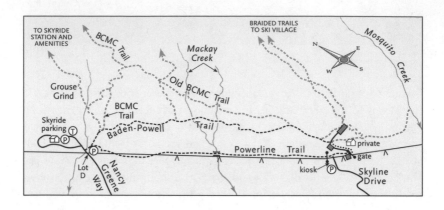

ACCESS

Transit: various to Grouse Mountain Skyride

Vehicle: From Highway 1/99 (the Upper Levels Highway), take Exit 14 (Capilano Drive) and head north to its end to make your way to the Grouse Mountain Skyride area at the top of Nancy Greene Way. Park in Lot D to the right.

Car GPS entry: Capilano Road & Nancy Greene Way (North Vancouver District)

Trailhead: 49° 21.866′ N, 123° 5.443′ W

THE BEST VIEWS in this circuit lie to the west, where Hollyburn Mountain, Mount Strachan and The Lions dominate the horizon; these are most advantageously seen while walking west along B.C. Hydro's power line right-of-way. This circuit, therefore, travels east on the Baden-Powell Trail from the Grouse Mountain Skyride area to Skyline Drive, then loops back under the power line.

Lot D is a no-charge lot where parking may be difficult, as it is also the beginning of the extremely popular Grouse Grind. The shared trailhead for

This deteriorating cedar is still useful to wildlife.

the Baden-Powell (B-P) and Grouse Grind trails at the northwest corner of Lot D can hardly be missed. There is a stretching area with bottled-water vending machines, large advisory signs and a gated fence that is locked after hours and in the winter. Just beyond the gate, a large sign directs Grouse Grinders to the left (for a near-vertical climb to facilities more than 800 m above) and B-P trail hikers to the right. Within 250 m, you will pass—and ignore—two consecutive junctions, the first related to the Grind and the second, the BCMC Trail. Stay on the B-P Trail, with its distinctive orange fleur-de-lys markers, as it climbs steadily and unrelentingly over rough, rooty terrain for 25 to 30 minutes, before reaching the junction with the old BCMC cabin site and Larsen Trail. (The British Columbia Mountaineering Club based their hiking, skiing and social activities at the cabin from 1910 to 1966. No visible traces remain.)

Now the trail drops, rises and drops again to cross the two branches of Mackay Creek. Landslides and rushing waters have washed away the bridges, so particular care is required when crossing, especially when wet. Carry on, gradually descending through open understorey and past large burned-out snags to the next significant fork, where you keep right (left goes to Mosquito Creek), emerging in a few minutes at a bend on Skyline Drive. Walk down the road to a gate, beyond which is an information kiosk and very limited parking (should you wish to start from here). Pass the next gate onto a gravel track, which you follow for about 30 minutes along the power line right-of-way, enjoying the views where they are not obstructed by the ever-growing vegetation as you complete your circuit.

MOSQUITO CREEK

Return: 8 km (5 mi)   **Allow:** 2.5 hours

Surface: packed, paved   **Elevation gain:** 210 m (690 ft)   **High point:** 240 m (787 ft)

Rating: easy   **Season:** all year

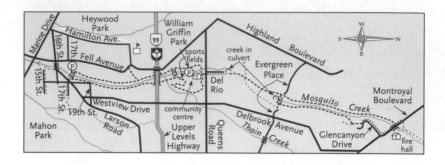

ACCESS

Transit: various along Marine Drive to Fell Avenue; Route #232 along Queens Road West

Vehicle: From Marine Drive in North Vancouver, turn north onto Fell Avenue and park near 17th Street.

Car GPS entry: Marine Drive & Fell Avenue

Trailhead: 49° 19.456′ N, 123° 5.613′ W

NUMEROUS CREEKS RUN down the slopes of the North Shore mountains, and their ravines provide pleasant outings in a modified, natural setting. Mosquito Creek has been altered to protect properties from flood damage, and now the wide, hard-surfaced path beside the rushing waters is an inviting destination.

From the trailhead on 17th Street, stay on the west side of Mosquito Creek to head upstream. Within a minute or two, you'll notice a side trail passing through a fence and across a small watercourse on your left. You may follow this diversion over boardwalks and on a narrow footpath that wanders through a small eco-sensitive wetland. Since the mid-1990s, this area has been improved to restore habitat for spawning salmon and other wetland flora and fauna. (Please remember that lively dogs can do damage

Rapids on Mosquito Creek.

that we may not readily observe.) Back on the relatively level multi-purpose path, you continue, then pass under the Upper Levels Highway, where you begin rising to William Griffin Park and Community Recreation Centre (and alternative parking) on Queens Road. Look for the row of cut stones cleaved by growing trees, a dynamic art sculpture that changes slowly over time through natural forces. For a short outing, this is a convenient place to turn back.

Before continuing upstream, note the creek falling over a short drop behind an enclosed area. This is where the water exits from its journey through a pipeline, begun approximately 1 km (0.6 mi) above. Now, cross Queens Road to Del Rio Drive, opposite the William Griffin Park sign, and proceed to its end, where the trail resumes. Initially, you travel through a thinly treed area, overgrown with ivy, to a paved crosspath and a bridge on your right at Evergreen Place. Below the bridge is the pipeline intake that carries the creek to where you saw it emerge earlier. Without crossing the bridge, you continue through a surprisingly wide, landscaped valley for about 15 minutes to the fire-charred substructure of the bridge on Montroyal Boulevard. This is your turnaround point, as the deteriorating trail continuing upstream has sloughed and is now closed.

To vary your downstream return with a "woodsy" experience, climb the steps to Montroyal Boulevard, cross to the east side, then go right on Glencanyon Drive to its end. Enter the woods on the right-hand trail to descend on a rough track, popular with dog walkers, until you arrive at the path from Evergreen Place, where you cross the footbridge to join your outward route.

MAHON PARK

Return: 5 km (3.1 mi) **Allow:** 1.5 hours

Surface: trail **Rating:** easy to moderate **Season:** all year

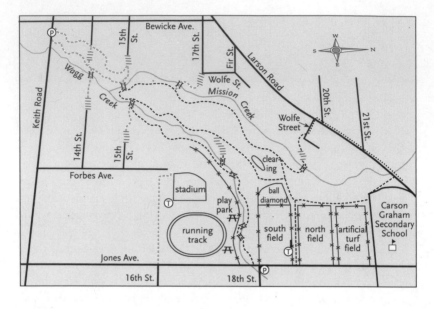

ACCESS

Transit: Route #240 and #255 on Keith Road

Vehicle: Make your way to Jones Avenue and West 18th Street. Park in the lot on the northeast corner. Street parking is available elsewhere.

Car GPS entry: Jones Avenue & West 18th Street

Trailhead: 49°19.519′ N, 123°4.896′ W

KNOWN AS THE "jewel of the city," this little park, named for Edward Mahon, a pioneering visionary of conservation, offers a breath of nature. Large trees and two pretty streams in a ravine mute the surrounding city noise. Numerous bridges sport fragments of running verse, such as "step into a forest" and "a creek flows at your feet."

On foot, cross Jones Avenue to the trailhead opposite the parking lot, then pause at the information kiosk to learn about the cultural and natural

A peaceful forest stream.

history of the area. As you enter the forest, descending a well-made trail against a steep slope, you might consider the contrast of this natural environment with that on the playing fields above. As you cross the bridges back and forth over Wagg Creek, avoid the one leading west (right) up a long flight of stairs; instead, continue downstream on the creek's left bank and cross on the bridge below West 15th Street. Going left over another bridge leads you quickly to the Keith Road exit, but your route turns hard right onto a trail that climbs gently out of the ravine to the crest of the ridge between Wagg and Mission Creeks. Watch the left-side slope for the cedar tree with a rock amongst its roots. Do you think of a mother bird hugging its egg? Pass a descending set of stairs—the flight mentioned earlier—and you soon arrive at a flat clearing. Playing fields are a short distance beyond. Keeping the ball diamond on your right, walk between the south and north fields and exit onto Jones Avenue, not far from your vehicle.

It's hard to do two loops on three trails without repeating one of the legs, so this might be a good time to rest by the sports track. If you choose to continue, you could retrace either your descending or ascending track to arrive back at the trail junction below West 15th Street. Now, with Mission Creek at your left and ignoring a bridge, follow the trail uphill for 10 minutes to a fork: right leads to the familiar fields and back to your starting point, left to Wolfe Street via a stairway beside an enormous stump. Choosing the latter path up to Wolfe Street, go left to Larson Road, turn right, walk 250 m to a substantial path leading to Carson Graham School, follow the service/bike road to a gate, then turn right onto a narrow path west of the playing field. This goes between the north and south fields and so back to your vehicle.

LYNN HEADWATERS LOOP

Lynn Loop: 5.2 km (3.2 mi) **Allow:** 1.5 hours

Debris Chute return: 9 km (5.6 mi) **Allow:** 3 hours

Surface: road, unimproved trail **Elevation gain:** 200 m (655 ft)

High point: 380 m (1245 ft)

Rating: easy to moderate **Season:** most of the year

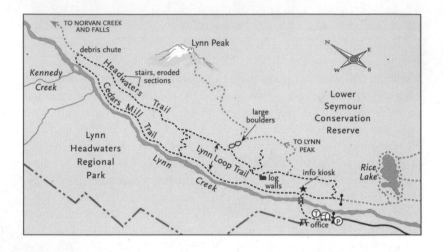

ACCESS

Transit: Route #228 to Lynn Valley Road at Dempsey Road adds 3 km (1.9 mi) return to your walk

Vehicle: From Highway 1/99 (Upper Levels Highway), take Exit 19 and travel north on Lynn Valley Road to a park gate (note the hours). Follow the narrow road to the last parking lot.

Car GPS entry: Lynn Valley Road & Dempsey Road (North Vancouver District)

Trailhead: 49° 21.578′ N, 123° 1.680′ W

YOU MAY CUSTOMIZE your own outing here at Lynn Headwaters Regional Park: an easy return stroll along Lynn Creek on the Loop and Cedars Mill Trails to a wide clearing opposite Kennedy Creek Valley; a moderate workout on a rough forest trail with noticeable elevation changes to the same clearing; or a shorter loop combining the two. Note that this is a popular destination, and, on a busy day, you may have to park up to 1 km (0.6 mi) from the trailhead.

From the picnic area, cross Lynn Creek Bridge to an information kiosk where the easy upstream walk begins to the left. To follow the more demanding route, go right for some 5 minutes to the signed Lynn Loop trailhead heading left into the trees. Along the way are moss-covered trees and tangles of blowdowns, trees toppled in strong windstorms. Within 15 minutes, you pass the trailhead to Lynn Peak on your right then, a little later, a possible (signed) side trip up a short, steep track that rises 70 m (230 ft) to a rocky outcrop with a broken view across Burrard Inlet. Still later, another side path to the right takes you to a pair of huge boulders, or erratics, deposited well over 10,000 years ago by a retreating glacier. Next comes a point of decision: you may complete Lynn Loop by dropping steeply—note the pair of enormous cedar stumps flanking a staircase—to the Lynn Creek Trail, where you turn left downstream, or you may continue north another 2 km (1.2 mi).

If you continue, now on the Headwaters Trail, you gradually start descending, occasionally on a staircase. The trail crosses small watercourses and one or two debris torrents, potentially dangerous during high runoff. A largish creek, which you cross on stepping stones, marks your return junction where you go left. (Headwaters Trail continues a further 2.3 km/1.4 mi north to Norvan Falls.) Descend to a large clearing with a superb view to the wild country north of Grouse Mountain; access to Lynn Creek, where you might want to dawdle; and the head of the riverside Cedars Mill Trail, your return route.

Travelling downstream, you pass the long-vanished Cedars Mill, where only a few pieces of rusted machinery remain, the T-junction with the Lynn Loop connector, and wire coils, remnants of wood-stave pipes that once carried water to North Vancouver. And so back to your vehicle.

Reluctant to leave? You could add the Rice Lake loop (Walk 28), which begins 1.5 km (0.9 mi) along the road from the Lynn Creek Bridge.

RICE LAKE

LSCR lake circuit: 3 km (1.9 mi)   **Allow:** 1.5 hours

Including Lynn Creek circuit: 6 km (3.7 mi)   **Allow:** 2 hours

Surface: packed trails   **Rating:** easy   **Season:** all year

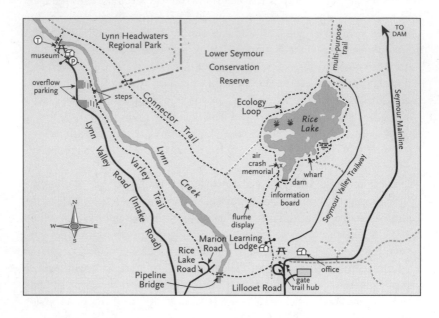

ACCESS

Transit: LSCR and Lynn Valley: Route #228 Lynn Valley Road at Dempsey Road, walk 150 m north to Rice Lake Road, cross the bridge at its end and follow a gravel road to the information kiosks.

Vehicle to LSCR: From Highway 1/99 (Upper Levels Highway), take Exit 22A (Capilano College/Lillooet Road) and drive 5 km (3.1 mi) north on Lillooet Road to park.

Car GPS entry: Lillooet Road & Monashee Drive (North Vancouver District)

Trailhead (Learning Lodge): 49° 21.096′ N, 123° 0.978′ W

Vehicle: To begin in Lynn Valley, drive to the north end of Lynn Valley Road and proceed through a gate to a parking lot; all lots link to Varley Trail. Note that all gates are closed at night.

Car GPS entry: Lynn Valley Road & Dempsey Road (North Vancouver District)

Trailhead (Varley): 49° 21.561′ N, 123° 1.677′ W

Moments of reflection at lakeside.

RICE LAKE IS a "well-groomed" destination, with its wide paths and stops of interest: a flume and shinglebolt display, a plane-crash memorial and a large, wide fishing wharf. This description begins from the Learning Lodge at the Lower Seymour Conservation Reserve (LSCR) with the walk around Rice Lake, then describes an optional stroll to nearby Lynn Creek.

Your trail begins at the Learning Lodge, northwest from the parking lot, past a gatehouse and north from the information kiosks. From the Learning Lodge, bear left on a wide, gravel path that soon branches right to Rice Lake. Immediately on your left is a display about local logging activities more than a century ago and about the lake's more recent role as a reservoir. Next, the memorial to a 1947 plane crash will catch your attention before you come to the unannounced, short Forest Ecology Loop Trail. Continue around the lake, ignoring a broad multi-purpose trail leading to the north, until you arrive at the Douglas Mowat Memorial Special Fisheries Wharf. Rice Lake is stocked regularly with rainbow trout for local anglers (licence required).

Back on the main trail, turn left to return to your starting point or right to continue an additional 1.5 km (0.9 mi) to the bridge over Lynn Creek and the decrepit water intake dam at Lynn Headwaters Regional Park (see also Walk 27). To complete the circuit, proceed to the southeast end of the upper parking lot to read about Frederick Varley, the Group of Seven artist who lived and painted in the area, then join the trail named for him. Note that staircases along the route lead to parking lots above. Twenty minutes later, you emerge onto Marion Road and immediately meet Pipeline Bridge over Lynn Creek, the upper reaches of Lynn Canyon. Five minutes more, up the road with the unusual street lamps, and you're back at your vehicle.

TWO-CANYON LOOP

Short circuit: 4.8 km (3 mi)

Long circuit: 8 km (5 mi)

Surface: packed, rough

Rating: moderate to challenging

Allow: 1.5 hours

Allow: 3 hours

Elevation gain: 140 m (460 ft)

Season: most of the year

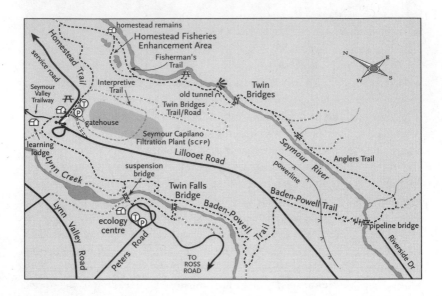

ACCESS

Transit: Route #229 to Peters Road at Duval Road; walk east on Peters Road to the Lynn Canyon Ecology Centre to join the route.

Vehicle: From Highway 1/99 (Upper Levels Highway), take Exit 22A (Lillooet Road), turn north at the first light onto Lillooet Road, continue to a gate, then drive 3 km (1.9 mi) to the Lower Seymour Conservation Reserve parking lot.

Car GPS entry: Lillooet Road & Monashee Drive (North Vancouver District)

Trailhead: 49° 21.026′ N, 123° 0.832′ W

THIS LOOP TAKES you past rocky shores, roaring waterfalls and moss-covered artifacts of human activity in two adjacent watercourses, Lynn Creek and Seymour River. Conservation-minded visionaries created Lynn Creek Park in 1911. The Seymour River's Lower Seymour Conservation

Reserve (LSCR) is managed for water storage and delivery infrastructure and to provide educational and recreational opportunities. (Gates are closed at night.)

Begin your outing at the information kiosk at the northwest corner of the parking lot, then find your trail at the lot's northeast corner, between works-yard fences. It soon crosses a service road, then enters open forest on the wide Twin Bridges Trail. The first junction, left, leads you to Homestead Trail, which descends gently to the Seymour River, where you turn right onto the Fisherman's Trail (left connects with Walk 30). Fern-festooned gate frames and water's-edge foundations evoke imagined historical activities. Present-day activities on your right may draw you through the Fisheries Enhancement Area, after which you may take a side trip along a substantial trail leading to the river. Look for the remains of a stone fireplace hidden in the growth next to a huge mossy stump. Next, watch for a tunnel on the right, cut for the passage of a waterline, and soon thereafter you reach the bridge across Seymour River, a replacement for the original twin bridges—note the foundation of one with a water gauge. For the shorter outing, turn right without crossing the bridge to return to your vehicle via the Twin Bridges Road.

Alternatively, continue downstream along the old water-main road, which, in places, is cut into the canyon walls. At a junction, angle sharp right, descend beside the old iron pipe and cross the bridge over water roaring below. The trail now rises 110 m (360 ft) up stairs (just over 100) and switchbacks to the power line clearing. Continue west on the Baden-Powell Trail, cross Lillooet Road and stay with the Baden-Powell Trail through open forest until, just above Lynn Creek, you turn right to descend to the valley floor. Next, follow boardwalks, rough trails and seemingly endless stairs back up to Twin Falls Bridge. From here, the trails on either side of the river each lead to the popular Lynn Canyon suspension bridge. The ecology centre and amenities lie on the west side, an alternative starting point.

The eastside trail heads upstream to arrive, within 20 minutes, at the Learning Lodge grounds and your parking lot beyond the gatehouse.

FISHERMAN'S TRAIL

Return: 13 km (8 mi)   **Allow:** 4 hours

Surface: trails, paved road   **Rating:** easy   **Season:** most of the year

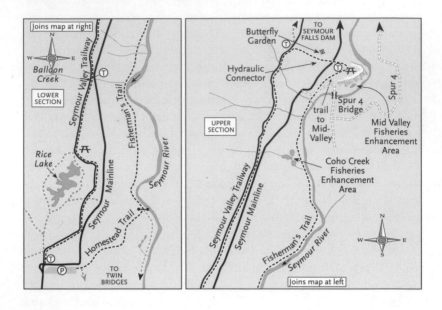

ACCESS

Transit: Route #228 to Lynn Valley Road and Dempsey Road; walk north to follow Rice Lake Road to a bridge, cross this and walk to the Lower Seymour Conservation Reserve parking lot, about 800 m.

Vehicle: From Highway 1/99 (Upper Levels Highway), take Exit 22A (Lillooet Road), turn north at the first light onto Lillooet Road, continue to a gate (closed at night), then drive 3 km (1.9 mi) to the parking lot.

Car GPS entry: Lillooet Road & Monashee Drive (North Vancouver District)

Trailhead: 49° 21.026′ N, 123° 0.832′ W

THIS TRAIL, ONE of many in the Lower Seymour Conservation Reserve (LSCR), provides a pleasant walk through forest and along the riverbank, with views of Mount Seymour and its neighbours from an unusual perspective. It finishes on a purpose-built, paved recreational road.

Area information is available at a kiosk at the northwest corner of the parking lot and at the gatehouse just beyond. Your trail begins at the northeast corner, between works-yard fences. Initially, you follow a narrow passage beside a high fence to a service road, which you cross to enter open forest on the wide Twin Bridges Trail. A moment later, go left on the Homestead Trail and descend gently about 100 m to meet the Fisherman's Trail, where you turn upriver at a wooden gate (downriver leads to Walk 29). The well-made path rolls along through maturing second-growth conifers hiding large moss-covered stumps; from time to time it wanders beside the riverbank. In places, lengths of boardwalk have been installed to protect the fragile, boggy environment. Bridges facilitate crossing the several streams, some of which become quite swollen during heavy rains, even causing small mudslides from the slopes above. One such unmarked stream drains the hidden Coho Creek Fisheries Enhancement Area, one of several in the LSCR. After about 75 minutes, you arrive at a junction with the service road. Cross this to begin a steady ascent to the mid-valley destinations. Within 10 minutes, and after rounding a bend on a gravel road, a picnic and viewing area greets you—a good spot to study both mountain and valley.

To return, you may retrace your steps or complete your circuit on a route of quite a different character: the Seymour Valley Trailway, a multi-use, paved recreational road that is popular with cyclists and rollerbladers. To reach the trailway, take the Hydraulic Connector Trail from the northeast corner of the picnic area. A short diversion to the Butterfly Garden, a one-time RCMP bomb disposal site, is worth a look in season.

Along the 5.5 km (3.4 mi) of the trailway that make up your return journey are picnic tables, toilets and signed stops of interest, one of which was the site of an experimental balloon-logging operation in 1967. Another signed stop, near a side trail leading to Rice Lake (Walk 28), provides information about homesteading in the area. Finally, you arrive at the Learning Lodge and other facilities, including the gatehouse. The parking lot, and the end of your journey, is just a few paces beyond.

MAPLEWOOD FLATS

Return: 3.3 km (2 mi) **Allow:** 1 hour

Surface: packed **Rating:** easy **Season:** all year

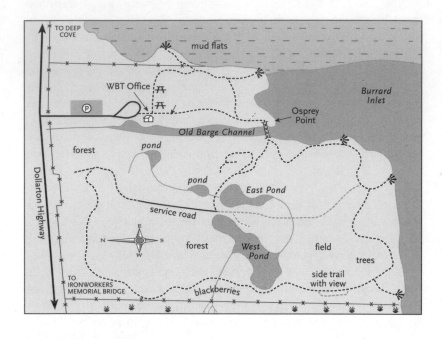

ACCESS

Transit: Route #212 or #C15 to the 2500-block of Dollarton Highway

Vehicle: Maplewood Flats is located about 2 km (1.2 mi) east of the Ironworkers Memorial Bridge. Drive along the Dollarton Highway and park either within the gates (note the hours) or on the street outside.

Car GPS entry: 2645 Dollarton Highway (North Vancouver District)

Trailhead: 49° 18.429′ N, 123° 0.213′ W

THIS LITTLE WILDERNESS retreat, hidden amongst industrial and urban activities on North Vancouver's bustling waterfront, provides an easily accessible opportunity to enjoy birdsong and wildlife viewing throughout the year. Well over 200 bird species have been sighted, as well as mammals small and large. Sightings are noted on a board outside the Wild Bird Trust (WBT) of British Columbia office. The conservation area is operated by the WBT on land that was once an industrial site, until public interest groups initiated actions to restore the degraded land to a natural state, including a meadow, ponds, woods and shoreline, and preserve a remnant of the once-common waterfront wetland ecosystem on the north shore of Burrard Inlet. The land is now leased to Environment Canada, whose Pacific Environmental Science Centre occupies an area at the sanctuary's entrance.

Start your walk at the WBT office, then head south towards Burrard Inlet and Osprey Point. You may be lucky enough to spot an osprey, whose population has been slowly growing since the conservation area was established. Note the breeding boxes for purple martins on the old pilings, once used for mooring. Proceed to the bridge over the Old Barge Channel, pause to watch the activities below, then at the fork continue left, the more interesting direction. The trail meanders through woods, approaches the shoreline, where occasional benches are placed at viewpoints, pauses at a salt marsh backdropped by industrial activity, then reaches a pond fringed with water-loving plants where several waterfowl are in residence.

Beyond the pond, you enter an area of forest, where the ubiquitous wild blackberry is overrunning flowering shrubs and ferns. (The berries are delicious in season, if you can pluck them from amongst the thorns.) After a small piece of paved service road, you swing to the left on a trail passing between two ponds and continuing to yet another left fork. This leads to a miniature summit, where once-fine views are now obstructed by towering cottonwood trees. Descend and walk left to recross the bridge over the Old Barge Channel. The eastern part of the conservation area is quite small, with paths leading to viewpoints, where you may observe the intertidal marshes and the vast mud flats that stretch out across the bay at low tide. Finally, the path returns you to the WBT office, where there are a few picnic tables.

The WBT sponsors free guided walks and other activities. For more information, call 604-924-2581 (limited hours) or visit the website: www.wildbirdtrust.org.

BRIDLE PATH

Return: 11.5 km (7.1 mi)   **Allow:** 4.5 hours

Surface: rough, packed   **Elevation gain:** 125 m (410 ft)   **High point:** 260 m (850 ft)

Rating: moderate   **Season:** most of the year

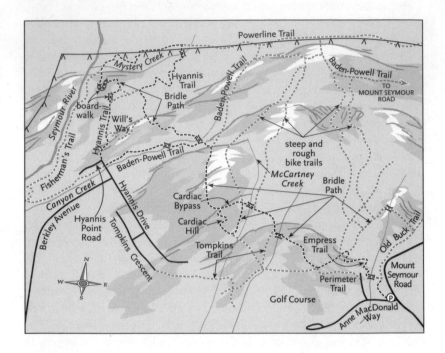

ACCESS

Transit: Route #C15 to Indian River Drive at Mt. Seymour Road; walk 300 m north to Anne MacDonald Way.

Vehicle: From Mt. Seymour Parkway, turn north onto Mt. Seymour Road, drive 850 m to Anne MacDonald Way and park in the lot near the junction.

Car GPS entry: Mt. Seymour Parkway & Mt. Seymour Road (North Vancouver District)

Trailhead: 49° 19.384′ N, 122° 58.325′ W

THE BRIDLE PATH, created on the remnants of logging tracks in the days when horse riding was fairly popular, is today a busy multi-use trail, largely maintained by mountain bikers. Be prepared to step aside for bikers and runners.

Begin your walk by crossing a footbridge near an information kiosk then, about 130 m along, turn left onto the signed Empress Bypass Trail. Ignoring trails to the right, ascend this well-groomed bike path for 800 m to meet the wide Bridle Path, where you turn left. As you travel, watch for orange markers on trees, some with text and directional arrows. Just beyond a bridge, a side trail, which you do not take, leads to Tompkins Crescent. Soon you cross McCartney Creek Bridge, then arrive at a four-way junction. To initiate a 500 m semi-loop, go downhill on Bridle Path, then, on meeting another trail, turn sharp right on Cardiac Hill, which rises to meet Cardiac Bypass, your homebound shortcut. Next, at a well-signed junction, go left where the Baden-Powell and Bridle Path trails overlap for 70 m, then right onto Bridle Path.

Over the next 1 km (0.6 mi), you descend slightly to where Bridle Path goes right to cross Canyon Creek, cross boardwalks over bog, navigate through a tangle of signed trails, pass Will's Way and eventually arrive at Hyannis Trail. Turn right here and continue about 500 m to cross Mystery Creek Bridge, then ascend to Powerline Trail. Now, go left (west) for about 5 minutes to a gated trail by a pylon, where you go left and down the side of the shady Mystery Creek ravine to Fisherman's Trail, beside the Seymour River.

Now you are at your low point, but not for long. Go left to recross Mystery Creek (right leads to Walk 29), then, 100 m along, turn left onto Bridle Path, to ascend to the south rim of Mystery Creek ravine. From the rim, the trail levels in a stretch of old forest. Going right at the next T-junction, then left over a boardwalk, brings you back onto Hyannis Trail and soon thereafter to the Hyannis Point trailhead. A short walk on Hyannis Drive takes you to the Baden-Powell trailhead on the left. Here, you follow an aging trail, closely watching for Baden-Powell Trail signs at forks, until you regain the point where Bridle Path heads right.

Returning, you may follow the Cardiac Bypass shortcut, thus completing that loop and, from here, arrive back at the start within 30 minutes.

HISTORIC MUSHROOM LOOP

Return: 6.4 km (4 mi)   **Allow:** 2.5 hours

Surface: rough, packed, road

Elevation gain: 275 m (900 ft)   **High point:** 570 m (1870 ft)

Rating: moderate   **Season:** May to early November

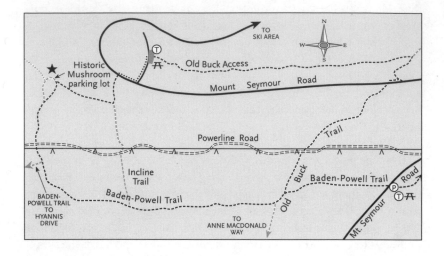

ACCESS

Vehicle: From Mt. Seymour Parkway in North Vancouver, go north on Mt. Seymour Road. About 2.5 km (1.6 mi) from the entrance to Mt. Seymour Park, park at a small lot opposite the Baden-Powell trailhead.

Car GPS entry: Mt. Seymour Parkway & Mt. Seymour Road (North Vancouver District)

Trailhead: 49° 20.300′ N, 122° 57.385′ W

DURING THE 1930S AND 1940S, the "mushroom," a large roofed-over stump at the end of a driveable road with a parking area, served as a rendez-vous point, message board and trailhead for mountain enthusiasts. Today, a somewhat mouldy information board with historic photos helps you imag-ine those days. Of further interest is the history of the Baden-Powell Trail, which stretches 48 km (30 mi) across the North Shore mountains, from Horseshoe Bay to Deep Cove. The Boy Scouts and Girl Guides of B.C. built it in 1971 to celebrate British Columbia's centenary.

The historic Mushroom Lot information board.

From the parking lot, cross Mt. Seymour Road and enter the forest westbound. The trail rises gently to reach, within a few minutes, an intersection with the Old Buck Trail. Here, drop left a few paces to regain the Baden-Powell Trail by going right, over a bridge. Carry on for 20 to 30 minutes, ignoring any side branches that are used by mountain bikers, until the Baden-Powell Trail veers sharp left, but your route continues straight ahead. Shortly thereafter, cross the power line cut, and before long you reach the historic mushroom site. Today, only remnants of the "mushroom stump" remain and nothing of the former parking lot.

Continue onward until you reach another junction, where you turn left to ascend a steepish slope over a number of horizontal logs, well sculpted by water and use, set into the trail. In a few minutes, you reach the road, cross it and head downhill a few paces to the entrance to the Vancouver Picnic Area. Once part of the original road up Mount Seymour, this is a comfortable place to relax and enjoy the amenities before continuing.

The next part of your route is the most pleasant, as it descends gently to the junction with the Old Buck Trail. Turn right onto this former logging road, which leads to the highway; cross and head uphill to regain the trail. As you cross the power line, you may glimpse the tops of Buntzen and Eagle Ridges, the only view available on this walk. Re-entering the forest, you continue to descend. Watch for the sharp turn left onto your original trail, which will take you back to your starting point. (All junctions are well signed.)

For a walk taking another hour or so, you may start lower on the mountain, going left off Mt. Seymour Road onto Anne MacDonald Way, then immediately right into a parking lot at the Old Buck trailhead. From here, the Old Buck Trail rises 215 m in 2.3 km (1.4 mi) to meet the Baden-Powell Trail.

THREE CHOP/OLD BUCK LOOP

Return: 7.7 km (4.8 mi) **Allow:** 2.5 hours

Surface: rough trail **Elevation gain:** 545 m (1788 ft) **High point:** 764 m (2507 ft)

Rating: moderate to challenging **Season:** June to November

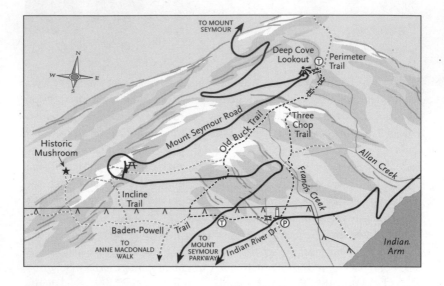

ACCESS

Vehicle: From Mt. Seymour Road at the Parkgate Shopping Centre, go north for 600 m then sharp right onto Indian River Drive. After 700 m, go left on Indian River Crescent, which soon becomes Indian River Drive. Just beyond the 2 km marker, park opposite a B.C. Hydro access road.

Car GPS entry: Mt. Seymour Parkway & Mt. Seymour road (North Vancouver District)

Trailhead: 49° 20.296′ N, 122° 56.820′ W

LOCATED ON THE lower slopes of Mount Seymour, this walk in the woods avoids the high-use areas of the provincial park and can be enjoyed while higher trails (Walks 35, 36 and 37) are still snowbound. The highlight is an expansive view from Deep Cove Lookout on Mt. Seymour Road.

Begin your walk to the right of the gate on the service road, climbing to arrive in short order at the power line right-of-way, where the trail lies

Bridge repair after a washout on Allan Creek.

directly in front of you. As you pass underneath the wires towards the forested slope ahead, keep left at a fork on a rough path and ascend steadily in fairly old second-growth trees, until you come to Francis Creek; this is easy to cross, with care, most of the year. After the creek crossing, the grade steepens and the trail is eroded, but eventually relief comes just as the forest cover becomes deciduous, with berry bushes and ferns crowding in on the trail. Then you work left to join the Old Buck Trail, some 2 km (1.2 mi) from the start.

Now turn right on the Old Buck Trail, a rehabilitated logging road, continuing on its gentler grade, with bridges and fine views of many little waterfalls along the way. The appearance of a large rockslide on your left signals the Mt. Seymour Road immediately above. At a junction, you turn left over a final bridge with a view both up- and downstream of the falling waters of Allan Creek. Soon you arrive at Deep Cove Lookout on Mt. Seymour Road, at first a seemingly anticlimatic destination. Walk around the perimeter, however, and there before you lies the wide sweep of the Fraser Valley and its delta, from Mount Baker to the southern Gulf Islands across the Strait of Georgia. Unfortunately, trees now obstruct the view of Deep Cove itself.

Returning from the lookout, take the Old Buck Trail, staying with it as it swings gradually west across the face of the mountain, bridging numerous streams. Ignoring all forks, continue directly down to Mt. Seymour Road, cross it, walk 50 m uphill to pick up the route again, keep going to the power line and cross that as well. Then continue down to the Baden-Powell Trail, going left when you reach it (right connects with Walk 33). Within 10 minutes, you'll cross Mt. Seymour Road again, and within another 20 minutes, descending an easy grade through attractive forest, you'll be back at your vehicle.

GOLDIE AND FLOWER LAKES

Two-lakes loop: 4 km (2.5 mi)   **Allow:** 1.5 hours

Surface: improved, mainly rough   **Elevation gain:** minimal   **High point:** 1020 m (3345 ft)

Rating: moderate   **Season:** June to October

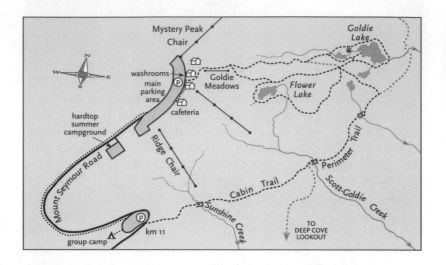

ACCESS

Vehicle: Travel along Mt. Seymour Parkway to Mt. Seymour Road at the Parkgate Shopping Centre; go north and drive to the top parking lot.

Car GPS entry: Mt. Seymour Parkway & Mt. Seymour road (North Vancouver District)

Trailhead: 49° 21.969′ N, 122° 56.872′ W

WOULD YOU LIKE a cool walk in the forest on a hot day? Goldie Lake makes an attractive destination, and you could include Flower Lake as well to extend your outing. Both Goldie and Flower are subalpine lakes with marshy shores that are slowly being invaded by surrounding plant life. They are situated near the ski runs in the popular Mt. Seymour Provincial Park.

The trail begins at a large signpost located behind the first-aid building, near the Magic Carpet tow in the Goldie Meadows beginners' ski area. Follow the signs to the wide, well-marked path through forest for 560 m to a junction, the right arm of which leads to Flower Lake (320 m), which

Measuring the upturned root ball on a fallen tree.

you can save for later. Continue on the main path about 200 m farther to another junction. Watch the signs carefully, because in this area there is a confusion of junctions and trails amongst the marshes and ponds that form the western side of Goldie Lake. Goldie Lake lies to your left, nestled in a shallow basin; you may make the 1 km (0.6 mi) loop of the lake in either direction. Note the variety of flowery plants and sedges that thrive in the marshes, beyond which the sometimes muddy trail lies close to the lake's edge. Note also that trees and shrubs are smaller here than lower on the mountain because of the harsher growing conditions.

At one of the trail crossings west of Goldie Lake, a signpost indicates the Perimeter/Flower Lake junction. The route to Flower Lake includes a stepping-stone creek crossing when water levels are high. The trail wanders through forest and eventually meets, at a signed junction, an optional return to the parking lot. However, you continue past the end of Flower Lake and back to the first Goldie-Flower junction, the one you noted early in your outing. From here, turn left and ascend the gentle slope back to your vehicle.

The Cabin/Perimeter Trail provides a somewhat strenuous challenge (and additional time), best approached from Mt. Seymour Road. Watch for a large parking lot on a hairpin turn at km 11; the route begins at the Old Cabin Trail across the road. Be aware that this 1.6 km (1 mi), sinuous trail requires careful attention to footing and occasional use of hands, especially in wet weather. It takes you to the Goldie Lake junction and the lake circuits. To return, either retrace your route or continue to the upper parking lot then walk beside Mt. Seymour Road for 1.5 km (0.9 mi) to your vehicle.

DOG MOUNTAIN AND DINKEY PEAK

Dog Mountain return: 5 km (3.1 mi)   **Allow:** 2 hours
Return via Dinkey Peak: 6 km (3.7 mi)   **Allow:** 2.5 hours
Surface: rough, packed trails
Rating: moderate   **Season:** June to October

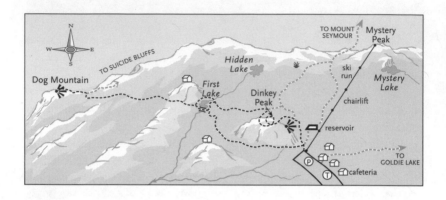

ACCESS

Vehicle: From Mt. Seymour Parkway, turn north onto Mt. Seymour Road at the Parkgate Village Shopping Centre. Drive to the top parking lot.

Car GPS entry: Mt. Seymour Parkway & Mt. Seymour Road (North Vancouver District)

Trailhead (kiosk): 49° 22.053′ N, 122° 56.950′ W

PANORAMIC VIEWS OF city, mountains and expanses of water are your reward at the end of this trail. Despite its name, Dog Mountain is actually just a bluff, reached with little elevation gain. Ease of access makes this a very popular outing, which, unfortunately, has resulted in deterioration of the trail bed. It is definitely an "eyes-on-the-ground" surface as you pick your way over deeply exposed roots and through ever-widening muddy patches.

Start your walk at the far end of the parking lot by the information kiosk and, keeping left, head uphill briefly, watching for a signpost directing you to First Lake and Dog Mountain. After some 20 minutes, you arrive at pond-size First Lake, set in a picturesque wooded basin overlooked by a

Dinkey Bluff overlooking the Mount Seymour parking lot.

search & rescue cabin perched on a bluff above. Crossing at the lake's outlet, note the trails that join from the right; these can provide a variation of your return route. Again, you travel through forest over a tangled trail, staying left at a lesser fork—be alert to stay right on your return—until you arrive very shortly at the rocky outcrops and bluffs. Here, you can see Mount Baker watching over the Fraser Valley, neighbouring North Shore mountains, the mountains of Vancouver Island to the west, the sprawl of Metro Vancouver below and the Seymour River Valley at your feet.

To return via Dinkey Peak, a bluff that overlooks the parking lot below and Mount Baker in the distance, watch for the signed fork to Dinkey Peak at First Lake. Follow the gently rising trail to yet another junction, this one providing the option of a brief walk, left, to join the Mount Seymour main trail (see Walk 37) or a longer detour, right, over Dinkey Peak. For the latter, continue over the first rocky knobs, which form the actual "peak," then descend on a trail until you are surprised by a sturdy staircase on your right leading onto a bluff and your viewpoint. When you are ready to move on, return to the trail below the staircase and continue downhill a short distance to the main trail, where you turn right and descend to your vehicle.

Should you wish to avoid Dog Mountain and only reach the Dinkey Peak viewpoint, proceed up the main trail from the parking lot for just over 500 m to a signpost pointing the way. Similarly, a few paces farther along the main trail takes you to another posted trailhead and access to First Lake.

MYSTERY LAKE AND PEAK

Return: 4.2 km (2.6 mi) **Allow:** 2 hours
Surface: rough trail **Elevation gain:** 200 m (655 ft) **High point:** 1220 m (4000 ft)
Rating: moderate **Season:** July to October

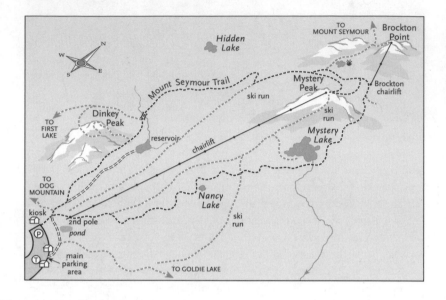

ACCESS

Vehicle: From Mt. Seymour Parkway, turn north onto Mt. Seymour Road at Parkgate Village Shopping Centre. Drive to the top parking lot.

Car GPS entry: Mt. Seymour Parkway & Mt. Seymour Road (North Vancouver District)

Trailhead (kiosk): 49° 22.053′ N, 122° 56.950′ W

MYSTERY LAKE, THOUGH close to the Mount Seymour ski slopes, rests in an appealing setting, with rocky places to sit and enjoy the peace of nature.

From the kiosk at the far end of the parking lot, head briefly up the main trail, then, just past the Mystery Peak chairlift terminal, at a signed junction, make your way towards the second chairlift pole, which stands just beyond a pond. Near this pole, a narrow trail goes into the trees and immediately starts rising. Your climb continues over rough ground and through

Mystery Lake after the first snowfall of the year.

the coniferous forest for about 15 minutes until you reach Nancy Lake, an attractive little body of water best viewed from the boardwalk on its uphill side.

A few minutes later, the trail crosses a wide ski run then re-enters the trees, where orange markers indicate the route. The trail, which also serves as a rather eroded creek bed during heavy rains and melting snow runoff, becomes stonier as it continues to rise for another 10 minutes or so. That's when you hear the sound of Mystery Creek, signalling that the lake is not far. The trees gradually thin, and your surroundings become more subalpine as you near your objective in its rocky basin.

After a break at the lake, you could retrace your steps, but the more pleasant way is to continue forward. Follow the track north on the lake's east side, rising slightly, dropping, then rising again to the foot of the Brockton Point chairlift and a signposted junction. From here, you can continue round to the main Mount Seymour Trail. If, however, you want to enjoy the expansive views from Mystery Peak, you walk about 100 m west, then go left to climb and circle around to the summit and the upper terminus of the Mystery Peak chairlift. When ready to descend, continue your circuit of the summit by going north on the Velvet ski run (signed), which swings around to meet the main Mount Seymour Trail, where you go left and down.

Some 240 m below the Mystery Lake junction on the main ski run, you arrive at another signpost, this one pointing to the Mount Seymour Main Trail. This original, well-used trail provides a more "woodsy" alternative to the wide ski-run swath for the remaining 1.2 km (0.7 mi) to the parking lot. En route, and not far from the parking lot, you pass the two ends of the Dinkey Peak Loop Trail (Walk 36), which may entice you to a final view before arriving back at your vehicle.

BADEN-POWELL TRAIL (DEEP COVE)

Return from Panorama Park: 5.3 km (3.3 mi)　　**Allow:** 2.5 hours

Surface: rough　　**Elevation gain:** 200 m (655 ft)　　**High point:** 225 m (740 ft)

Rating: moderate　　**Season:** all year

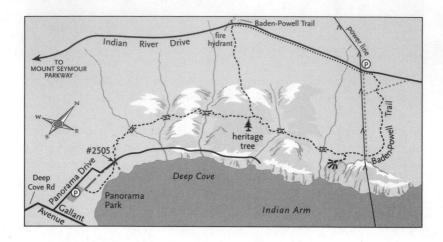

ACCESS

Transit: Routes #211, 212, C15 to Deep Cove

Vehicle: Make your way to Deep Cove via Dollarton Highway or Mt. Seymour Parkway and, off Deep Cove Road, to Panorama Park on the left near the water. Parking will be tight on a nice day, but there are a variety of options nearby.

Car GPS entry: Mt. Seymour Parkway & Dollarton Highway (North Vancouver District)

Trailhead: 49° 19.781′ N, 122° 56.978′ W

A LANDMARK BLUFF overlooking Deep Cove and visible from the town-site's Panorama Park is the destination of most trail users, but it is possible to continue farther on the Baden-Powell Trail to make a longer loop. Panorama Park, itself a popular recreation area fronting Indian Arm, is actually a little south of your trail's beginning, but the view from the park makes this a worthwhile starting point.

On foot, you may descend to the waterfront and rise again to Panorama Drive. Look for the trailhead up the driveway at house number 2505, where a set of stairs takes you into the forest. After swinging right, continue to

Misty view of Deep Cove from the great bluff.

follow the fleur-de-lys tags on the trees that mark the Baden-Powell route, as you cross numerous bridges and climb several sets of stairs. Within about 25 minutes, you arrive at two landmarks: a track left heading uphill, a possible return route, and some 5 m off the trail to your right, a heritage Douglas-fir tree with a small label on the trunk.

After another 15 minutes or so, you reach a viewpoint on the right, the great bluff visible from Deep Cove. This is an ideal spot to rest and contemplate the scene before you: the waters of Indian Arm across to Belcarra on the left, Burnaby Mountain ahead and Deep Cove below on the right. A short distance farther is a power line stretching across the water, its final pylon to the west of Indian Arm standing on a rocky eminence. Here is another return point.

If you do wish to continue, follow the Baden-Powell Trail into the forest and uphill beyond the power line right-of-way, where it climbs to meet Indian River Drive. Now, make your way west for 500 m until, at the road's high point, beside a small water tower, the Baden-Powell Trail goes off right, heading for Mt. Seymour Road, while you go a few metres farther, then turn downhill opposite a fire hydrant. (There is a pullout suitable for parking under the power line, should you wish to begin your outing here and avoid the congestion of Deep Cove on a sunny summer weekend.) The track into the woods is the one you passed on your outward journey, and it drops straight down to join the main trail opposite the heritage tree. Turn right, once more on the Baden-Powell Trail, for your return to Deep Cove.

INDIAN ARM PARKS

Five-park circuit: 4.5 km (2.8 mi)   **Allow:** 1.5 hours

Cates Park return: 10.5 km (6.5 mi)   **Allow:** 3 hours

Surface: trail, paved   **Rating:** easy   **Season:** all year

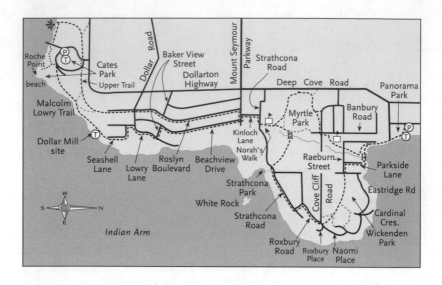

ACCESS

Transit: Route #212 to both Cates Park and Deep Cove

Vehicle: Make your way via Dollarton Highway or Mt. Seymour Parkway to Deep Cove and, off Deep Cove Road, to Panorama Park on the left near the water. Parking will be tight on a nice day, but there are a variety of options nearby.

Car GPS entry: Mt. Seymour Parkway & Dollarton Highway (North Vancouver District)

Trailhead: 49° 19.648′ N, 122° 57.020′ W

A CLUSTER OF five little parks near Deep Cove in lower Indian Arm makes a fine destination for a short outing. You may extend your excursion by trekking along residential streets with harbour views to Cates Park, which is located beside Dollarton Highway farther south and is a family-oriented destination in its own right. Or you may combine the shorter walk with Walk 38.

From Panorama Park, head south past buildings at the water's edge and bend around the bay, passing through the woods of Deep Cove Park to cross a footbridge. Turn south on Parkside Lane to Raeburn Street, go left to cross Lockehaven Road and enter Wickenden Park. Continue east amid tall trees, staying right where the boardwalk forks, left up some steps and right again to emerge above Roxbury Road. This you follow a short distance before jogging left onto Strathcona Road, which takes you to the attractive Strathcona Park in its little bay. From it, you travel westwards across Noble Bridge to Myrtle Park, where you must decide whether to return or continue to Cates Park.

To return, stay left to make a clockwise circuit of Myrtle Park and emerge on Cove Cliff Road near Banbury Road, on which you go north briefly before turning right on a path behind Cove Cliff Elementary School. Ignoring a bridge on your right, traverse a playground on the way to a small parking lot and thus to Raeburn Street. Cross this and walk north on a track flanked by a creek on your right. Back in Deep Cove Park, a left turn leads to your starting point.

To include Cates Park in this excursion, go left after Noble Bridge, left again through a screen of trees, left again close to Seycove Secondary School, straight past the parking lot to Norah's Walk, right on Strathcona Road, left on Kinloch Lane, left on Mt. Seymour Parkway, then immediately right onto Beachview Drive with its vistas. Follow this to Baker View Street, where you go left to Lowry Lane with a little park, right on Dollar Road, then left again onto Beachview, left, then finally right on Sea Shell Lane to Cates Park. The remains of a beehive sawdust burner from the (Robert) Dollar Mill established in 1916 meet you at the entrance. Posted maps illustrate a loop of trails and other facilities where you may wander to enjoy the highlights of the park.

To vary your return, exit the park on the Upper Trail then walk back on Roslyn Boulevard; return to Kinloch Lane across Mt. Seymour Parkway, thence to Myrtle Park. Here, loop left and return to Deep Cove via the return route described above.

POINT GREY/WRECK BEACH

Trail 7 to Acadia Beach one-way: 4.5 km (2.8 mi)   **Allow:** 1.5 hours

Surface: rough, sand   **Rating:** easy to moderate   **Season:** all year

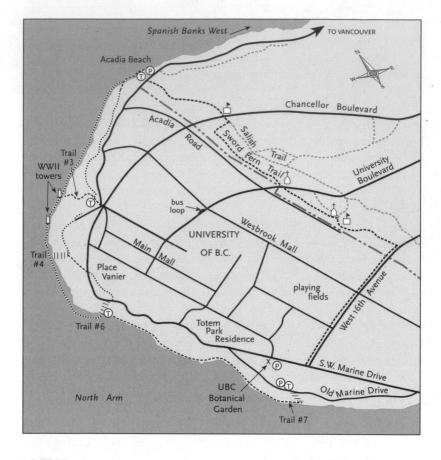

ACCESS

Transit: From the UBC Bus Loop, take Route #C20 to West Mall and Stadium Road. Walk through the Botanical Garden parking lot then 200 m left to Trail 7.

Vehicle: Park near the Trail 7 sign on Old Marine Drive, which forks off SW Marine Drive halfway between West 16th Avenue and Wesbrook Mall.

Car GPS entry: SW Marine Drive & West 16th Avenue

Trailhead (Trail 7): 49° 15.154′ N, 123° 15.036′ W

GEOGRAPHIC AND CULTURAL characteristics combine to make this walk unique. Part of the Pacific Spirit Regional Park, Point Grey is where river meets ocean, and travel on the beach is determined by the height of the tide (check www.tide-forecast.com for Point Grey). As well, Wreck Beach is a popular summer destination for nude sunbathing. Several stairways connect the beach to the road, allowing you the option of shortening your walk.

After checking the map at the trailhead information kiosk, your outing begins with a 55 m descent beside a creek to a rough track. Turn right, and for the next 1.5 km (0.9 mi), you pass through woods to avoid the river's marshy edge. You also pass many pockets of sandy beach tucked in amongst logs—an area particularly popular with nude sunbathers in season—as you continue to the "heart" of Wreck Beach at Trail 6. Visitors should behave with discretion.

Here, the long North Arm Breakwater marks the mouth of the Fraser River, and your route begins to curve northward. (Trail 6 offers a shortcut back to your transportation. From Place Vanier Residences at the top, go right along sw Marine Drive.) Continuing around the bend, you pass spectacular actively eroding cliffs that are fully exposed to fierce storms. Although protective berms have been built and cobblestones dumped on the beaches, winds and waves continue to scour away below while unseen internal forces loosen the cliffs from above. (Trail 4 offers a shortcut on this stretch, leading up to the Museum of Anthropology [MOA] and NW Marine Drive. Turn right to return to your transportation.)

Ahead stands the first of two searchlight towers that were part of the Canadian military's defence system at Point Grey Fort during World War II. Finally, after about 20 minutes of rocky terrain, which may be slippery, you exit the clothing-optional zone and soon reach the Acadia Beach parking lot. (Trail 3, at the second tower, climbs to Marine Drive, where you turn left to reach Acadia Beach on an easy path.)

Several options exist for your return. To remain on trails, cross NW Marine Drive to Salish Trail, which leads up to Chancellor Boulevard, where you cross then turn right onto Sword Fern Trail. At 16th Avenue, turn right to reach your vehicle. To find a bus or to explore the UBC campus, walk up NW Marine Drive for 15 minutes to Chancellor Boulevard, where you can catch a #C20 bus back to your starting point or wander back at will through campus, taking in parts of Walks 42 or 43 along the way.

CHANCELLOR WOODS

Short circuit: 3.9 km (2.4 mi)   **Allow:** 1 hour

Long circuit: 6 km (3.7 mi)   **Allow:** 2 hours

Surface: trails   **Rating:** easy   **Season:** all year

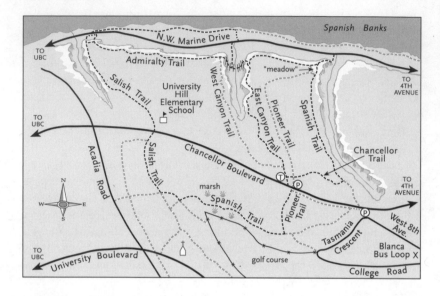

ACCESS

Transit: various routes to Blanca Loop. On 8th Avenue, walk 700 m west to Tasmania Crescent, then, 100 m farther, go north to join the route at Spanish Trail.

Vehicle: On West 4th Avenue, head west past Blanca Street near the University of British Columbia and continue 800 m west of Drummond Drive to an obvious roadside parking area.

Car GPS entry: West 4th Avenue & Blanca Street

Trailhead: 49° 16.251′ N, 123° 13.761′ W

THE NORTHERN SEGMENT of Pacific Spirit Regional Park, extending from Chancellor Boulevard to Spanish Banks, contains a number of trails, mostly in forest. The area features a considerable variety of trees, some quite deep ravines and, optionally, the beach. The trail system lends itself to circular walks; two that start from the same point are described here.

From the information kiosk at the trailhead, head east into the forest along Chancellor Trail, a connector to Spanish Trail, which then leads north amongst tall second-growth Douglas-fir, cedar and hemlock growing on the flats above Spanish Bank Creek. After some 20 minutes of gentle descent, you meet a junction with a stile; the track behind the stile leads to Pioneer Trail and the site of a pioneer homestead of which only a small "meadow" remains. From here, an unmarked trail connects to the Admiralty Trail below.

From the junction at the stile, continue downhill to another stile, at which the Admiralty Trail goes left. (From here, you can also drop down to Marine Drive and the beach.) Admiralty Trail follows the edge of the bluffs until you meet the junction with East Canyon Trail, which leads back to the trailhead to complete the shorter outing. This route follows the ravine's edge fairly closely, though it is sometimes forced away from the main canyon by washouts.

The longer loop continues straight on from the East Canyon Trail junction and winds down to the depths of the ravine, where another option presents itself. The more challenging route climbs back up over what may seem like endless stairs, but these eventually land you on a continuation of the easy Admiralty Trail along the bluffs—which afford winter views of Burrard Inlet and beyond—until it meets the Salish Trail.

The second option from the ravine's floor is to cross NW Marine Drive, walk left along the beach, ascend to the Acadia Beach parking lot (see Walk 40) and, a few paces beyond, recross the road and pick up the Salish Trail. This broad packed-gravel path ascends gently to University Hill Elementary School and Chancellor Boulevard. Use the pedestrian crossing and stay with Salish Trail south to its intersection with Spanish Trail, where you go left. This track goes through deciduous scrub and crosses a marsh before entering pleasant, open forest. Finally, going left on Pioneer Trail takes you back to Chancellor Boulevard and your transportation.

UBC GARDENS TOUR

Return: 5 km (3.1 mi)   **Allow:** 2 hours

Surface: paved; trail   **Rating:** easy   **Season:** all year

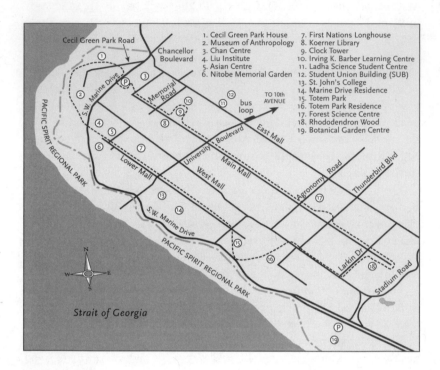

1. Cecil Green Park House
2. Museum of Anthropology
3. Chan Centre
4. Liu Institute
5. Asian Centre
6. Nitobe Memorial Garden
7. First Nations Longhouse
8. Koerner Library
9. Clock Tower
10. Irving K. Barber Learning Centre
11. Ladha Science Student Centre
12. Student Union Building (SUB)
13. St. John's College
14. Marine Drive Residence
15. Totem Park
16. Totem Park Residence
17. Forest Science Centre
18. Rhododendron Wood
19. Botanical Garden Centre

ACCESS

Transit: Numerous buses service UBC. From the UBC Bus Loop, walk west along Student Union Boulevard, cross East Mall and join the walk at the clock tower.

Vehicle: Make your way to NW Marine Drive at UBC and the Rose Garden parkade near the Chan Centre.

Car GPS entry: 6278 Marine Drive NW (Rose Garden Parkade)

Trailhead (outside parkade): 49°16.169′ N, 123°15.415′ W

GARDENS AND ATTRACTIVE treed avenues have fortunately been left intact as the large campus—actually, a city within a city—undergoes continual change and growth. This walk links some natural highlights; you could, in fact, begin anywhere along the circuit and adapt it to your own inclinations. (To assist your route-finding, see www.maps.UBC.ca/map and parking.UBC.ca). This walk also links nicely with Walks 40 and 43.

From the parkade, cross NW Marine Drive, go right a few paces then cut left beside a parking lot and between buildings to reach Cecil Green Park Road. Cross this and find your way behind some buildings to Cecil Green Park, with its attractive grounds and fine view. Next, go west and south along the clifftop opposite the Museum of Anthropology, continue past Haida House with its totems and follow a wooded path to exit on NW Marine Drive opposite the Liu Institute. The path continues a few paces to the right across the road to Lower Mall, and almost immediately you arrive at the Nitobe Memorial Garden. Behind the walls (entrance fee) lies a miniature Japanese landscape. Opposite this garden sits the Asian Centre with its commemorative Pacific Bell in a pagoda; take a diversion on Memorial Road to visit it. Your next stop is the First Nations Longhouse, built amongst trees that were once part of a larger arboretum.

Continuing south along Lower Mall, you cross University Boulevard, pass St. John's College and the Marine Drive Residences, then cross the northern jog of Agronomy Road. Now cross diagonally through Totem Park, an open woodland of red cedar and Douglas-fir, then wend your way east (left) through the residence grounds to West Mall. Here, you go right to reach Larkin Drive, on which you soon go right into Rhododendron Wood, which, despite its name, is another woodland of cedar and fir. Stroll along the path to its end, then jog left to the broad pedestrian Main Mall Greenway, where you turn left again and begin your return journey.

The first stop of interest here is a community garden followed by a carved wooden arch, Hungarian style, at the Forestry complex. Note the adjacent pole, carved from an 800-year-old Western red cedar that was blown down in Stanley Park during a major storm in 2006. Thereafter, continue strolling along Main Mall until you reach the clock tower in the grounds of the Irving Barber Learning Centre, which hugs the original library building built of stone.

From here, continue north for another minute or two to the lovely Rose Garden, with its balcony views of the garden itself, the entrance to Howe Sound and the mountains beyond. Now you need only descend some steps to arrive at the parkade entrance, thus completing your loop.

UBC BOTANICAL GARDEN

Return: 4 km (2.5 mi) **Allow:** 2 hours

Surface: mulch paths **Rating:** easy **Season:** all year

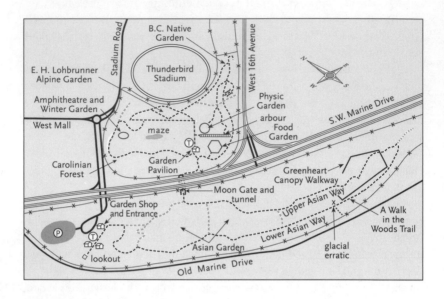

ACCESS

Transit: Numerous buses service UBC. At the UBC Bus Loop, transfer to Route #C20 and alight at West Mall and Stadium Road

Vehicle: Make your way to the junction of SW Marine Drive and Stadium Road, which is just northwest of the intersection of SW Marine Drive and 16th Avenue. Turn southwest into the lot, which offers free parking for garden visitors.

Car GPS entry: SW Marine Drive & Stadium Road

Entrance gate: 49° 15.236' N, 123° 15.034' W

THE UBC BOTANICAL Garden is a world-class facility, a hidden gem where you can wander the endless paths covering the garden's 31.5 ha (78 ac), stroll through an eclectic variety of lovely thematic gardens, learn about the hidden powers of medicinal plants and take a tour on the Greenheart Canopy Walkway. The garden has served as a valuable teaching and research centre since 1916. After paying your admission fee and collecting the garden map, you enter a world of tall trees, massed rhododendrons and magnolias, and a

Just one of many varieties of dogwood trees.

variety of exotic shrubs and climbing vines. It is a wonderful place to walk on a hot day, its shady paths abloom with a profusion of primulas, Himalayan blue poppies and Asiatic dogwood. But each season has its beauty, and you will want to experience them all. (You may have an advance taste of the gardens at www.botanicalgarden.UBC.ca.)

To progress through the maze of trails, make your way to Lower Asian Way, then stay with it as it heads south, making little forays aside to points of interest. (Plants are labelled with metallic tags.) Note the large rock in a meadow; this erratic, left by a receding glacier on the slopes of Hollyburn Mountain, was donated and transported here. Next, you come to A Walk in the Woods Trail, a 20-minute loop through second-growth forest, which is relatively undisturbed but for the canopy walkway overhead.

The Greenheart Canopy Walkway is a 308 m aerial adventure offering a unique visual perspective on the gardens. Exit the walkway onto Upper Asian Way and continue west to the Chinese Moon Gate. This guards the tunnel under sw Marine Drive and the path to the North Gardens. On the other side of the tunnel, from the balcony of the Garden Pavilion, you can view the layout of the grounds and plan your next wanderings. Close in, to your right, is the Food Garden, with its amazing array of espalier-trained apple trees, a long wooden arbour with a fine display of climbing plants and vines, and the Physic Garden, a re-creation of a medieval garden of medicinal plants. To the northeast, various trails lead into and around the B.C. Native Garden, which contains indigenous plants, shrubs, trees and bog. Travelling west, you pass a hothouse and the E.H. Lohbrunner Alpine Garden, with its international collection. Farther along on your circuit, you will see a maze built into the Great Lawn, come upon the Winter Garden at the amphitheatre, pass through the Carolinian forest of hardwoods and find other treasures as you make your way back to the entrance.

MUSQUEAM/FRASER RIVER

Return: 8 km (5 mi)   **Allow:** 2.5 hours

Surface: road, packed, bridle trail   **Rating:** easy   **Season:** all year

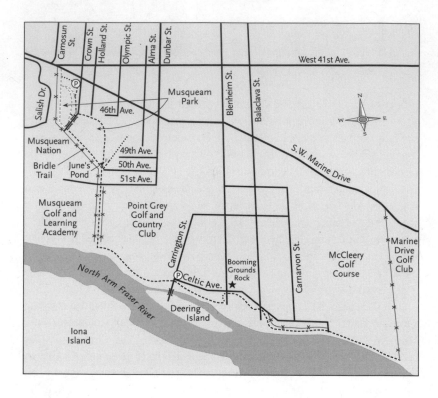

ACCESS

Transit: Routes #41 and #49 at SW Marine Drive and Crown Street

Vehicle: Drive to Crown Street south of SW Marine Drive, just east of its junction with 41st Avenue. A few parking slots jut into Musqueam Park.

Car GPS entry: SW Marine Drive & Crown Street

Trailhead: 49° 13.970′ N, 123° 11.633′ W

OVER THE CENTURIES, this former wetlands has supported wildlife, First Nations life, immigrant farmers, a cannery, ship-building, forestry activities and now golf courses and residences. This walk provides a taste of each.

From your vehicle, either on the roadside or within the forest, head south until, at the foot of Crown Street, you enter the Musqueam Reserve (private land). Cross two closely situated bridges, and at the second, turn left onto a bridle trail that runs behind houses and briefly beside a stream. (Bridle trails can be very muddy.) Continue across a large covered water main, keeping right, and cross 51st Avenue, still on the bridle path, which now runs between the Musqueam Golf and Learning Academy on your right and the Point Grey Golf and Country Club on the left. How many golf balls can you spot in the deep drainage ditch? Then comes the river, with views up, down and across to Iona Island; log booms lining the shore; and planes using the airport just beyond. Before long, you arrive at Carrington Street (where there is parking) and the bridge to Deering Island, the west end of which is a park where there are benches and a small shelter with historical information. To think that this island sold for four dollars in 1900!

Back on the mainland, continue eastwards past stables to your left and a slough to your right, on which are moored pleasure craft below the island houses. At the next street end (Blenheim) you encounter the "Booming Grounds Rock," a large boulder inscribed with memories of the life of a boy growing up on the booms. Then you are forced onto Celtic Avenue for a block or so to Balaclava Street, where you follow a public path between a works yard on your right and new housing on your left, built on land previously occupied by different owners who built boats and ships until 1994. Still heading upstream and stopping at the info-boards, you come to a stretch with views over the pleasant, public McCleery Golf Course then an "End of Trail" sign at the Marine Drive Golf Club grounds.

Now, you retrace your steps until, having turned north at the Musqueam Golf Academy, you go half right on the water-main path just beyond June's Pond where a plaque commemorates her work to protect the Musqueam Park wetlands. Proceed across a wide grassy field to its northern edge to cross to 46th Avenue. When 46th ends at Holland Street, go straight ahead on the little lane to Crown and back to your vehicle via road or wooded trail.

HASTINGS MILL TO SPANISH BANKS

Return: 6 km (3.7 mi)   **Allow:** 2 hours

Surface: paved   **Rating:** easy   **Season:** all year

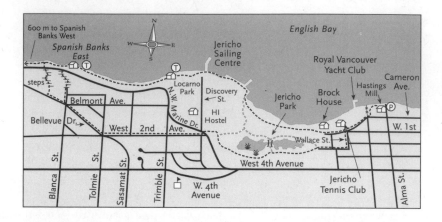

ACCESS

Transit: various routes along West 4th Avenue to Alma Street, then as below

Vehicle: From West 4th Avenue, drive north on Alma Street to Point Grey Road, turn west and park in a strip-lot beside Hastings Mill Pioneer Park.

Car GPS entry: West 4th Avenue & Alma Street

Trailhead: 49° 16.362′ N, 123° 11.130′ W

BRING ALONG YOUR swimming kit (in season!) on this walk, which features a touch of history, sandy beaches, well-groomed paths, lawns and copses of trees. Once home to a First Nations village, then a logging camp known as Jerry's Cove—hence Jericho—then a base for the Department of National Defence (a few buildings remain), water and beach make this a popular destination nowadays.

On foot, go to the north end of Alma Street to see the Hastings Mill Store Museum (limited hours). This 1865 structure was built in Gastown and served as the first post office and community centre on Burrard Inlet. A lucky survivor of the 1886 Gastown fire that nearly levelled that settlement, it was barged to its present location in 1930.

The Hastings Mill Store, built in 1865.

Starting at the museum, cross the park to Point Grey Road and head west past the Royal Vancouver Yacht Club, the Jericho Tennis Club and the Brock House Senior Centre (once the Brock family home), before angling towards the beach and a small Parks Board pavilion. From now on, you see the North Shore mountains across the inlet on your right and Bowen Island more or less ahead. Continuing past the Jericho Sailing Centre and half left towards a grove of trees, you reach the pavilion at Locarno Beach. A further 600 m on, travelling amongst dog walkers, cyclists and beach-goers, you reach the Spanish Banks East pavilion. Should you wish to continue yet another 600 m to the pavilion at Spanish Banks West, you will meet the boundary of Pacific Spirit Regional Park at Spanish Bank Creek and the beginning of that park's web of trails (see Walk 41).

To add an interesting variation to your return route, cross NW Marine Drive immediately behind the Spanish Banks East pavilion to a set of stairs. This ascends the steep, 30 m bank to the foot of Blanca Street, and a short walk uphill leads to a five-way intersection. Alternatively, another set of stairs, steeper and longer (45 m), climbs the hill from a point farther west, about halfway along the parking lot. You must keep a sharp eye to spot either set. The second set emerges on Belmont Avenue. Turning left along this street of majestic homes takes you to the aforementioned five-way intersection. Go half right onto Bellevue Drive and along West 2nd Avenue, passing the Aberthau Community Centre, a former family residence. Cross NW Marine Drive to Jericho Park, then make your way back to Hastings Mill Pioneer Park and your starting point.

KITSILANO/FALSE CREEK

Granville Bridge return: 7 km (4.3 mi)   **Allow:** 2 hours

Surface: paved   **Rating:** easy   **Season:** all year

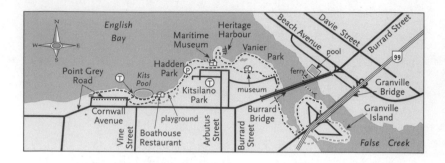

ACCESS

Transit: various routes on Cornwall Avenue to Trafalgar Street; begin at the west end of the walk

Vehicle: At the north end of Arbutus Street in Kitsilano, park in the pay lot near the playground. If full, there are other lots to the east.

Car GPS entry: Arbutus Street & Cornwall Avenue

Trailhead parking lot: 49° 16.578′ N, 123° 9.085′ W

ARE YOU LOOKING for a walk with the option of other sideline activities? You could happily spend several hours at this popular destination that offers a lovely walk with great views as well as swimming, history and culture. You can determine your own walking distance, as this part of the path is but a small section of the 30 km (18 mi) Seaside Bicycle (and walking) Route that stretches between Stanley Park and Spanish Banks (Walk 45).

From the beach at the parking lot described, walk east around the point to arrive at Hadden Park. Here you can explore Kits Point, the Heritage Harbour and the Maritime Museum, which houses the RCMP schooner *St. Roch*. This vessel, built in 1928, was the first to navigate the Northwest Passage in both directions and the first ship to circumnavigate North America. Outside the museum sits the *Ben Franklin*, a historic submarine. Continuing on takes you around Vanier Park on a bulge of land that marks the entrance to False Creek on its southern side. Have a kite? This is a good place to fly

Heritage Harbour and the Maritime Museum.

it. Like Shakespeare? This is the home of the popular Bard on the Beach theatre during the summer. Next, you pass under the 1932 art deco–style Burrard Bridge, and shortly thereafter, you arrive under the Granville Street Bridge. From here you may retrace your steps or, with more time, extend your walk by continuing left under the bridge to Granville Island, where there is a wonderful market and a host of shops to explore.

If you still want to continue along the Seaside Route, hop on a ferry (fare required) at Granville Island to cross False Creek and join the path that parallels Beach Avenue to Stanley Park. This will double your distance, but turnabout is always an option, as is a return by bus. (This walk links to Walk 47 at Granville Island.) Eventually, back at your starting point, you may continue your walk by heading west past the heated saltwater Kits pool to find a narrow path that runs unobtrusively below houses and above the beach. At its end, a flight of stairs rises to Point Grey Road, here a quiet residential street below whose houses you have just travelled. A return by the path or a stroll along Point Grey Road to rejoin the Seaside Route takes you back to the park and your transportation.

FALSE CREEK

Return: 8 km (5 mi) **Allow:** 2.5 hours

Surface: paved **Rating:** easy **Season:** all year

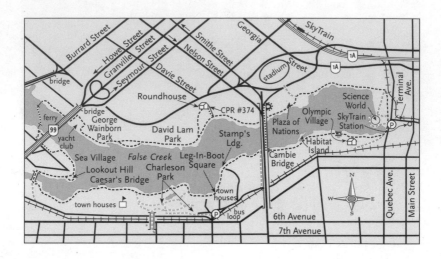

ACCESS

Transit: SkyTrain to Main Street at Science World, numerous buses

Vehicle: Travel to Science World at Terminal Avenue and Quebec Street. Park in the Science World lot on the west side of Quebec, south of Terminal.

Car GPS entry: Terminal Avenue & Quebec Street

Trailhead: 49° 16.388′ N, 123° 6.160′ W

THE TERM "URBAN wonderland" aptly describes this walk around False Creek, which encircles what was once Vancouver's clanging industrial core. Strolling the seawall provides stunning views, green spaces, artistic décor, glimpses into history, a mini-ferry ride and the eclectic Granville Island. Note that, as a circle walk, there are various access points.

Beginning your outing in a counter-clockwise direction from Science World and rounding the end of the inlet, you pass the Plaza of Nations outdoor amphitheatre and stroll along the edges of Yaletown, Vancouver's trendy, renovated former warehouse district. Next, having passed under the Cambie Street Bridge, you may take a side trip to the Roundhouse

A ferry on False Creek fronting Vancouver's West End.

Community Centre, which displays artifacts of early railroading days, including Engine #374, which pulled the first transcontinental train into the city in 1887. Farther along, a bilingual poem in English and Chinook, a settlement-era trading language, is inscribed on the seawall handrail of David Lam Park. Watch for great blue herons at the water's edge; regenerated habitat in False Creek has attracted the return of these gangly birds. Your next experience is a ride across the water to Granville Island on one of the mini-ferries that you've seen darting about while you were walking; board one (fare required) at the foot of Hornby Street. See www.theaqua bus.com for accessibility information.

To continue your route left from the ferry landing, the most attractive way is the waterside walk past shops and the Sea Village of floating homes to Lookout Hill. Of course, you may want to explore the Granville Island Market and other attractions first. West of Lookout Hill, you cross a footbridge to make your way along the south shore of False Creek, from which your view now takes in the reflective downtown high-rises set against the North Shore mountains.

Continuing along the seawall, you pass residential and light commercial areas then suddenly notice an old wooden framework at the water's edge, sheltered by brambles. This is the last tangible link with what once was: it marks the site of a shipyard where ships were built for World War 1, then later, where steel was fabricated for Vancouver bridges and buildings and for structures all over the world. Next, you may visit Habitat Island, an ecohabitat project designed to be a sanctuary for birds and marine life where once stood a railway yard and lumber mill. Finally, after crossing a contemporary metal bridge as you pass Olympic Village, where the athletes lived during the 2010 Winter Olympic Games, it is but a few minutes back to Science World, your transportation and your exit from this urban wonderland.

CANADA PLACE TO BROCKTON POINT

Return: 12 km (7.5 mi) **Allow:** 3 hours

Surface: paved **Rating:** easy **Season:** all year

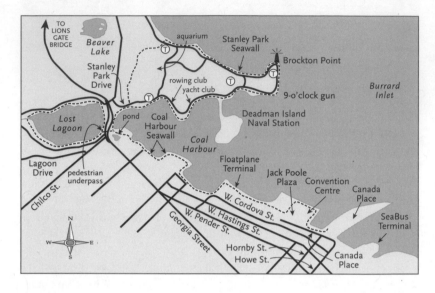

ACCESS

Transit: SkyTrain or SeaBus to Waterfront Station; various bus routes to Canada Place

Vehicle: Parking downtown may be difficult, and pay parking is in effect throughout Stanley Park.

Car GPS entry: Howe Street & Canada Place

Canada Place: 49° 17.277′ N, 123° 6.834′ W

FROM THE SEASCAPE-COLOURED glass towers of downtown to the deep-green forest of Stanley Park, from cruise ships to a historical cannon and lighthouse, from busy floatplane berths to quiet ponds, this walk is a feast for the eyes and the mind. And once in Stanley Park, you could wander at will then return by bus.

From your transportation, walk to the front of Canada Place at the foot of Hornby Street. Adorned with five "sails" symbolizing the area's rich maritime connections, this multi-use facility with an interpretive centre is itself worth exploring. Perhaps a cruise ship will be in dock. Next, head west and

The Brockton Point Lighthouse overlooking Burrard Inlet.

follow the seawalk to stroll around the perimeter of the Convention Centre, noting the 2.4 ha (6 ac) green-roof system that nourishes indigenous plants. On the centre's west side, climb the steps to Jack Poole Plaza and the impressive cauldron that held the Olympic flame in 2010. Back on the lower level, you take a promenade into history as you travel along the Coal Harbour Seawalk with its historical information boards. Runners jog by, floatplanes come and go, and yachts doze in the marinas. The Devonian Harbour Park and pond at the head of Coal Harbour owe their existence to activists who saved it from upscale development. As you approach the causeway, note the pedestrian underpass that leads to Lost Lagoon, a diversion for later.

Now, changing direction, you proceed along the south shore of Stanley Park towards Brockton Point, first passing an information booth, then a naval base on Deadman Island, once a First Nations funerary site. Vancouver's unique nine-o'clock gun, a muzzle-loaded naval cannon cast in 1816 that has been fired almost daily since 1898, sits on the southern "elbow" of Brockton Point. Three hundred metres along stands Brockton Point's iconic, fully functioning red-and-white lighthouse, the current structure completed in 1915. From here, wide-ranging views take in the cityscape, ships in the harbour, industrial activities across the water and mountains forming the northern skyline.

The next section stretches 1.3 km (0.8 mi) in view of the Lions Gate Bridge before you turn inland at Lumberman's Arch, near a waterplay area. You pass behind the aquarium en route to the information booth you passed earlier. Retrace your steps on the seawall to the pedestrian underpass noted previously; this provides access to a pleasant 1.8 km (1.1 mi) circuit of Lost Lagoon Bird Sanctuary and its summer fountain. Finally, return through the underpass and back towards the city, perhaps varying your route as you wish.

THE 3-C CIRCUIT

Return: 5.5 km (3.4 mi)   **Allow:** 1.5 hours

Surface: paved, packed   **Rating:** easy   **Season:** all year

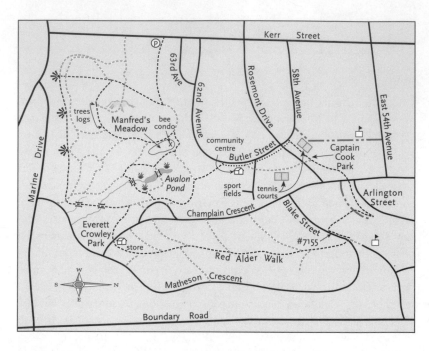

ACCESS

Transit: Route #26 to Rosemont Drive and Butler Street or to Champlain Crescent and Matheson Crescent

Vehicle: From Kerr Street in southeast Vancouver, park in a lot south of East 63rd Avenue.

Car GPS entry: Kerr Street & 63rd Avenue

Trailhead: 49° 12.719′ N, 123° 2.472′ W

LOCATED IN THE southeastern corner of Vancouver, the three Cs are Everett Crowley, Captain Cook and Champlain Heights Parks. Your walk loops through all three, beginning in the first. Note the information kiosk with a map at the parking lot.

Discovering Everett Crowley Park is a happy surprise. Located on slopes overlooking the north arm of the Fraser River and the farmlands of Richmond, with Mount Baker beyond, this park is one of Vancouver's largest. The site has experienced logging, farming, quarrying and, for 25 years, was a dump for Vancouver's garbage. However, since the park was established in 1987, it has been returning to a more natural state, attractive to birds and wildlife, and people out for a breath of nature.

From your vehicle, walk to the first major intersection, where you turn right on a wide, gravel path. As the path turns east, continue down to the parallel mulch trail, which offers brushy viewpoints best enjoyed in the leafless winter. In about 650 m, the trail bends north onto a concrete path and ascends behind residences to a T-junction. Turn right to reach and cross Champlain Crescent, then turn left between a convenience store and bus stop. Now follow Red Alder Walk north, rising gently and ignoring side paths, for about 900 m until you exit on Matheson Crescent opposite a field. Cross at the crosswalk and walk 150 m left to a narrow footpath just past the "Kanata Co-op 7155 Blake Street" sign. Turn right onto this path then right again briefly, then bend left to join a path paralleling Arlington Street. Cross Champlain Crescent and proceed along a greenway, the woods of Captain Cook Park on your right. Emerging onto Butler Street, turn left and continue past Champlain Heights Park to its end, where your route again leaves the streets to re-enter Everett Crowley Park at its northeast corner.

Bear left when the trail branches and gradually descend, catching glimpses of Avalon Pond below, then turn right to approach the water on a gravel path. The pond was named for Vancouver's last working dairy, owned by the Crowley family and sold in 2011. A footbridge over Kincross Creek at the mouth of the pond provides the best view. Turn right to follow the water-side mulch path to its end, ascend left then go right on the main gravel path. Now, bearing left and sharp left, watch for Manfred's Meadow (unsigned), a grassy field also on your left. Pause here to rest, observe and read about the bee condo. Next, your trail curves right past a regenerated area with log borders, then right to a large planter on the corner where you return to your vehicle.

VANCOUVER FRASER FORESHORE

Return: 8 km (5 mi)   **Allow:** 2.5 hours

Surface: packed, paved   **Rating:** easy   **Season:** all year

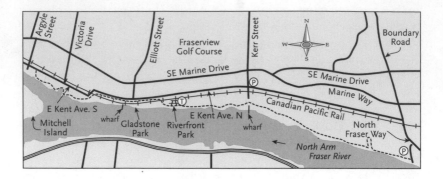

ACCESS

Transit: Route #116, Boundary Road at Kent Avenue. Walk south to trailhead.

Vehicle: From the south end of Boundary Road, which divides Vancouver and Burnaby, cross the railway tracks south of Marine Way. Go straight ahead onto a secondary road where Boundary Road bends into North Fraser Way. Park at the end.

Car GPS entry: Boundary Road & Marine Way

Trailhead: 49° 12.087′ N, 123° 1.413′ W

THIS TRAIL, PART of a riverside greenway being developed along the north shore of the Fraser River, features log booms, wharfs and birdlife on one end; a variety of residential styles and development on the other; and a picnic site and playground halfway along.

From the parking lot, head west on the trail beside a chainlink fence. (Walk 70 goes east.) As of 2013, the first 1.5 km (0.9 mi) of trail lies between this fence and a string of log booms on the river's edge. This once-busy industrial and log-sorting area now throbs with the sounds of trucks and diggers relentlessly converting sheds and works yards into residential complexes and manicured grounds. Kerr Street marks the transition to the future. Here, there is a restaurant, a parking area (an alternative access point), a wharf and a boardwalk; it's a nice place to pause. Here, also, the bike and pedestrian paths separate.

Kerr Street's wharf and boardwalk.

Some 700 m later, you arrive at the picnic site and playground, after which the path swings around a works yard and closely parallels the railway tracks, turning back to the water at Gladstone Park. The *Langara II* fishing lodge moors here for the winter; in summer, it is towed to Haida Gwaii for use by sports fisherfolk. A short wharf marks the west end of the narrow Gladstone Park; limited parking is available.

Until now, you will no doubt have noticed the noise and activity on the far side of the Fraser, the traffic running along River Road in Richmond. Beyond that road is a strip of industrial concerns and then farmland. Your next 800 m, however, follow a seawall-like path of paving stones. The path, which wanders in front of flower gardens, sculpted lawns and attractive townhouses, offers places to sit or lean and watch the river traffic and activities. The river channel here narrows as it splits around Mitchell Island then passes beneath the Knight Street Bridge. The island was originally three separate ones—Mitchell, Eburne and Twigg—divided by channels that have filled in over time and is named for its first pioneer settler and farmer. Alexander Mitchell also advocated successfully for construction of the first Fraser Street Bridge in 1893 to connect Vancouver and Richmond. The bridge was opened for ship traffic with a hand crank. Today, the island is home to industrial activities but also a 0.4 ha (1 ac) park with a fishing pier.

Before you reach the Knight Street Bridge, however, your route ends abruptly and without fanfare at a roadside where you turn to retrace your steps to your starting point.

SEA ISLAND

Return: 9.5 km (5.9 mi)   **Allow:** 3 hours

Surface: packed, paved   **Rating:** easy   **Season:** all year

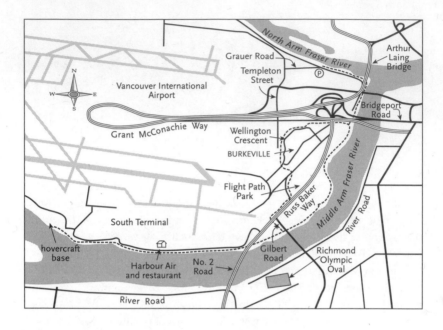

ACCESS

Transit: various buses or SkyTrain to Bridgeport Station, then #C92 to the Seair Seaplanes terminal and do the walk in reverse

Vehicle: Cross the bridge to Sea Island on Grant McConachie Way, turn right on Templeton Street, then right on Grauer Road and park in a small lot on the dyke.

Car GPS entry: Templeton Street & Grauer Road

Trailhead parking: 49° 11.968′ N, 123° 8.571′ W

SEA ISLAND IS well known as the home of Vancouver International Airport. Less well known is that a pathway skirting the eastern end of the island takes the walker past a variety of scenery and points of interest and includes the option of a meal or beverage at the turnaround point.

From your vehicle, walk east on the dyke along the North Arm of the Fraser River to the northeast corner of the island, noting the log booms

The seaplane wharf.

and other river activities as you go. As you approach the corner, you arrive at a stop of interest, Eburne, one of the earliest communities in Richmond and a former agricultural hub. Then you meet the first two of four bridge underpasses. Now heading south along the Fraser's Middle Arm and under two more bridges, you pass between the Delta Hotel and a marina with its pavilion supported above the water on posts, then past the large glass building that houses the aerospace technology campus of the British Columbia Institute of Technology. Shortly thereafter, cross Gilbert Road and note the impressive Richmond Olympic Oval across the river, built for the 2010 Winter Olympics. Also impressive on a clear day is the vista, with the mountains of the Lower Mainland forming a fine backdrop. The Harbour Air seaplane base and associated restaurant with its river views lies another 20 minutes along. From here, you may opt to continue 1 km (0.6 mi) farther to the end of the road, where an old hovercraft rests on the Coast Guard grounds.

On your return journey, when you reach Gilbert Road, turn left to the traffic lights on Russ Baker Way, cross to the far side and go right, along the fence and around its corner. You are now opposite Flight Path Park, designed for the comfort of plane spotters. Stay left, however, and follow Wellington Crescent between the airport facilities and private housing. This rather unique settlement is Burkeville, a 300-home subdivision built by the Canadian government in 1943 to house armed forces personnel and employees of the Boeing Aircraft plant. At a sharp fork, angle right on Wellington Crescent and follow this to emerge on Miller Road. Turn right and continue to Russ Baker Way, cross this and keep to the pedestrian/bike path north of the Delta Hotel, heading towards the water. Just as the path approaches the bridge access ramp, descend to the right to rejoin your outward route under the bridge. Your starting point is now 1.2 km (0.7 mi) distant.

LULU ISLAND DYKES

Middle Arm and West Dyke one-way: 9 km (5.6 mi) **Allow:** 2.5 hours
Terra Nova Loop: up to 3 km (1.9 mi) **Allow:** 1 hour
Surface: packed dyke, improved trail (Terra Nova) **Rating:** easy **Season:** all year

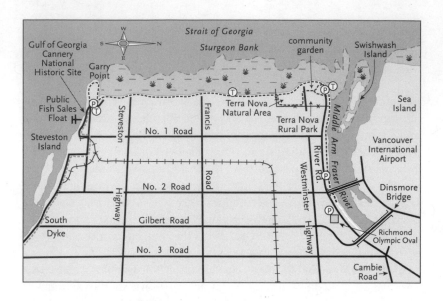

ACCESS

Transit: Route #C94 to River Road and Hollybridge Way near the Richmond Olympic Oval. Walk to the dyke and head left, downstream.

Vehicle: Pay parking is available under the Olympic Oval; enter from Road C off River Road, just south of the No. 2 Road Bridge. Limited parking is available on River Road west of Lynas Lane.

Car GPS entry: Road C & River Road

Trailhead: west of Lynas Lane 49° 10.403′ N, 123° 9.956′ W

Terra Nova: 49° 10.473′ N, 123° 11.882′ W

THE WEST END of Richmond's Lulu Island, opposite Vancouver's international airport, is an inviting setting for watching both birds and aircraft. As well, the Terra Nova Rural Park and Natural Area provide a diversion between the dykes on the northern and western banks of Lulu Island. With these options, you can tailor your outing as you wish. (If you prefer not to walk back, either carry bus fare or park a second vehicle in Steveston.)

Beginning near Lynas Lane, climb onto the dyke, pause at the viewing platform overlooking the Middle Arm of the Fraser River, then head downstream. (The walk from the Olympic Oval to Lynas Lane is about 800 m.) An enhanced marshland area with a variety of birds lies close at hand, and Sea Island (Walk 51) lies beyond. As you travel westwards, you can see Point Grey, the North Shore mountains and the islands of Howe Sound. Within less than an hour, you arrive at the Terra Nova reclamation projects, on the point where the Fraser River meets the Strait of Georgia (parking available).

The Terra Nova Rural Park contains historic buildings, community gardens and a picnic area. The Terra Nova Natural Area, separated from the park by the residential end of Westminster Highway, protects former farmland as old-field, or grassland habitat, to maintain the environment required by raptors and other birds and species. (Dogs are not allowed in this area.) A network of trails wanders through the two preserves. The southern trail in the Natural Area meets the west dyke.

The popular West Dyke Trail, with its distant views and occasional benches, stretches from Terra Nova to Garry Point Park. It borders Sturgeon Bank, a rich estuary and an important bird-nesting habitat that is part of the Pacific Flyway. More than 1 million birds migrate through the area annually. Towards the south end of your walk, a line of radar-reflecting towers warns passing ships of the proximity of the mud flats. On the landward side, housing developments have replaced farm crops.

Next, you reach a lagoon and Garry Point Park, the end of your walk. However, the village of Steveston, reached by following Moncton Street, is worth exploring before you head back. (Walk 53 continues from here.) The #401 bus leaves from Chatham Street east of 2nd Avenue; get off on Westminster Highway at Lynas Lane, walk north to River Road then left to your vehicle, or right to return to the Richmond Oval.

STEVESTON GREENWAYS

Return: 15 km (9.3 mi)   **Allow:** 4 hours

Surface: packed, paved   **Rating:** easy   **Season:** all year

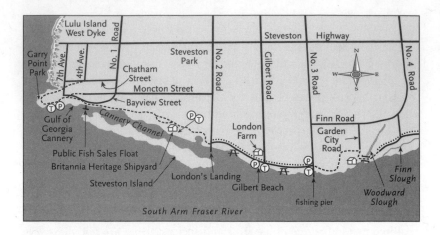

ACCESS

Transit: Route #410 to 7th Avenue and Chatham Street

Vehicle: Make your way to Garry Point Park in the village of Steveston in the southwest corner of Richmond. The walk description starts here, but you may start your outing at any point along the route.

Car GPS entry: 7th Avenue & Chatham Street

Trailhead: 49° 7.503′ N, 123° 11.532′ W

LIFE AND WORK along this south shore of Richmond's Lulu Island in the first half of the 20th century can only be imagined today through the remaining historical buildings, rotting wooden pilings lining the shoreline and numerous information plaques planted along the route.

Go out to Garry Point (links to Walk 52) for a few minutes to see the sculpture of a net-mending needle, a tribute to the fishermen who lost their lives at sea, to feel the winds and to look over the waters that once teemed with uncountable quantities of salmon. Now turn back and follow the paved lane heading east from the facilities and leading to the Gulf of Georgia Cannery. Inside, the displays take you through fish processing from

Britannia Shipyard's heritage building.

catch to canned product. Past the bronze cannery workers out front, angle right to Bayview Street and the beginning of the Steveston Greenways/ Richmond Trails walk. Alternatively, you could stroll along Moncton Street for two or three blocks before jogging over to Bayview. You might climb the viewing tower at the foot of No. 1 Road and imagine your surroundings as part of a vast wetlands area, harvested by First Nations peoples long before the arrival of the attractive and colourful homes of today.

Other sights along your way include the Britannia Heritage Shipyard, where people once lived and worked in their own ethnically defined zones; sailboats and working boats at anchor; the London family farm with its 1888 house and gardens open for viewing; farmland; and a fishing pier at the foot of Gilbert Street, to the east of which is an off-leash area for dogs. A large packing plant on the waterfront is the only obstacle to be skirted; on its east side, continue straight ahead to the waterfront and the pumphouse at Woodward Slough. In 5 minutes, you arrive at Dyke Road; this parallels Gilmour Island, which forms the southern side of Finn Slough, the name referring to the narrow channel of water and to the community that dates from cannery days, when a group of Finnish immigrants settled here. The individualized wooden dwellings on stilts amongst the brush and tidal flats provide a living snapshot into the past and face a tenuous future.

From here, as you retrace your route, you may stop to rest at any of the many clusters of picnic tables and benches along the way and perhaps wonder what changes will affect this area over the next 100 years.

DEAS ISLAND REGIONAL PARK

Return: 4.4 km (2.7 mi)   **Allow:** 1.5 hours

Surface: packed, paved   **Rating:** easy   **Season:** all year

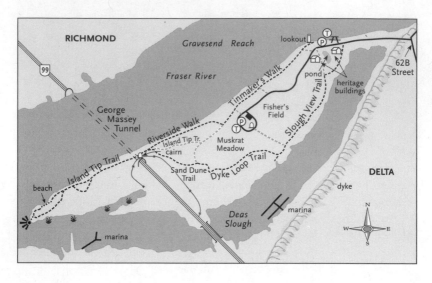

ACCESS

Transit: Route #640 to River Road at Deas Island Road

Vehicle: Make your way to River Road and Deas Island Road in Delta, turn east beside a gravel business and drive along the dirt causeway to a parking lot.

Car GPS entry: Deas Island Road & River Road

Trailhead: 49° 7.596′ N, 123° 3.522′ W

NAMED FOR THE tinsmith and cannery owner who purchased the island in 1873, this 120 ha (300 ac) park is now connected to Delta by a causeway small enough not to detract from the land's island status. It is a popular bird-watching destination and features three historic buildings relocated here in the 1980s for preservation. The heritage, one-room Inverholme Schoolhouse is near the parking area; next is the Victorian-style Burrvilla, whose attic is a summer nursery for bats; and next again is the Delta Agricultural Hall, now the park's operation centre. To your right, at the Tinmaker's Walk trailhead, are a commemorative tablet and a lookout tower, which

The Burrvilla heritage home.

mark the site of Deas's long-demolished cannery. The tower provides fine views of activities on the river.

Walking downriver, you pass another parking area then arrive at a fork, the left arm of which, Dyke Loop Trail, takes you back by Deas Slough to your point of departure. By staying right on Riverside Walk, however, you veer closer to the river, being joined quite soon and in quick succession by Island Tip Trail and Sand Dune Trail, which are combined horse and hiking trails. Soon, you travel over the southern entrance to the George Massey Tunnel, where vehicles emerge from or disappear under the Fraser River on Highway 99. Your trail west stays close to the river now as you make for the island's tip, passing a little beach en route.

From there, you look south across the mouth of Deas Slough, with its marina lying just to the south of Ladner Marsh. Southwest lies Kirkland Island, a navigation beacon marking its shallow waters. North, of course, is the river, and Lulu Island beyond, the shoreline marked by commercial and industrial operations, such as freight terminals and the B.C. Ferries refitting dock.

On your return across the tunnel, go right on Sand Dune Trail, where you experience a sample of dune ecology, then join Dyke Loop Trail. Where this meets Slough View Trail, you have views across Deas Slough, a popular site for rowing. To complete your circular tour of the park, stay right on Slough View Trail, where a left fork leads to the picnic area at Fisher's Field. Continue along the sandy route until, just behind Burrvilla, you keep right again and cross the bridge on Tidal Pond Trail, the pond replete with vegetation and a blaze of colour in summer. All too soon, you emerge at the picnic area near where you began your outing.

BRUNSWICK POINT

Return: 9.8 km (6.1 mi) **Allow:** 2.5 hours

Surface: packed dyke **Rating:** easy **Season:** all year

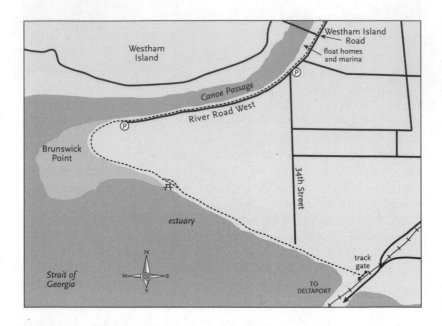

ACCESS

Vehicle: Make your way to River Road West in Ladner. Some 600 m beyond the road to Westham Island and the Reifel Migratory Bird Sanctuary, find a small parking area on the dyke opposite 34th Street.

Car GPS entry: River Road West & Westham Island Road

Trailhead: 49° 4.480′ N, 123° 7.844′ W

THIS OUTING TAKES you along a dyke that separates rich delta marshland abundant with plants and birds from rich agricultural land nourished by its deltaic under-burden. It also contrasts reminders of the one-time cannery industry at Brunswick Point with the modern-day coal and container terminals at Deltaport. Be sure to take your binoculars, and be prepared for brisk winds.

Your walk begins on the shore of Canoe Passage, the southernmost arm of the Fraser River and part of the immense Fraser River Estuary. (The far banks are on Westham Island, which adjoins Reifel Island, home of the George C. Reifel Migratory Bird Sanctuary. Part of the Pacific Flyway, the estuary is a key stopover for more than 1 million migrating birds.) About 1.7 km (1 mi) along the dyke, you reach the end of the road, an alternative place to park. A few minutes later, you find a "garden" of ragged-top pilings, often occupied by cormorants drying their outspread wings. The Brunswick Cannery, one of many that existed along the Fraser River Delta, operated here from 1897 to 1930, after which the premises were used for other fishing-related purposes until its demolition in 1983.

Continuing around the point, you pass two sets of benches, beyond which a horse track drops off the dyke and enters high brush. Hidden in here is a sheltered picnic table, about midway to your turnaround point. Look for eagle nests across the road in a line of trees planted as a windbreak. If you were an eagle soaring overhead, you would see how the powerful Fraser River continuously reshapes the underwater landscape. Its burden of silt fills in channels and adds to the flats, which extend seawards for about 6 km (3.7 mi) before dropping off into deep waters in the Strait of Georgia. Also watch for large flocks of dunlins, which overwinter here, their white bellies and dark backs alternately contrasting as they swoop and swarm over the marshlands to confuse their predators.

The towering cranes of Deltaport loom larger on the horizon as you approach 34th Street, unfortunately separated from the dyke by a deep ditch. This makes a good turnaround point, or you could continue to a gate 700 m farther. Your return walk rewards you with an unobstructed 360-degree view of the mountains surrounding the Lower Mainland, from southern Vancouver Island to Mount Baker and the Fraser Valley, and around to the North Shore and the Sunshine Coast, with high-rises on Kingsway Ridge in the foreground.

BOUNDARY BAY DUO

North Section return: 8.5 km (5.3 mi)   **Allow:** 3 hours

South Section return: 4.5 km (2.8 mi)   **Allow:** 1.5 hours

Surface: dykes, both; sandy trail, south only   **Rating:** easy   **Season:** all year

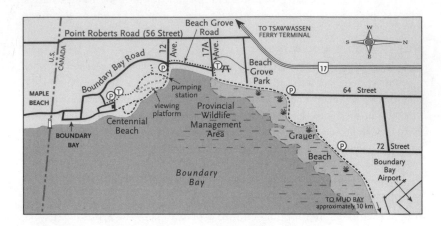

ACCESS

North Section—Transit: Route #603 or #C84 to 16 Avenue and Braid Road. Join route one block north on 17A Avenue.

Vehicle: Make your way to Highway 10 (Ladner Trunk Road) and 72 Street or, to halve the distance of your walk, to 64 Street.

Car GPS entry: 72 Street & Ladner Trunk Road

Trailhead at 72 Street: 49° 3.588′ N, 123° 1.453′ W

South Section—Transit: various routes on 12 Avenue to Morris Crescent

Vehicle: From 56 Street (Point Roberts Road) in Tsawwassen, go east on 12 Avenue and drive to a small parking lot at road's end.

Car GPS entry: 56 Street & 12 Avenue

Trailhead at 12 Avenue lot: 49° 1.480′ N, 123° 3.492′ W

BOUNDARY BAY IS of international importance to migrating and wintering birds. Waterfowl and shorebirds are common; hawks and eagles hunt small mammals; and, in winter, you might spot a snowy owl. Fabulous marine and mountain views are an added attraction. The north section is a

A snowy owl.

straightforward multi-use dyke walk at the edge of farmland; the south section includes Centennial Beach, a wildlife reserve and several trails.

To walk the north section, turn right onto the dyke, which hugs the shoreline of Boundary Bay, its daily character determined by weather and tide, before it arrives at Beach Grove Spit and the beginning of housing. At the spit, the trail follows a short lane to the corner of 17A Avenue and Beach Grove Road. A few steps up 17A, there is a park with picnic tables and facilities, a nice place to relax before your return. However, if you are keen to continue to the south section, follow Beach Grove Road for 15 minutes to the dyke, remembering that this diversion will add considerably to your return distance.

To walk the south section, from the 12 Avenue lot, walk on the Dyke Trail towards the water, noting a pumping station on your right. As you continue and the dyke becomes indistinguishable from the beach, a trail veers inland, heading towards the facilities at Centennial Beach. An optional loop on the left provides information on dune ecology. To vary your return and enjoy some undeveloped marshland, head towards the park entrance road. From here, follow a rough track just outside the park boundary and walk north, a ditch to your left and a narrow strip of bush separating you from the parking lot on your right (accessed from Boundary Bay Road). Soon, you join the Savannah Trail that leads back to the main Raptor Trail. Thereafter, keep left until, close to the main dyke, you veer right to meet it by the pumping station you noted earlier. (The maze of trails available to explore will not lead you too far astray.) From the pumping station, proceed to your vehicle.

WATERSHED PARK TO MUD BAY

Return: 14 km (8.7 mi)   **Allow:** 4 hours

Surface: packed, paved, trail   **Rating:** easy   **Season:** all year

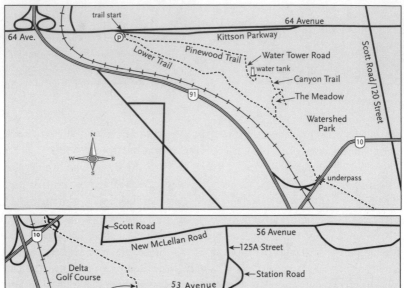

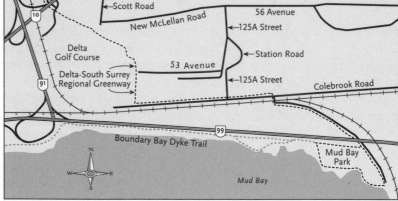

ACCESS

Transit: Route #340 to Kittson Parkway at McKenzie Drive (in Delta), then walk 400 m west to the trailhead

Vehicle: Make your way to 64 Avenue in North Delta or Surrey. It is the northern boundary of Watershed Park and provides access to Kittson Parkway, which you follow to the westernmost Watershed Park sign, 800 m east of Highway 91, or 1.8 km (1.1 mi) west of Scott Road. Park off the road on the south side.

Car GPS entry: 11200 Kittson Parkway, Delta

Trailhead: 49° 7.126′ N, 122° 54.949′ W

IF YOU LIKE both forest and shoreline, then this walk is for you. Beginning in Watershed Park, you travel through second-growth coniferous forest, through swampland with its largely unseen creature activities, past overgrown pastureland and along a road between railway tracks and blueberry fields before you arrive at Mud Bay with its abundant birdlife.

There are several park entrances off Kittson Parkway; this walk begins at the westernmost one, where a short, narrow trail descends to encounter the obvious Lower Trail onto which you turn left. This you follow past various small trail and road diversions used by mountain bikers, runners and dog walkers. After 2 km (1.2 mi), you pass under Highway 10, then continue between neglected pastureland and steep slopes until, at a high chainlink fence, you are directed south. Here, a raised path, the Delta–South Surrey Regional Greenway, bounded by scrubby trees, leads through swampland; the views and bird watching are best when the trees are leafless. Your arrival at Colebrook Road (go left) marks the beginning of a 2 km (1.2 mi) roadside trek past agricultural land until you cross the railway tracks and pass under Highway 99 to arrive at Mud Bay (parking). As you cross the tracks, note that the rails from the U.S. join the Canadian line here.

An extension of Boundary Bay, Mud Bay is a delta formed by the Serpentine and Nicomekl Rivers. The tidal marshes and eelgrass beds support millions of migratory birds that stop or overwinter here, making it a birder's paradise. A looped dyke trail, with many benches, looks across the bay to Blackie Spit close in and to Point Roberts and Tsawwassen in the distant right.

Well rested, you must retrace your steps to Watershed Park, but there you can vary your return. Six hundred metres beyond the Highway 10 underpass, turn right up a wide, stony road. Very quickly, you arrive at the Meadow, a gently sloping grassland with benches and a viewpoint overlooking Mud Bay, where you just were. From the north side of the Meadow, follow woodsy Gravity Bowl Trail for a few paces, then go left onto Canyon Trail. This contours the hillside until it exits onto Water Tower Road near a water tank, and 150 m up the hill, where an artesian well once supplied cool refreshment on hot days. From here, follow the Pinewood Trail for the final 900 m back to the start.

ELGIN HERITAGE TRAIL

Long circuit: 7 km (4.3 mi) **Allow:** 2 hours

Short circuit: 3.3 km (2 mi) **Allow:** 1 hour

Surface: packed, unimproved **Rating:** easy **Season:** all year

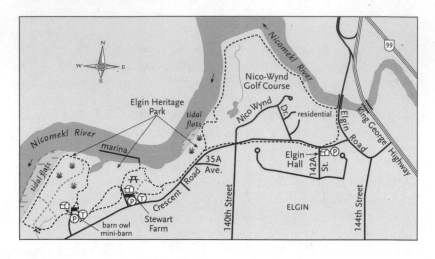

ACCESS

Transit: Route #352 to Crescent Road at 142A Street

Vehicle: Make your way to King George Boulevard in South Surrey (Exit 10 off Highway 99) and follow signs to Crescent Road. Park at the old Elgin Hall at 142A Street, noting the time restrictions.

Car GPS entry: 142A Street & Crescent Road

Parking: 49° 4.023' N, 122° 49.645' W

THIS PLEASANT STROLL winds along the calm waters of the narrow Nicomekl River, around a golf course, through a historic farmyard, past tidal flats and marshes, and through an inviting second-growth forest.

After parking at the community hall, read the information board about local history and then cross busy Crescent Road to its north side. Head right, towards the gas station, then left on Elgin Road until you see a cairn marking the trail's beginning (49° 4.120' N, 122° 49.526' W). Here, a paved path fronts colourful townhouses; look for an eagle's nest not too far along and

Nicomekl River.

pause at the various information boards. Soon, you'll have to be alert for flying golf balls, but this is also a great area for bird watching as you stroll past the tidal flats beyond the golf course.

Next, at a fork in the trail, bear right to the riverside lawns lying between the marina—which caters mainly to self-propelled craft—and the buildings of a historic farm and its restored 1894 Victorian mansion. The Stewart family settled here in the late 19th century and developed a productive hay farm. Leaving the buildings for closer examination later, continue past the parking lot through a forested area with many large native trees and some remnant stumps. Beyond a second parking lot, your route follows dykes and boardwalks around marshes and across tidal sloughs, habitat for a variety of birds from the patient great blue heron and majestic bald eagle to the tiny wren. Across one wet meadow, you spot an intriguing building on stilts, a wee barn to house barn owls that no longer have access to real barns.

Finally, your path takes you back to the heart of Heritage Park, the Stewart Farm, where tours are available in season. Guides in Victorian costume provide tours of the house and grounds, including agricultural tools and machinery displays. Once your curiosity is satisfied, make your way back to your vehicle, following the trail that parallels the highway until it swings away, at which point you emerge onto Crescent Road for the 7- or 8-minute walk to Elgin Hall.

If you prefer a shorter loop, you could park at Stewart House (or in the lot just west) and from there content yourself with a walk of about 3 km (1.9 mi) within the park.

SOUTH SURREY URBAN FORESTS

Sunnyside Acres and Crescent Park, each circuit: 3 km (1.9 mi) or less   **Allow:** 1.5 hours

Surface: unimproved trail   **Rating:** easy   **Season:** all year

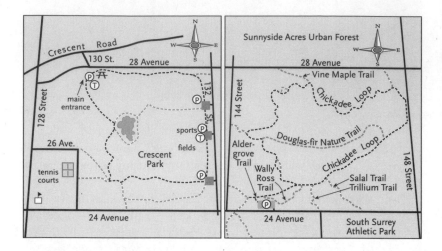

ACCESS

Sunnyside Acres—Transit: Route #352 to 148 Street at 26 Avenue

Vehicle: Drive to 24 Avenue in South Surrey, then to the Sunnyside Acres parking lot on the north side, between 148 and 144 Streets.

Car GPS entry: 144 Street & 24 Avenue

Trailhead: 49° 2.768′ N, 122° 49.274′ W

Crescent Park—Transit: various routes to 128 Street at 26B Avenue

Vehicle: Drive to 28 Avenue and 132 Street, then continue west through forest to Crescent Park's main entrance.

Car GPS entry: 132 Street & 28 Avenue

Parking: 49° 3.148′ N, 122° 51.820′ W

LOOKING FOR A shady walk on a hot summer's day? Consider these little oases, similar yet different in character. Sunnyside Acres is an urban forest rescued from development by the local heritage society; Crescent Park has picnic and sports facilities as well as trails.

An attractive pond in Crescent Park.

Starting from Sunnyside Acres, at the information kiosk look for the Interpretive Trail Map, a guide to numbered stops, and begin on the Stellar's Jay Trail. Go right on Alder-grove, noting in passing the short, wide Wally Ross Trail to your right. Next, you come to a junction with Chickadee Loop Trail, which you join, going right. Keeping left (side trails to the right lead to streets), and enjoying the shade of Douglas-fir trees, you very soon pass the Douglas-fir Nature Trail, a little track that disappears into the trees on your left. Then you enter an area with a more open canopy and an abundance of shrubs. When your path emerges onto busy 148 Street, you go left for a minute or two, before re-entering the forest. Keeping left at main intersections and ignoring all unofficial tracks, make your way past windfalls—some old, some recent—and great cedar stumps, relics of the forest logged a century ago. Then the western end of the Douglas-fir Nature Trail emerges on your left as you continue right and, finally, back at the Chickadee Loop–Alder-grove Trail T-junction, right again, retracing your outward route the short distance back to your car.

For a short stroll to the heart of Crescent Park from the main entrance, take the path to the right behind the washrooms. This leads through a wide clearing and picnic area and to a little pond with waterfowl, circled by several trails. For a ramble round the perimeter of the park, go left at the entrance on a bridle trail through fine second-growth forest, until you emerge to pass several sports fields and their associated parking lots along 132 Street. At the third of these, the walkway leads westwards; keep right at forks and continue to the central pond and its picturesque little bridge, on the near side of which lies the return path to your vehicle.

CONFEDERATION PARK/CAPITOL HILL

Combo circuit: 6.2 km (3.9 mi)

Nature loop: 2.7 km (1.7 mi)

Capitol Hill circuit: 5 km (3.1 mi)

Surface: packed, roads, unimproved trail

Elevation gain: 150 m (500 ft)

Rating: easy to moderate

Allow: 2.5 hours

Allow: 1 hour

Allow: 1.5 hours

High point: 200 m (655 ft)

Season: most of the year

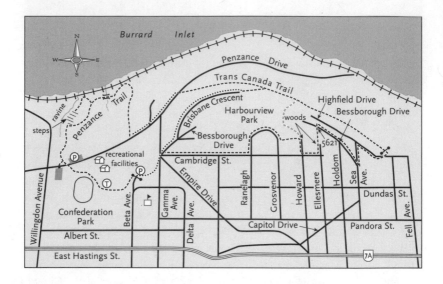

ACCESS

Transit: various routes on Hastings Street to Beta Avenue; walk 300 m north on Beta

Vehicle: From Hastings Street, drive north on Beta Avenue to the parking lot at the end.

Car GPS entry: Hastings Street & Beta Avenue

Parking: 49° 17.079′ N, 122° 59.827′ W

THIS EXCURSION EXPLORES the wilderness retreat that is hidden between bustling Hastings Street and the waters of Burrard Inlet. It begins in the "civilized" part of Confederation Park, descends through its wild side to sea level, then finishes with the ascent of Capitol Hill 200 m above, providing a good workout. The plentiful, ever-changing vistas make it all worthwhile.

A view along the Confederation Nature Trail.

Start by passing through the gate in the parking lot, walk beside the fence abutting the picnic grounds and play park, then go right at the sports track. Beyond the skateboard park, cross Penzance Drive and find the Confederation (Penzance) Nature Trail loop at the left edge of the parking lot. The trail begins with a sustained descent through forest, across a pipeline right-of-way and past the top of a staircase to a fork. Keep left and left again to explore the valley below, and perhaps ascend the 106 stairs. Return to the fork and cross the footbridge, then follow the trail as it bends around and rises stiffly back to Penzance Drive. (For a shorter route, turn back at the road, or, to ascend Capitol Hill only, begin here.)

To visit Capitol Hill, turn left and walk 330 m to a pedestrian crossing. Here, you join the Trans Canada Trail, which, rising gently, skirts Capitol Hill then exits at a gate onto Cambridge Street, where you turn sharp right. Ascend to Highfield Drive, walk left on Sea Avenue then sharp right on Bessborough Drive, enjoying, as you rise, the views over Burrard Inlet. Opposite house number 5621, enter the forest. Immediately go left and uphill on a track that exits onto Ellesmere Avenue. Turn right onto Cambridge, then right again onto Howard Avenue, where you'll find a pleasant track leading through the woods to Harbourview Park, the summit of Capitol Hill.

After pausing to celebrate your ascent, continue round the curved Grosvenor Crescent to again turn west on Cambridge. Now you may enjoy expansive views south and west as you descend steeply, cutting through a tiny park atop a reservoir and arriving at Gamma Avenue. Here, jog left then right to descend a lane between houses and woodland. A left turn at the bottom returns you to your starting point, where you might enjoy a picnic. Refreshed, you might then want to check out the variety of facilities available in Confederation Park.

BURNABY MOUNTAIN/SFU

Short circuit: 5 km (3.1 mi)

Long circuit: 8.5 km (5.3 mi)

Surface: unimproved trail, packed, road

Elevation gain: 180 m (590 ft)

Rating: easy to moderate

Allow: 2 hours

Allow: 3 hours

High point: 340 m (1115 ft)

Season: most of the year

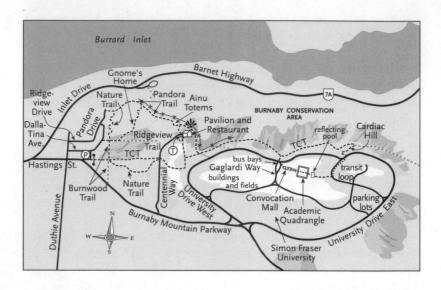

ACCESS

Transit: Routes #135 and #144 to Hastings Street at Duthie Avenue. Walk 250 m east on Hastings to the gated road.

Vehicle: At the east end of the curve where Hastings and Burnaby Mountain Parkway blend, turn north onto Dalla-Tina Avenue then immediately right. Park near a gate at the corner.

Car GPS entry: Hastings Street & Burnaby Mountain Parkway

Trailhead: 49° 16.825′ N, 122° 56.970′ W

SET IN THE midst of the Burnaby Mountain Conservation Area, Burnaby Mountain is a popular destination because of its spectacular views, its network of trails through second-growth forest and its proximity to the mountain-top Simon Fraser University (SFU) campus. This walk complements Walk 62.

On foot from the gate at Dalla-Tina Avenue, walk up the incline—where there are lots of salmonberries in season—to a Trans Canada Trail (TCT) sign, just past the Burnwood Trail crossing. Here, you may either continue directly up the multi-purpose pathway or take the more interesting nature trail to the right and ascend through forest to Centennial Way. Across the road, continue on the TCT past a towering rock with a plaque commemorating the 1967 Confederation Centennial plantation of rhododendrons, unfortunately now overshadowed by trees. A rising, wide sweep takes you to the TCT pavilion, your point of decision.

For the shorter walk, head north through open lawns and picnic sites, towards the Horizons Restaurant and the lovely rose garden beyond. Enjoy the fine views along Indian Arm and Burrard Inlet, and note the Kamui Mintara, the Ainu totems that commemorate Burnaby's friendship with its sister city, Kushiro, Japan. Follow the gravel path that loops below the totems to join the fence-side Pandora Trail into the woods. After 10 minutes, you reach the junction where Gnome's Home branches left. You may follow Gnome's Home or continue to descend on Pandora; either trail leads to the Ridgeview and Burnwood trails and then quickly back to your starting point.

For the longer walk to the SFU campus, head uphill from the TCT pavilion. Ignore a lesser trail to the right then, at an information kiosk and fork, stay right. This leads to University Drive, where you continue on the roadside pathway to the T-junction with Gaglardi Way, a bus hub. Cross here, bear left and climb a broad stairway to a courtyard with a fountain. Convocation Mall draws you in under its glass and trussed roof, thence more stairs lead to the Academic Quadrangle, a large reflecting pool and other points of interest, and finally to the bus loop opposite a pleasant cascade of waterfalls. From here, descend East Campus Road beyond University Drive to an information kiosk and the top of the steep, popular Cardiac Hill, which you descend to meet the TCT. Go left to return to the restaurant area, head towards the totems and proceed as for the shorter outing.

BURNABY MOUNTAIN SUMMIT LOOP

Return: 8 km (5 mi)

Surface: packed; unimproved trail

Rating: easy to moderate

Allow: 3 hours

Elevation gain: 150 m (500 ft)

Season: most of the year

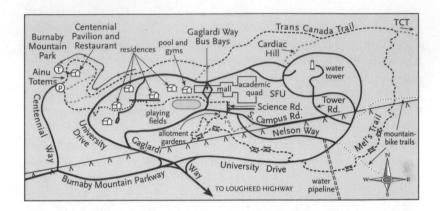

ACCESS

Transit: various routes to SFU University Drive; join walk on TCT

Vehicle: From Burnaby Mountain Parkway, turn north onto Centennial Way and drive to the Centennial Pavilion parking lot.

Car GPS entry: Burnaby Mountain Parkway & Centennial Way

Parking: 49°16.947′ N, 122°56.125′ W

BURNABY MOUNTAIN WEARS a crown of jewels: Simon Fraser University (SFU) sits at the top, a trail system for walkers and mountain bikers encircles it, and a lovely park with a picnic area and rose garden sits on the west shoulder (Walk 61), from which there are views of city, sea and mountain.

From your vehicle, wander over to view the Ainu totems, Kamui Mintara, then stroll beside the cliff-edge fence, enjoying the bird's-eye views and the rose garden. A few minutes beyond the children's playground, at an information board, stay left for a slow descent on the wide Trans Canada Trail (TCT) across the steep mountain slope. You pass through second-growth forest, cross several streams and get glimpses of the inlet below. Where you meet a large junction, keep left and continue downhill—uphill is

A floral eco-sculpture overlooking Burrard Inlet.

the well-named Cardiac Hill, a challenge for another day. The next junction, reached about 45 minutes from your start, is the dual-use Mel's Trail, with a curious little spring at its foot.

Here, you head up on a narrow track, well rutted by bicycles, to round the east flank of the mountain, climbing steadily until you reach the power line. Watch for the wreck of a blue Volkswagen bug below the trail and wonder how it got there. The trail now rises and falls, mainly through alder, and crosses a few streams on footbridges until suddenly you reach University Drive. Your route continues directly across the road, crosses more footbridges and leads to a meeting of several trails and a service road under the power line. Head left on the wide track for a dozen paces then right up a bike trail, negotiating a few obstacles, until you are confronted by a puzzle: Why is there a rusted-out trash barrel in this particular spot? Soon your answer appears in the form of an overgrown plaque dedicating (in 1972–73) a children's adventure playground, the nearby wooden structures now tilted and moss-covered. Continue over a curving bridge to exit the woods onto South Campus Road, cross this onto Science Road and proceed along it briefly before turning onto a sidewalk heading west beside the buildings.

After crossing Gaglardi Way, go diagonal left between the recreational complex and the sports fields, at the end of which you curve left briefly then go straight ahead, passing Chilcotin, Kitimat and Penticton Houses on their south sides. Round Quesnel House at its northwest corner to find your trail behind it, gently descending the escarpment to University Drive. Finally, cross this road onto a trail opposite then angle across the grassy field, passing the TCT pavilion en route to your vehicle.

BARNET TRAILS

Barnet and Cougar Creek return: 4 km (2.5 mi)   **Allow:** 1.5 hours

With Burnaby Mountain (return): 9.3 km (5.8 mi)   **Allow:** 3.5 hours

Surface: road, trail

Elevation gain: 265 m (870 ft)   **High point:** 335 m (1100 ft)

Rating: moderate to challenging   **Season:** most of the year

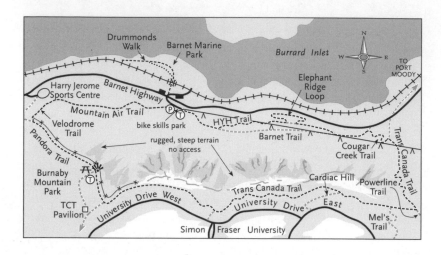

ACCESS

Transit: Route #160 Barnet Highway at 8300 block

Vehicle: Travelling on Highway 7A (Barnet Highway), turn south at the traffic lights at Takeda Drive (opposite Barnet Marine Park) into the parking lot of the Mountain Air Bike Skills Facility.

Car GPS entry: Barnet Highway & Takeda Drive

Trailhead: 49° 17.271′ N, 122° 55.318′ W

THIS COMBINATION OF trails on the north slopes of Burnaby Mountain forms an elongated shape, the two ends linking the "lowlands" to the "high-lands," providing a good aerobic workout. The upper part of the trail over-laps part of the two Burnaby Mountain/SFU walks, Walks 61 and 62.

On foot from the parking lot, follow a paved path eastwards outside the fence to the marked trailhead. Your trail rises to join the power line trail,

A few of the 500 steps on the Velodrome Trail.

which lies in the usual wide clearing, a productive habitat for salmonberry and blackberry bushes. You very soon arrive at the branch to Hang Your Hat (HYH) Trail, immediately before a mysterious set of swings overgrown by these same spreading bushes. Follow this attractive walking and biking trail as it winds through the forest and across several small, bridged creeks until a wide, bushy valley sloping down from the left gives way to a little ridge. Here, the Elephant Loop Trail provides a 20-minute diversion with a view of Burrard Inlet through the trees, though only once the leaves have fallen. Rejoining the main trail, you quickly reach the crest of a minor bump and a sign announcing the end of Barnet Trail and the beginning of Cougar Creek Trail. Leaving the power line, which heads uphill, you drop sharply, losing the little height you had gained, before you approach the highway briefly and swing away and up again, finally meeting the Trans Canada Trail (TCT) about 2 km (1.2 mi) from your start, a possible return point.

Continuing right and uphill on the TCT is more strenuous, as you start with the better part of 150 m of fairly steep trail to ascend to the information kiosk at the junction of TCT and Powerline Trail. Stay with the TCT all the way to Burnaby Mountain Park, with its picnic facilities and expansive views. Once rested, continue west, keeping close to the fence on the Pandora Trail for about 12 minutes until you reach the Velodrome Trail on your right. Upgraded in 2011, this trail drops 100 m on 500 steps (there is a bench halfway where you can take a breather) to link with, ironically, Mountain Air Trail.

Now you are on the home stretch: a 1.5 km (0.9 mi) walk through woodlands returns you to the parking lot and your transportation. When you are nearly there, and at a prominent, unsigned road junction, stay right. Left is a service road ending at a fence.

BURNABY MOUNTAIN SOUTH

Short circuit: 4 km (2.5 mi)

Long circuit: 7.7 km (4.8 mi)

Surface: packed, paved, mountain-bike trails

Elevation gain (short circuit): minimal

Elevation gain (long circuit): 145 m (475 ft)

Rating: easy to moderate

Allow: 1.5 hours

Allow: 2.5 hours

High point: 280 m (920 ft)

Season: all year

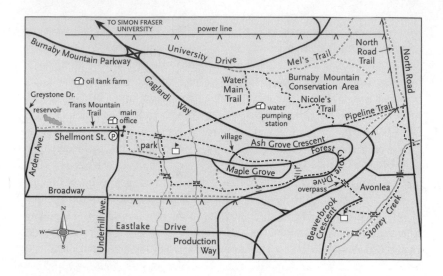

ACCESS

Transit: Route #136 to Forest Grove Drive at Underhill Avenue

Vehicle: From Lake City Way, cross Broadway onto Arden Avenue, turn east onto Shellmont Street and park near the gate. Alternatively, from the north, drive south on Duthie Avenue, east onto Greystone Drive, then left at Shellmont.

Car GPS entry: Arden Avenue & Shellmont Street

Trailhead at gate: 49° 15.978′ N, 122° 55.637′ W

THESE ROUTES TREAD the southeastern slopes of Burnaby Mountain, provide some aerobic workout and ramble along nature trails through residential and recreational areas. And you could add a "prewalk" by parking on Shellmont well west of the gate then following a pleasant off-road trail to the gate.

A fall day on the trail.

About 500 m beyond the gate, past the playing areas, you come to a fork. For the short circuit, walk straight ahead on the Trans Mountain Trail. At Ash Grove Crescent, cross onto a path below townhouses; this leads to Forest Grove Drive opposite Maple Grove Crescent. Cross Forest Grove and descend the wide stairway to a path just above the road's parallel lower section. Now, turn back west on this trail, which is joined by successive paths and stairs, as it gently ascends. Soon you come to a trail that crosses a pedestrian bridge high above a ravine of cottonwoods and continues to a T-junction at another gorge. Turn right, cross another bridge, then cross Forest Grove Drive again to arrive at a playground. A path beside a creek leads to your outward route, where a left turn leads back to the gate.

For the longer, more challenging route from the initial fork with the Trans Mountain Trail, take the narrow path leading left through brush. This takes about 5 minutes to ascend—with your ears alert for sounds of oncoming cyclists—to Gaglardi Way. Once across, climb to a water tower then continue on the Water Main Trail to join Mel's Trail on your right. Enter the woods and, within 5 minutes, cross a bridge then find the dual-use Nicole's Trail. (Continuing on Mel's Trail links to Walk 62.) Here, you descend, winding back and forth, wondering at the bikers' daring alterations, until you exit left onto the smooth Pipeline Trail. Next, climb gently to meet and cross Powerline Trail and, just behind two pipeline-related buildings, go right on the North Road Trail and descend to creek level, emerging left on North Road at the beginning of the Stoney Creek Trail (Walk 65). Follow this path, pass through a pedestrian underpass, then, at an information kiosk, cross a bridge to your right to walk beside a school and arrive at Beaverbrook Crescent. Turn right. After a few paces, go left to follow a paved pathway amongst trees, cross Gaglardi Way on an overpass, then cross Forest Grove Drive to the path just beyond the sidewalk. About 150 m to your left, join the short-circuit route to complete your return.

STONEY CREEK/SFU

One-way: 7.7 km (4.8 mi)

Surface: roads, improved trails

High point: 360 m (1180 ft)

Rating: moderate to challenging

Allow: 2.5 hours one way

Elevation gain: 310 m (1015 ft)

Season: most of the year

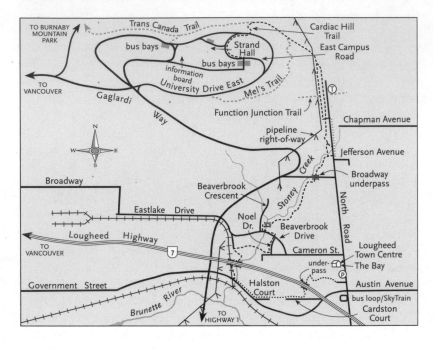

ACCESS

Transit: various routes to Lougheed Town Centre

Vehicle: Make your way to the Austin Road entrance on the south side of Lougheed Town Centre. Park near the southwest corner of The Bay (4 hours free).

Car GPS entry: Austin Road & Gatineau Place

Trailhead: 49° 15.000′ N, 122° 53.900′ W

THIS WALK PROVIDES something of a workout; it takes you uphill all the way from a busy shopping centre and along greenway paths to Simon Fraser University (SFU) on the summit of Burnaby Mountain. There, you may explore as you wish before walking down or riding the bus (Route #145 to Production Way, then hop onto the SkyTrain to travel one stop east to Lougheed Town Centre).

Begin your trek at the crosswalk at a bend in the parking lot's perimeter road west of The Bay. A few steps take you to a sidewalk (turn left) then a pedestrian tunnel under Highway 7 (Lougheed Highway) leading to Cardston Court, which soon becomes Halston Court. Turn right onto Government Street for about 300 m, then right into the trees and onto the wide, more tranquil path of Burnaby Mountain Urban Trail, here running alongside Stoney Creek, with its fine split-rail fencing. You pass under Highway 7 again before exiting onto the bottom of Eastlake Drive to turn right. Now, in short order, pass a ball field to Keswick Avenue, go left on Keswick, turn right onto Cameron Street, left again onto Noel Drive, then across and left on Beaverbrook Drive to its meeting with Beaverbrook Crescent. Here, you leave the streets for the last time until arriving at your destination.

Your track enters the trees at the street corner, where you drop to the creek and a bridge. Stay with the path through yet another tunnel, this time under Broadway, curve around a residential area, then step onto North Road just long enough to cross the bridge and dive back into the woods, now onto the dual-use North Road Trail. After walking for about 10 minutes and 500 m uphill, you arrive at a small pipeline building; jog left then immediately right onto the Powerline Trail. Surprisingly, about 650 m up the road, is a convenient outhouse. About 5 minutes later, you bear left at a fork to join the Trans Canada Trail and re-enter the trees (overlapping Walk 63).

Your steady slog continues for about 10 minutes before you head up the challenging Cardiac Hill Trail. Once at the top, however, your track almost flattens, or so it seems, as you make your way up University Drive East and East Campus Road to the bus loop. Here, you may rest and enjoy the water fountain, visit a café or further explore the campus (Walk 61) before making your way back down to your transport, by bus or by foot.

BURNABY LAKE

Long loop: 10 km (6.2 mi) **Allow:** 2.5 hours

Short loop: 5 km (3.1 mi) or less **Allow:** 1.5 hours

Surface: improved trail **Rating:** easy **Season:** all year

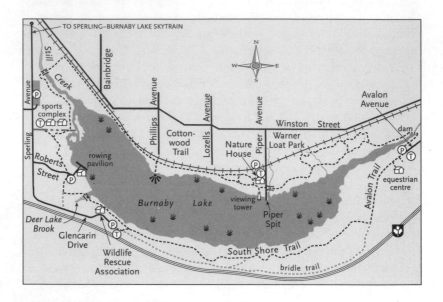

ACCESS

Transit: Route #101 to Cariboo Road and Avalon Avenue

Vehicle: To reach the Avalon Avenue lot at the east end of Burnaby Lake, from Highway 7 (Lougheed Highway) travel south on Brighton Avenue, east on Government Street, south on Cariboo Road, then west on Avalon Avenue to a parking lot.

Car GPS entry: Cariboo Road & Avalon Avenue

Trailhead: 49° 14.807′ N, 122° 55.093′ W

AN OASIS OF nature, the long, narrow Burnaby Lake is home to more than 200 species of resident or visiting birds as well as animals—look for trees gnawed by beavers. The park attracts runners, walkers, bird watchers and families who enjoy feeding the ducks and geese. The most interesting section for a short outing lies between the Avalon parking lot and the Piper Spit area. Information kiosks are located at parking lots and

Reflections along the marshy shore of Burnaby Lake.

trailheads. Occasional steps, especially at the dam, may be a small obstacle to strollers.

Circling the lake in a counter-clockwise direction gives you the choice of doing either the short or long loop. Heading right from the parking lot, you'll soon cross the Brunette River (Walk 67) on the Cariboo Dam, which was built to control water flow from the lake while managing fish access. Prior to dam construction in 1915, logs were floated along the lake and downstream to the Fraser River. A few minutes beyond the dam, there are two side loops to explore before you arrive at Piper Spit. Here, a wharf extends out to a beaver lodge, wild iris and other marshland plants thrive, and a variety of noisy waterbirds provide entertainment. If you want to feed the birds, bring grains, which are better for them than bread. Near the spit are the Nature House, a butterfly garden, a viewing tower and one more loop, where a sawmill once operated. (Limited parking is available at Piper Spit; this is the best access for strollers.)

The next leg of the trail stretches ahead for 2.3 km (1.4 mi), squeezed between railway tracks and lakeshore greenery, then makes a sharp turn to cross Still Creek before traversing the parking lot (an alternative starting point) and playing fields at the Burnaby Sports Complex. Continue south, cross the rowing pavilion parking lot, then regain your trail amongst black-berry bushes and shrubbery. Pause on the Deer Lake Brook bridge and in warm weather look for turtles busking on logs. The next 3.5 km (2.2 mi) along the Southshore Trail lie between the lake, near which farms once thrived, and the highway, where an electric tram once travelled. Board-walks traverse swampy sections made brilliant by the yellow swamp lan-terns (skunk cabbage) in spring. A few minutes past a clearing, go left on the broad multi-use Avalon Trail—where you may meet horseback riders from the equestrian centre—and so back to your starting point.

BRUNETTE RIVER

Return: 6 km (3.7 mi)   **Allow:** 2 hours

Surface: packed, paved   **Rating:** easy   **Season:** all year

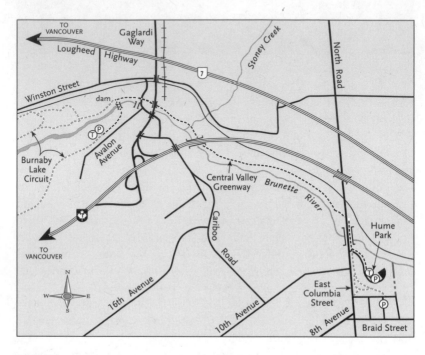

ACCESS

Car GPS entry: East Columbia Street & Holmes Street

Trailhead: 49° 14.316′ N, 122° 53.557′ W

Transit: Route #C9 to 600-block East Columbia Street, or go to the Braid SkyTrain Station bus loop and find a passage through the fence opposite, which takes you across railway tracks and onto a path, the Central Valley Greenway. Go left to arrive at Lower Hume Park in about 15 minutes. This will add 900 m each way to your walk.

Vehicle: Make your way to Hume Park off East Columbia Street, north of Braid Street in New Westminster. Drive past park facilities to a small parking lot. Or, to start from Burnaby, make your way to Cariboo Road, turn west onto Avalon Avenue and follow this to a parking lot at its end. From your vehicle, walk 200 m north (right) to cross the Brunette River on the Cariboo Dam and meet the route of the upstream walkers.

Car GPS entry: Cariboo Road & Avalon Avenue

Trailhead: 49° 14.807′ N, 122° 55.093′ W

Cariboo Dam and the fish ladder.

THE BRUNETTE RIVER, so named for the brown colour derived from the peaty soil with which its waters mix, flows from Burnaby Lake to the Fraser River. This attractive walk follows the banks of the river upstream from Hume Park, though you could also do the walk in reverse from Burnaby.

From Lower Hume Park, walk to East Columbia Street, cross at the pedestrian light, then head north over the bridge (where Columbia Street becomes North Road) to the service road on your left, the beginning of your excursion. Very soon, you arrive at an area of extensive enhancement work on both sides of the river that began in 2012 to extend and improve fish-spawning and -rearing habitat, and riparian and wildlife habitat. Keep an eye open for birdlife along the river, particularly for the great blue herons and the common kingfishers that frequent the area, looking for lunch. Seasonal water levels vary from a gentle flow, with tiny cascades over the two weirs, to swollen and rapid currents. As you stroll along, the sounds of nature compete for your attention with the dull drone of traffic. Compare this with the environment in 1859, when Robert Burnaby explored the river in its wilderness state, finding it tortuous, shallow and tangled with blowdowns.

After passing under the highway bridge, you come to Stoney Creek, where, thanks to the diligent efforts of volunteer streamkeepers, fish return to spawn. (Dogs, of course, have to rely on their owners to keep them out of the fish habitat areas, no matter how inviting a nice splash may be.) Next, you pass the entrance to a trailer park, follow the access road (Cariboo Place) to a crossing of Cariboo Road, then walk 250 m to the Cariboo Dam, with its fish ladder and nearby rest area. From here, you may continue up the right side of the water to the short loop on the Burnaby Lake walk (Walk 66), or you may return the way you came, enjoying the view from the opposite direction.

DEER LAKE PARK

Return: 7 km (4.3 mi)

Allow: 2.5 hours

Surface: packed; improved trail

Rating: easy

Season: all year

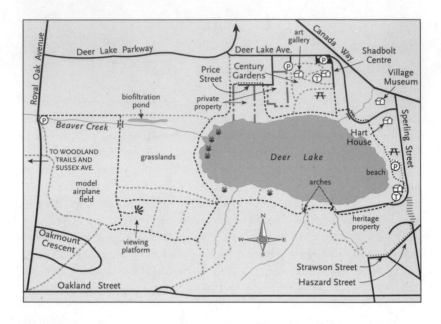

ACCESS

Transit: Route #144 to Deer Lake Avenue at Shadbolt Centre; join the trail at the lake.

Vehicle: For west-side access, drive north on Royal Oak Avenue and watch carefully for the entrance (right turn only) into a small lot at the bottom of the long hill.

Car GPS entry: Royal Oak Avenue & Buxton Street

Trailhead: 49° 14.298′ N, 122° 59.318′ W

DEER LAKE PARK offers walking trails, a beach and water-recreation facilities, broad views of the Lower Mainland's mountains and easy access to the beautiful Century Gardens and Burnaby's cultural hub.

Beginning your outing at Royal Oak, walk east beside Beaver Creek, the major feeder stream for Deer Lake, to the first junction, where you turn right onto a straight path. Immediately on your left is a side path with an information board explaining the nearby biofiltration pond; a few steps

Looking northeast across Deer Lake. *Photo: Paul Adam*

along on your right is a meadow for model airplanes. Surrounding grass-lands were once the site of a farm worked by inmates of Oakalla prison, which sat on the slope ahead, now occupied by housing. Continue walking up a rise, past two trails to your left, to a platform offering a wide view of the North Shore and Golden Ears mountains, with Deer Lake as foreground. Just above the platform, turn left and stay high until you reach a T-junction, where you turn downhill to meet the lakeside trail. Go right to travel along the south shore, where you'll traverse the edge of marshlands, walk under two arches on a boardwalk and pass in front of two city-owned heritage properties, the Eagles' Estate and Baldwin House, before turning left at an information board to reach the beach area with its many facilities. (To park and begin your outing here, turn south off Canada Way onto Sperling Avenue.) Some 300 m beyond the beach, the trail swings "inland" to cross a small creek on a bridge on Deer Lake Avenue, then immediately angles back towards the lakeshore.

Much of the north-side trail is on boardwalk with occasional benches. You may choose to make a side trip to explore Century Gardens and the Shadbolt Centre grounds, before you have to detour around private property. On a signed route, the trail makes a sharp turn north for 200 m to Price Street, travels 150 m west along Price, then heads south to rejoin the lake at its west end. Now, follow the boardwalk south through marshland to the junction of trails you crossed earlier. Here, for a variation on your return, choose one of the two lower trails heading west, turn uphill at its end, pass the viewing platform, continue uphill and right, then finally turn downhill, Royal Oak Avenue on your left.

Back on the flats, you may choose to extend your outing by passing under the roadway and wandering around woodland trails on the far side. Or you may choose to continue north back to your vehicle.

BYRNE CREEK RAVINE PARK

Return: 3.5 km (2.2 mi)   **Allow:** 1.5 hours

Surface: trail   **Rating:** easy to moderate   **Season:** all year

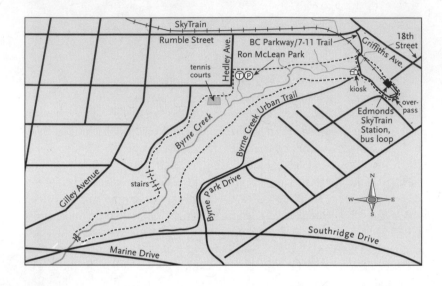

ACCESS

Transit: SkyTrain, buses to Edmonds Station

Vehicle: Park at Ron McLean parking lot, two blocks south of Rumble Street off Hedley Avenue in southeastern Burnaby.

Car GPS entry: Rumble Street & Hedley Avenue

Trailhead: 49° 12.691′ N, 122° 58.102′ W

BYRNE CREEK RAVINE Park, the "wilderness" portion of an urbanized watershed, provides a quiet oasis and pleasant escape from its busy surroundings, particularly on a hot day.

By transit, from the entrance of Edmonds SkyTrain Station, turn left and go through the parking lot by the bus loop to a path underneath the SkyTrain. Follow the path parallel to abandoned railway tracks, cross these to go left at a wide junction (signed B.C. Parkway/7-11), then immediately go right and walk between woods and townhouses for 500 m to the Ron McLean parking lot.

A shady creekside trail.

From the parking lot, walk downhill to the end of Hedley Avenue then turn right; the Byrne Creek Ravine Trail begins just beyond the tennis courts. Initially, the trail is level and bordered by deciduous shrubs and big-leaf maples, but then it drops about 75 m down dozens of steps to creekside. The creek water you see is collected by drains in the watershed and carried underground to the head of the ravine, where it is "freed" for a brief run. After flowing through more pipes, it winds up in the lowlands and artificial spawning grounds near the Fraser River (Walk 70). Today, Byrne Creek is cared for by streamkeepers who nourish salmon-spawning habitat. (Dogs who frolic in the water do unseen damage to this fragile resource.) In the 1870s, prime timber for ship masts was cut in the area, then floated down-stream to the Fraser River.

After crossing the creek on a footbridge, bear right to reach Southridge Drive, a noisy but brief interruption to your peace. Walk 10 m left to a short, steep embankment, which you climb to regain your trail. This path now braids its way along, well above the ravine, with views down the steep, veg-etated slopes, until you arrive at cement-and-stone foundations and large walnut trees. You could wander around here and try to picture what life might have been like before our population density forged the current envi-ronment: residential towers that you glimpse through the trees. Continue straight ahead, the towers and the paved Byrne Creek Urban Trail to your right, until you meet a T-junction with an information kiosk. Look down-stream from the nearby bridge to see the side channel–type fish ladder, built by streamkeepers to help juvenile fish on their upstream journey.

To return to Edmonds Station, turn right and follow a paved path for about 175 m to meet stairs leading up and over the SkyTrain tracks, then go left to the station. To return to Ron McLean Park, however, turn left at the kiosk and continue until, just before reaching the abandoned tracks, you turn left. This will lead you back to Ron McLean Park in short order.

BURNABY FRASER FORESHORE PARK

Return: 8 km (5 mi) **Allow:** 2.5 hours

Surface: packed; paved **Rating:** easy **Season:** all year

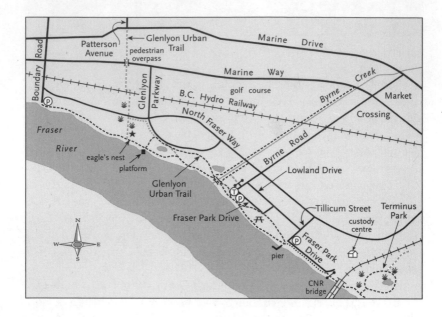

ACCESS

Transit: Route #116 to Boundary Road and East Kent Avenue North

Vehicle: The western entrance to this trail lies at the southern end of Boundary Road, the border between Burnaby and Vancouver. Keep right where the road bends east, south of the railway tracks.

Car GPS entry: Boundary Road & Marine Way

Trailhead (Boundary Road): 49° 12.078′ N, 123° 1.396′ W

THIS PLEASANT STROLL along the North Arm of the Fraser River offers places to watch activities on the river, an ecological reserve, and play and picnic areas.

From your vehicle, approach the river and turn left (Walk 50 goes right) on the dyke trail that lies between the tree-clad riverbank and, behind a row of trees on your left, light industrial businesses sitting on ancient peat bog. Dyke upgrading in early 2014 will have altered the appearance of this approach somewhat. In about 1 km (0.6 mi), a major trail enters from the north. Take a brief sidetrip about 200 m up this path and look for a large eagle's nest atop a cottonwood tree on the east side; perhaps its owners are nearby. Five minutes from this diversion, near the Glenlyon Creek dam, a viewing platform invites you closer to the river and the log booms. Soon thereafter, at Byrne Creek, a mounted picture frame outlines the scene.

Here, you may take a diversion. Turn upstream before the bridge and you'll quickly meet the picturesque Glenlyon Urban Trail. Curving right here leads towards North Fraser Way, a footbridge and a track down the east side of Byrne Creek back to the main trail. Or you may cross the road and walk northwards to Marine Way beside the placid, sometimes obscured watercourse that provides habitat for salmon spawn and fry under the guardianship of the Byrne Creek Streamkeepers.

Continuing on the main trail, over the next kilometre, you pass scattered picnic tables and extensive grassy fields lying between footpath and bike path, before arriving at a spacious platform ideal for relaxing. Shortly thereafter, you reach the archway at Tillicum Street. (Parking is available both at the picnic site, located near Fraser Park Drive off Byrne Road, and near the archway on Fraser Park Drive.) Now, walk along the gravel path to a gated, riverside trail. Within 5 minutes, you pass under the Canadian National Railway (CNR) bridge, with its centre span left open for river traffic, and arrive at the wide, unmarked junction to the Estuary Nature Area of the Fraser Foreshore Park, also known as Terminus Park. Here, there are more than 2 km (1.2 mi) of trails through a diversity of habitats, including restored wetlands and an old-field meadow.

Back on the main trail, continuing east for 500 m leads to an abrupt end at a waterworks bunker and shore access. Once back in the main park and, having crossed to the west side of Byrne Creek, you may vary your return route. Walk north to the Glenlyon Urban Trail (as you may have done earlier as a diversion) and this time turn left around a picturesque pond. At a second pond, a wide path through gateposts leads back to the riverside trail and your start.

EDMONDS/NEW WESTMINSTER QUAY

One-way from Edmonds Station: 7 km (4.3 mi)   **Allow:** 2.5 hours

Surface: paved   **Rating:** easy

Season: all year

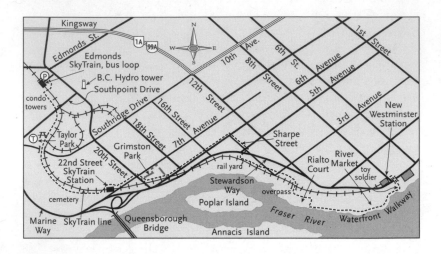

ACCESS

Transit: SkyTrain, buses to Edmonds Station

Vehicle: Park near the Edmonds SkyTrain station (in southeastern Burnaby).

Car GPS entry: Station Hill Drive & Station Hill Court

Edmonds station: 49°12.703′ N, 122° 57.528′ W

B.C. PARKWAY IS a 26 km (16.2 mi) multi-use pathway that roughly parallels the SkyTrain's Expo Line. This outing, along a portion of the parkway,
follows a decommissioned railway line, passes through a variety of residential and industrial environments, and ends at an urban esplanade and quayside market on the banks of the Fraser River in New Westminster. You may,
in fact, begin this circuit anywhere along the route, return to Edmonds Station on the SkyTrain after visiting the quay, then stroll back to your vehicle
on the pathway to complete your walk.

As you exit the Edmonds Station, turn right, walk less than 100 m to an
overpass on which you cross the tracks, then, across from the condo towers,

Fishing boats and tugs at New Westminster Quay.

turn left to join a wide, paved path, which is the B.C. Parkway. (Going right leads to Walk 69.) Follow the path across Southpoint Drive and past townhouses until, within 600 m, you reach Taylor Park. Once a landfill, the area has been transformed into a large multi-use attraction that is worth exploring. Visit the butterfly meadows near the bike park, and, in season, bring a pail to collect blackberries from the bushes that line the B.C. Parkway.

Next, cross Southridge Drive on an overpass and skirt the cemetery that lies tucked behind a cedar hedge, making a wide curve before arriving at the 22nd Street SkyTrain Station. Pass this on the uphill side and follow 7th Avenue to 20th Street, cross 20th and go right, then, after 80 m, turn left at a B.C. Parkway sign to reach Grimston Park. (As you make your way along, take the opportunity to look for views down the side streets.) Follow the path until you are blocked by Stewardson Way.

To continue, walk along 6th Avenue, past 16th Street, to Sharpe Street, where you turn right. Where Sharpe Street meets 5th Avenue on a bend, descend a ramp to Stewardson Way then go right 50 m to a controlled pedestrian crossing. Cross, then go left. Follow the sidewalk past industrial properties, then turn right on 3rd Avenue, cross the tracks on an overpass and turn left onto Quayside Drive. About 150 m along, you meet Rialto Court, onto which you turn right to reach the riverside.

Here, the whole atmosphere changes. Now you may stroll at leisure for about 1.5 km (0.9 mi) to River Market along a wooden esplanade lined with condos, information plaques and views. From its beginnings as a farmers' market in 1892, River Market has evolved—and continues to do so—into a family destination with a variety of diversions, eateries and shops.

Finally, at a children's play area overseen by a 9.8 m (32 ft) tin soldier (modelled on the Royal Engineers who founded New Westminster), cross the SkyBridge to the SkyTrain station, which is just beyond Columbia Street, for your return journey to Edmonds Station.

BELCARRA REGIONAL PARK DUO

Jug Island Beach return: 5.5 km (3.4 mi)
Burns Point return: 5.2 km (3.2 mi)
Surface: Jug Island—trail, packed; Burns Point—rough trail
Rating: Jug Island—moderate; Burns Point—easy

Allow: 2 hours
Allow: 2 hours

Season: all year

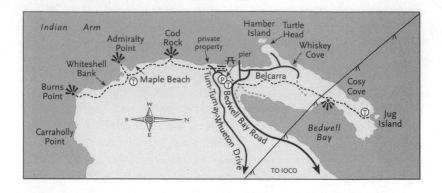

ACCESS

Transit: Route #C26 to Belcarra Bay Road at Midden Road (confirm route and schedule at www.translink.ca)

Vehicle: Follow Ioco Road in Port Moody alongside Burrard Inlet to First Avenue. Here, turn right then, at a fork, left onto Bedwell Bay Road. Pass the White Pine Beach Road, stay left and leave Bedwell Bay Road, following the sign to Belcarra Picnic Area. After 1 km (0.6 mi), you fork right and pass through a gate.

Car GPS entry: Ioco Road & Ungless Way

Jug Island (trailhead at road): 49° 18.812′ N, 122° 55.383′ W

Burns Point trailhead: 49° 18.734′ N, 122° 55.537′ W

SITUATED ON A point of land between Indian Arm and Burrard Inlet, this popular park is a magnet for picnicking and water activities. As well, there are two attractive walks in distinctive settings: a woodland walk along the spine of the peninsula to a delightful little beach at its north end and a ramble south near the shoreline at the mouth of Indian Arm. (Note that gates are closed when the park is at capacity.)

For Jug Island Beach, you may start from the north (far) end of the parking lot, cross Bedwell Bay Road, then walk a few paces left to find the

Looking north past Jug Island up Indian Arm.

trailhead, or you may start at the covered picnic tables on a signed trail leading into the forest to meet the trailhead across the road. At a junction to Bedwell Bay (a tidal flat, 35 minutes return), keep left on an old logging road working its way north along the ridge. After some 25 to 30 minutes, your route bends right onto a steeply rising, rocky track with stairs beside a mossy slab. A viewpoint nearby overlooks Bedwell Bay. Now the track levels briefly before dropping steeply to the secluded little beach with Jug Island just across the water, a pleasant spot to relax before you return.

For Burns Point, you start from below the concession stand on the south side of the parking lot. First cross a footbridge, then a road leading to private property, before your pleasant forest trail begins to rise a little above the waters of Indian Arm's southern reach. Small cleared areas with flower gardens gone wild were once home to squatters in the 1930s. Next comes Cod Rock, your first good viewpoint, followed by Periwinkle Notch, Maple Beach with its access trail, then a major junction at which the right fork takes you 100 m to Admiralty Point and expansive views.

Back at the junction, the trail becomes rougher, with ups and downs, until, after 1 km (0.6 mi), it reaches the rocky bluff of Burns Point, your destination, with its views up, down and across Burrard Inlet. At your leisure, you return the way you came.

SASAMAT LAKE/WOODHAVEN SWAMP

Sasamat Lake circuit: 3 km (1.9 mi)   **Allow:** 1 hour

Circuit with connector trail: 8 km (5 mi)   **Allow:** 3 hours

Surface (connector trail): trail, packed   **Rating:** easy   **Season:** most of the year

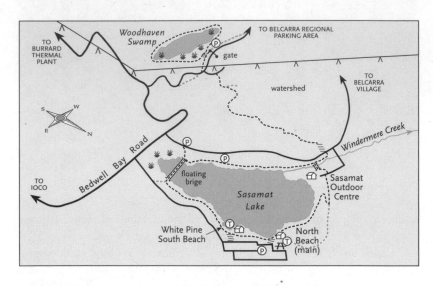

ACCESS

Transit: Route #150—seasonal

Vehicle: Follow Ioco Road in Port Moody alongside Burrard Inlet to First Avenue. Here, turn right then, at a fork, left onto Bedwell Bay Road. At a well-signed junction, turn right to White Pine Beach to park, preferably at the farthest lot. To walk the swamp trail only, drive towards the Belcarra Picnic Area and watch for a well-signed parking lot at Woodhaven Swamp.

Car GPS entry: Ioco Road & Ungless Way

White Pine Beach trailhead: 49° 19.500′ N, 122° 53.268′ W

Woodhaven Swamp trailhead: 49° 18.918′ N, 122° 54.352′ W

SASAMAT LAKE AND its two sandy beaches are so popular that on bright summer days only the early birds will gain access through the capacity-control gates. Nearby Woodhaven Swamp also makes a good destination. Before and during the Great Depression of the 1930s, loggers and shake

The swimming and fishing platform on Sasamat Lake.

cutters toiled here and shipped their products to Hastings Mill (Walk 45) in Vancouver.

The Sasamat Lake Trail begins at water's edge at the north end of the beach. Quite soon, it rises to an access road, where you turn left to meet the approach to the private Sasamat Outdoor Centre. Across this road, the trail resumes, dropping to and crossing the lake's outlet before coming to a T-junction. For the lake circuit, go left along the shore, paralleling Bedwell Bay Road above, until you come to the floating bridge with its swimming platforms, which cuts off the marshy southern foot of the lake. The pleasant trail continues through woods near the water with little bridges over side streams. Soon, you arrive at South Beach then North Beach and the completion of your walk.

Woodhaven Swamp can be reached by a connector trail (3.8 km/2.4 mi return) from Sasamat Lake or by driving to a parking lot adjacent to the swamp. From the lake circuit, turn right after crossing the outlet by the Sasamat Outdoor Centre, follow the creek downstream for about 200 m, then rise to road level at the Belcarra Village welcome sign, where a cross-walk leads to a flight of stairs. You now ascend between private properties, veer briefly to catch glimpses of the lake, cross a long bridge over a damp hollow and pass around the side of a bluff, after which the trail levels and comes to a power line access road. This, in turn, is joined by a bike path and emerges on the road to Belcarra Picnic Area directly across from the swamp. Cross the road and follow the bike path briefly to a small parking lot, where you descend stairs to the trail. The trail (1.2 km/0.7 mi) encircles the margin of this little wetland, a long boardwalk at its north end providing a place to pause. Finally, retrace your steps to Sasamat Lake to resume your course around its shore, perhaps finishing with a picnic or a swim.

BUNTZEN LAKE

Footbridge loop: 10.2 km (6.3 mi)

Penstock loop: 12.7 km (7.9 mi)

Surface: trail, packed

High point: 258 m (845 ft)

Rating: easy to moderate

Allow: 3.5 hours

Allow: 4.5 hours

Elevation gain: 100 m (330 ft)

Season: all year

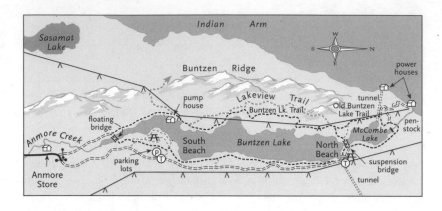

ACCESS

Transit: Route #C26—seasonal (confirm the route and schedule at www.translink.ca)

Vehicle: From Highway 7A (Barnet Highway), go north on Ioco Road, continue uphill on Heritage Mountain Boulevard, go right onto David Avenue at the traffic circle and follow signs left, then left again for Buntzen Lake. At a T-junction, go right on Sunnyside Road to the park's gate.

Car GPS entry: Ioco Road & Ungless Way

Trailhead at beach: 49° 20.377′ N, 122° 51.337′ W

BUNTZEN LAKE, WITH its two beaches and variety of hiking trails, is a popular destination for hikers, swimmers, self-propelled boaters and fisher-folk. Set in a deep mountain basin, the lake was created as a reservoir in 1903 to supply hydroelectric power to Vancouver, as it still does. (For more information about the area, see www.bchydro.com/community/recreation_areas.html.) Note that the gate is closed when the parking lot is full, a common summer occurrence; no neighbourhood parking is available.

The bridge across the south end of Buntzen Lake.

This excursion takes you around the lake. To begin, head to the beach from the parking lot, where your trail starts at a footbridge behind the washrooms. It rolls gently all the way to North Beach, with a few side trails providing access to the lake en route. (Returning from here gives an 8 km/ 5 mi walk.) Near the head of the lake, you step onto the road to cross an outlet spewing water into Buntzen Lake—consider that it comes from Coquitlam Lake through a tunnel hacked for 3.6 km (2.2 mi) through the towering Eagle Ridge above in 1903.

To complete the lake circuit from North Beach, you have two options: for the footbridge loop, cross the footbridge west of the picnic area and bear left to join the Buntzen Lake Trail; for the longer penstock loop, continue north on the road by McCombe Lake past the dam where you see the penstock carrying water to Buntzen #1 Powerhouse on Indian Arm below. Cross the penstock and follow the road about 150 m to a sign for the Old Buntzen Lake Trail. This loops through a very pleasant stretch of forest and past the water intake facility, before meeting the Buntzen Lake Trail from the footbridge and the biking and equestrian Lakeview Trail running parallel higher up the slope.

Now you descend into a hollow and climb up over the next bluff, with views of Swan Falls and the scar left by a large rockfall across the lake. In forest again, the track undulates, crossing and recrossing the power line right-of-way, before eventually bringing you back to the lake level beside a pumphouse. From here, you walk south on the service road for 1.2 km (0.7 mi) to cross the long metal bridge spanning the lake's southern extension and surrounding wetlands. Your final lap winds through another attractive stretch of forest back to your starting point.

SHORELINE TRAIL

Return: 6 km (3.7 mi)   **Allow:** 2 hours

Surface: rough trail, paved   **Rating:** easy   **Season:** all year

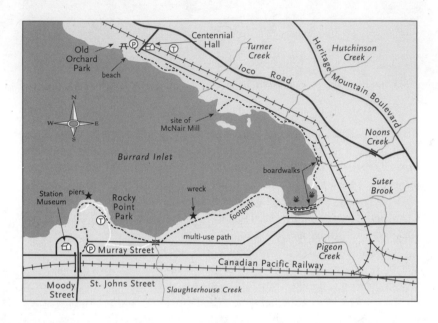

ACCESS

Transit: Route #C25, C26 to Murray Street at Hugh Street

Vehicle: From Highway 7A (St. Johns Street), turn north at the Moody Street intersection, follow the curve around and turn left on Murray Street, then left into the parking lot east of the underpass.

Car GPS entry: St. Johns Street & Moody Street

Trailhead at bridge: 49° 16.797′ N, 122° 50.865′ W

LYING MOSTLY SECLUDED from busy roads and urban activities, this trail provides glimpses into shoreline activities in the late 19th century: remnants of sawmills and shingle mills, a steel mill and brickyards that fuelled the growth of Port Moody. Built to suit both those who prefer a natural footpath and those who require a smooth surface, the twinned trails between Rocky Point Park, off St. Johns Street in Port Moody, and Old Orchard Park,

Remnants of early sawmill activity contrast with high-rises in the distance.

on the opposite shore off the Ioco Road, form a rough horseshoe around the head of Burrard Inlet. (Alternatively, you could park at Old Orchard Park and hike the trail in the opposite direction.)

You might start your outing with a visit to the Port Moody Station Museum, located west of the road underpass. It holds artifacts of First Nations origin and of European settlement days, and has available the descriptive brochure *Heritage Tour of Inlet Trail*. From the parking lot, the trailhead begins at a footbridge at the northeastern end of the grassy fields. The foot-trail and hardtop paths diverge at the bridge over Slaughterhouse Creek, whose name evokes the days when a slaughterhouse operated here in the 1920s. As you head into the trees, fir and cedar being prominent, note the final remains of a long-ago shipwreck on the shore. Stop at Pigeon Cove to imagine thousands of band-bailed pigeons migrating in the spring and fall, an attraction for hunters until the 1970s. Winding boardwalks and bridges take you over the mud flats and sedges that mark the head of Burrard Inlet. Next, watch for a short detour to the water, where a grassy area and small platform with a bench offer fine views down the inlet and of shoreline birdlife.

Soon thereafter, at Noons Creek, another side trail rises to the Noons Creek Fish Hatchery, which is managed by the Port Moody Ecological Society. Continuing on your way, you may spot scraps from early industrial activity. At Old Mill Site Park, you might explore the remains of one of the cedar mills that once dotted this part of the coast: the cement foundations of a beehive lumber-waste burner and rotting stanchions that once supported busy wharves and mill buildings. Benches and information boards dot the trail. Finally, your trail ends at Old Orchard Park, an attractive picnic area with a beach, children's play area and toilets available in a hall across the tracks. To return, you could choose the more direct and evenly graded multi-use path that runs between the railway tracks and the footpath.

COQUITLAM CRUNCH PLUS

Return: 5.7 km (3.5 mi) **Allow:** 2 hours

Surface: packed, paved **Elevation gain:** 244 m (800 ft) **High point:** 278 m (912 ft)

Rating: moderate to challenging **Season:** all year

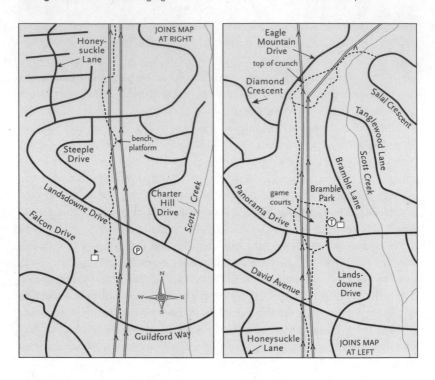

ACCESS

Transit: Routes #150 and #160, on Guildford Way to Eagleridge Drive, #C27 on Lansdowne

Vehicle: From Barnet Highway (Highway 7A), drive north on Lansdowne Drive, cross Guildford Way, then, 150 m past Scott Creek Middle School, turn left onto a dirt road near a patch of trees. Continue to the parking area.

Car GPS entry: Lansdowne Drive & Guildford Way

Trailhead parking lot: 49° 17.119′ N, 122° 48.917′ W

REFLECTING ITS NAME, this hillside walk provides a pleasantly steady, aerobic ascent with distant views on a clear day. The Crunch is but one portion of the 13.5 km (8.4 mi) Eagle Ridge Greenway that connects Westwood Plateau to the Fraser River. The slope is south facing and the entire corridor is without shade, so it will be hot on a sunny summer's day.

If travelling by transit, walk 200 m west on the north side of Guildford to reach your trail under the power line, then proceed 200 m to the parking lot. From here, the path begins steeply, opposite a school playground. There are signs that advise about safety precautions around power lines, since the route follows B.C. Hydro's transmission corridor. Within moments, you cross Lansdowne Drive for the first time, and just before the 0.5 km signpost, you may pause for relief at a viewing platform with a bench. Continuing upwards, there are a few sets of path-side steps that offer a change of pace. More relief comes when the slope begins to lie back close to the second crossing of Lansdowne Drive.

North of David Avenue, the midway point, the path swings around a fenced off-leash area before arriving at a fork. Either way works. Going right leads to a crossing of Panorama Drive opposite Bramblewood Elementary School. You can then go straight ahead, past the sports facilities, and swing left at the tennis courts to rejoin the trail beyond. If you go left and up the stairs, stay right of the game courts, then go left on Panorama Drive (past a bus-stop bench), before crossing to Bramble Park. Within another 500 m you reach the top of the Crunch (no bench) at Eagle Mountain Drive, about 45 minutes from your start. You can now reward yourself with a stroll through a strip of woods beside Scott Creek, the sound of nature in your ears and a soft path underfoot. Take a refreshing pause on the bridge over the creek before you exit onto Salal Crescent, your turnaround point.

Returning the way you came, you can extend your woodland moments by staying left at a junction until the gravelled trail reaches the transmission line clearing. Follow the path upwards to rejoin the Crunch, then head down to your starting point, enjoying the views en route. (Alternatively, to save your knees, you could catch the #C27 bus at Panorama Drive, which will take you down Landsdowne Drive to your start.)

RIDGE PARK LOOP

Return: 5 km (3.1 mi)

Surface: rough, improved trails

High point: 415 m (1360 ft)

Season: most of the year

Allow: 2 hours

Elevation gain: 130 m (425 ft)

Rating: easy to moderate

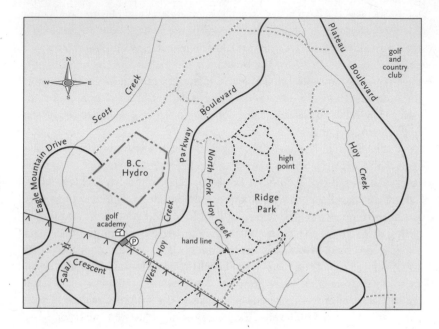

ACCESS

Transit: Route #C29 to Parkway Boulevard at Salal Crescent, opposite the parking lot

Vehicle: Travelling on Parkway Boulevard in Coquitlam, arrive at the Westwood Plateau Golf Academy under a power line, with a parking lot opposite. Park here.

Car GPS entry: Parkway Boulevard & Panorama Drive

Trailhead: 49° 18.308′ N, 122° 48.332′ W

RIDGE PARK LOOP, which winds through second-growth forest around, or over, a prominence in the centre, makes a good destination on a hot day. It is one of many trails and greenbelts that have been developed on or near Westwood Plateau since the Westwood Motorsport Park was closed in 1990 to give way to residential development.

A well-seasoned log bench.

From the parking lot, begin your walk on a gravelled path under the power line, where you might pause to enjoy the view across the Fraser River to mountains in the distance before entering the trees. Where the power line starts to drop rather steeply, go left onto an obvious trail into the forest. After about 250 m, there is a sharp switchback, which you follow down. There is also a rough, narrow trail that joins the corner here, your return track. Soon you arrive at another sharp switchback, which, in turn, leads to a crossing of the North Fork of Hoy Creek on two bridges. (Tracks to the right along the way lead to residential areas.) The trail now lies on a dyke of moss-covered, crushed rock until, just beyond a wooden bridge, it meets a junction. Go right and begin a stiff climb of 180 m (590 ft) over the next 2 km (1.2 mi). There are a few short downhill bits for relief, however.

After some 20 minutes of climbing, as your trail makes a large curve left, you begin to get glimpses through the trees of a golf course and houses. Now, approaching the high point on the main loop, you come to a fork where the left leads up and over the hilltop while the right contours around below. A map board and a mossy log bench, one of a few built along the loop, mark the top. From here, you may choose either a quick plunge or a more leisurely zigzagging descent to meet the main trail.

You then walk roughly parallel to and above the golf fairways for a short time before turning away and dropping quickly for 800 m to another junction with a map board. Now you go right to meet the most challenging part of the trip, another crossing of the North Fork of Hoy Creek, this time stepping carefully through the creek bed using a sturdy handline. A few paces later, you are back at the initial switchback and en route to the parking lot. If you wish to avoid this creek crossing, keep left on a track continuing down to the main trail, where you turn right and ascend the switchbacks.

COQUITLAM RIVER/
TOWN CENTRE PARK

Return: 9 km (5.6 mi)   **Allow:** 3 hours

Surface: trails, paved   **Rating:** easy   **Season:** all year

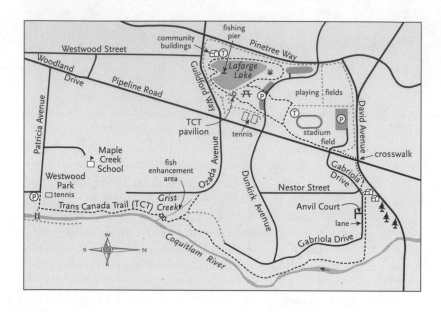

ACCESS

Transit: various routes to Lafarge Lake, then do the walk in reverse

Vehicle: Make your way to Highway 7 (Lougheed Highway) and Hastings Street, 200 m west of Coquitlam River Bridge. Drive 700 m north on Hastings to Patricia Avenue, turn right and park on the street at the end.

Car GPS entry: Hastings Street & Lougheed Highway

Trailhead: 49° 16.591′ N, 122° 46.723′ W

THIS WALK FOLLOWS the Coquitlam River and skirts a residential area, then makes its way through a large urban park with all its seasonal amenities and culminates with a pleasant circuit of Lafarge Lake. The lake provides a nice place to rest before you must return. Most of the route follows the Trans Canada Trail (TCT), so the distinctive signs help keep you on track.

Your path begins near the tennis court on Patricia Avenue and almost immediately reaches a bridge over the Coquitlam River. Look, but do not cross (Walk 79 lies on the other side); instead, turn left on the TCT and continue through mostly deciduous, then mixed forest with some large conifers and cottonwoods. In spring, the cottonwoods' sweet smell (sometimes called Balm of Gilead) scents the air; there are a variety of plants in the undergrowth. After about 10 minutes, you cross the bridge over Grist Creek, which is a protected salmon habitat area (sorry, Pooch, no swimming). As you proceed up the Coquitlam River, occasional side trails provide access to the water's edge.

After about 2 km (1.2 mi), you leave the riverside and turn westwards on a lane to emerge on Gabriola Drive, where, a few paces to your left and opposite Nestor Street, a TCT sign beckons. A short track between houses leads to the busy intersection of David Avenue and Pipeline Road. Cross Pipeline Road at the light to a bench at the corner of a park opposite. After resting and getting your bearings, follow a paved path in the trees parallel to Pipeline Road, passing expansive sports fields (with concessions and facilities) on your right, then continue past the playground and parking lots to Lafarge Lake. This area, a former gravel quarry, was donated to the city when quarry operations ceased. Although the lake with its fountain is not suitable for swimming, it is popular with fisherfolk. Turn right to circumnavigate the lake, skirting the wetland environment at the north end and passing community facilities at the southwest side. Now, choose between the paved multi-use path or the Lakeside Nature Trail, which winds up and down close to the water and passes the fishing pier. Both will take you to the TCT pavilion (kiosk), from which you start your return walk.

Follow the TCT trail that rises to meet and cross Pipeline Road, turn left (north) to find the right-of-way near the intersection that leads you back to the Coquitlam River Trail and retrace your steps back to your vehicle.

TRABOULAY POCO TRAIL: COQUITLAM RIVER

Return: 10.5 km (6.5 mi)   **Allow:** 3 hours

Surface: paved, packed   **Rating:** easy   **Season:** all year

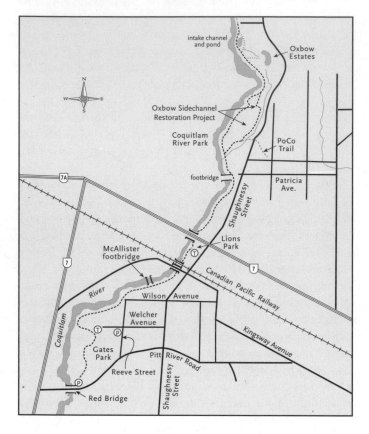

ACCESS

Transit: Route #C36 to Reeve Street at Hawthorne Avenue. Cross Reeve to the parking lot.

Vehicle: From Pitt River Road, drive north on Reeve Street, just east of the Coquitlam River. At Welcher Avenue, go west to the Gates Park parking lot.

Car GPS entry: Wilson Avenue & Reeve Street

Trailhead: 49° 15.479′ N, 122° 47.532′ W

THIS WALK BEGINS along the Traboulay PoCo Trail between street and stream, then continues into the woods where fish and wildlife habitat has been extensively regenerated. It is but one section of a network of connecting trails that are yours to explore (see also Walks 78 and 82).

From the northwest corner of the parking lot, walk 150 m left (west) on Welcher Avenue to a path leading left; follow this to join the wide, paved trail where you go right. You may either curve around the edge of the busy playing fields where the river itself makes a sharp bend behind the screen of trees, or you may cut across the fields on a walkway that goes past change rooms. This is a popular area for people of all ages, many of whom spend a few minutes at the various exercise stations along the route to Lions Park and the children's playground. Lions Park lies between the Canadian Pacific Railway tracks and Highway 7 (Lougheed Highway). Along the route, an interesting series of signs notes historical highlights going either forward or back in time, depending on your direction of travel. Benches are available for resting.

Beyond the Lougheed Highway Bridge, the path's surface changes to a narrower, less smooth track as it enters a wooded environment with more opportunities to view and approach the river. About 1 km (0.6 mi) farther along, and just past the Patricia Avenue footbridge (which links to Walk 78), you come to Coquitlam River Park, where the federal Department of Fisheries and Oceans, along with local groups, has reclaimed historic stream channels, ponds and wetlands. The area is an easily negotiable maze of old roads and trails through mixed forest. Ignoring the PoCo Trail to the east, continue straight ahead; you may keep more left, nearer the river, en route north and make a narrow loop on your return.

Soon, you'll pass a fenced-off stream (to keep dogs out) where you might see salmon fighting their way upstream to spawn in the fall. An information board describes the Oxbow Sidechannel Restoration Project. Next, you pass Oxbow Lake, surrounded by private residences, then shortly thereafter the northern end of the restoration project at the intake channel flowing into a dyked pond. Your turnaround point lies a short distance beyond, at the Elizabeth Drive road-end.

Returning, stay gently left south of Oxbow Lake to see another part of the wetlands restoration works. And so back to Gates Park, where views of the Golden Ears mountains dominate with best advantage.

COLONY FARM REGIONAL PARK

Return: 8 km (5 mi) **Allow:** 2.5 hours

Surface: packed, road **Rating:** easy **Season:** all year

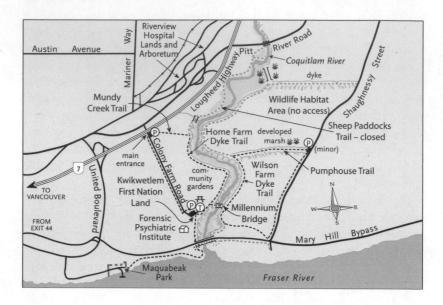

ACCESS

Transit: Route #177 to Cape Horn Avenue at Colony Farm Road

Vehicle: From Highway 7 (Lougheed Highway), turn south on Colony Farm Road (traffic lights) and park just across the tracks. Alternatively, drive 1 km (0.6 mi) farther to park.

Car GPS entry: Colony Farm Road & Lougheed Highway

Trailhead at first lot: 49° 14.369′ N, 122° 48.810′ W

COLONY FARM REGIONAL PARK is a work in progress. For more than 70 years, from 1904, residents of the onsite mental health hospital operated it as a renowned produce and dairy farm. Straddling the lower Coquitlam River near its mouth with the Fraser, the fertile land is now being restored with tidal flows and habitat enhancement to support an increasing variety of waterlife, wildlife and birds. Walking the dykes in this oasis of tranquility provides opportunity for mental relaxation.

From the top parking lot, your trail parallels Colony Farm Road on its west side to another parking lot, a picnic area and community gardens. Birding enthusiasts may want to explore along the lush dyke that runs south between river and ditch to the meeting of the Coquitlam and Fraser Rivers 600 m from the second parking lot. Otherwise, pass to the east side of the gardens and follow the trail there north alongside a ditch to a small bridge. Cross this to the Home Farm Dyke, then go right to cross the Coquitlam River over the arching Millennium Bridge. Turn right again to make a counter-clockwise circuit, beginning on an attractive section of the PoCo Trail that winds westwards amongst trees with a wetland on one side and old farmlands on the other. When Shaughnessy Street looms ahead, turn left onto the verge for the least attractive part of your journey and know that a pleasant reward awaits you after about 20 minutes.

An information kiosk welcomes you back into the park on the Pumphouse Trail and immediately the variety of wetland life attracts your attention. Farther along, you arrive at a pumphouse that controls water levels in the ditches. Go left and head downstream to return over the Millennium Bridge to complete this loop.

Now you turn north along the meandering Home Farm Dyke Trail, with its views to distant mountains. At the next junction, you may proceed 200 m to a closed gate (the trail beyond is eroding) to read the information boards about land rehabilitation plans, but the route back to your transportation turns left onto Mundy Creek Trail.

You now have the option of visiting Western Canada's first arboretum, established in 1912, on the Riverview Hospital grounds across the highway from your parking lot. The approach road leads to heritage buildings set amidst extensive lawns and a collection of native and exotic trees, originally about 1,900 of them. One enjoyable stroll would be up Fern Crescent to the Backyard Trail and Finnie's Garden, which began in 1951 as a horticultural therapy program for the mentally ill residents. The Riverview Horticultural Centre Society now maintains the grounds and runs tours. See www.rhcs.org.

WOODLAND WANDERS

Return: 9.6 km (6 mi) or less
Surface: rough trails
Elevation gain: 375 m (1230 ft)
Rating: moderate to challenging

Allow: 4 hours

High point: 700 m (2300 ft)
Season: April to November

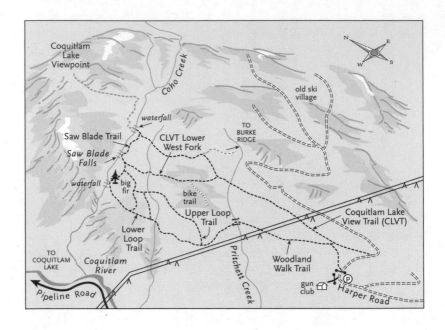

ACCESS

Vehicle: From Highway 7 (Lougheed Highway), drive 5 km (3.1 mi) north on Coast Meridian Road to Harper Road; turn right, drive 2 km (1.2 mi) to the gun club entrance. Park near the gate.

Car GPS entry: Coast Meridian Road & Harper Road

Trailhead: 49° 18.222′ N, 122° 44.945′ W

WATERFALLS, MASSIVE STUMPS, an enormous Douglas-fir tree and occasional logging artifacts mark the highlights of this wander through the woods, though the silence is sometimes disturbed by staccato from the nearby gun range. This walk has been considerably revised from previous editions, with the addition of Saw Blade Falls and, in part to compensate for the twinning of the power line (2013), some rerouting. The network of trails is maintained by the Burke Mountain Naturalists, see www.bmn.bc.ca.

At the road gate, a mountain-bike trail enters the woods and climbs for 10 minutes to a signed junction where the fork to the power line and Coquitlam Lake View Trail (CLVT) is on your right. (Walking on the road from the gate adds 500 m to your distance.) Your route, the Woodland Walk Trail, heads left on one of the many abandoned logging roads that lace the hillside of Burke Mountain. Reaching the power line road, go left, cross Pritchett Creek Bridge and very soon watch for the signed (new) trailhead to the Upper Loop Trail.

The trail gently ascends past enormous stumps in second-growth forest, the sight of their springboard notches evoking images of old-fashioned logging operations. Pass a T-junction to the Lower Loop Trail and continue onward. The next signed right turn leads to a viewpoint and Saw Blade Falls, but you continue a few paces downhill to where the Upper and Lower Loop Trails meet. Go right for about 15 minutes to see an impressive Douglas-fir and the attractive Woodland Walk Falls.

Now you have a choice: return to the aforementioned junction then back to your vehicle via either of the loop trails, or from near the falls, ascend steeply for 15 minutes to a rocky viewpoint. After resting, continue following signs and ascending, now less steeply, to CLVT's Lower West Fork. At last, within 100 m and taking care on the narrow path, you approach the outstanding Saw Blade Falls.

Now, another choice. The CLVT's Lower West Fork contours pleasantly for 1.6 km (1 mi) then meets the CLVT, which descends directly to your vehicle. (The easiest access to Saw Blade Falls is up the CLVT then fork left here, 1.2 km/0.7 mi from the power line.) Alternatively, from near Saw Blade Falls, follow the Saw Blade Trail that ascends through the woods for 1.2 km (0.7 mi) to arrive at yet another waterfall on Coho Creek, which here flows across the CLVT. Much smaller, this waterfall is at its best during spring runoff. Now, being on the CLVT, you descend directly to your vehicle.

DEBOVILLE SLOUGH/
NORTH PITT RIVER

Return: 12 km (7.5 mi) **Allow:** 3.5 hours

Surface: packed dyke **Rating:** easy **Season:** all year

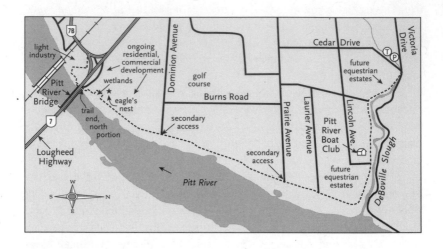

ACCESS

Transit: Route #C38 to Victoria Drive at Rocklin Drive

Vehicle: Make your way to Victoria Drive and drive east to its end at Cedar Drive in northwest Port Coquitlam. Park in the nearby lot.

Car GPS entry: Victoria Drive & Cedar Drive

Trailhead: 49°17.125′N, 122°44.014′W

THIS PORTION OF Port Coquitlam's 25 km (15.5 mi) Traboulay Trail (also part of the Trans Canada Trail) begins along a tranquil slough, then follows the banks of the Pitt River, with its views of mountains and river activities. The landscape is undergoing rapid reconfiguration as acres of farmland are being converted to equestrian estates, residential blocks and shopping malls.

From Cedar Drive, the trail wanders for 2 km (1.2 mi) along the banks of DeBoville Slough. Once an important hunting and harvesting area for the

Lush wildlife habitat lines the banks of DeBoville Slough.

Katzie First Nation, the wetlands were dyked by settlers a century ago to save the lands from floodwaters backing up the Pitt River from tidal water in the Fraser. Now the slough provides habitat for fish, wildlife and birds, including great blue herons, mute swans and waterfowl. The graceful swans like to frequent the Pitt River Boat Club area in the slough.

Heading south along the Pitt, occasional benches face the river for your enjoyment as you stop to take in the views, watch the boats or contemplate life itself! Across the river are the dykes of Chatham Reach (Walk 85). Near Laurier Avenue, you can see a large greenhouse complex; elsewhere are productive fields and pastureland. A tidal wetland area has been constructed about 700 m south of Dominion Avenue to compensate for commercial and residential development nearby. Just as your trail veers right to begin its way around this wetland, look for an eagle's nest high in a cottonwood tree on your right. On the far side of the wetland, the trail swings north, then bends back to parallel itself as it approaches the Pitt River Bridge underpass. Here, this section of the Traboulay Trail ends and the next section, the South Pitt River Trail, begins. (Other sections of the Traboulay Trail are included in Walks 79 and 80.)

Before you begin your return journey, however, you may give in to your curiosity and continue about 800 m farther, where you'll find yourself, surprisingly, amidst a hidden patch of industrial activity, once so commonly seen along waterways. Variously coloured piles of organic matter, woodchips and asphalt bits are bounded by the river, train tracks and highway, on the other side of which a shiny new shopping complex is being constructed (2014). Where the trail descends into a tunnel under the train tracks is a good turnaround point.

MINNEKHADA REGIONAL PARK

Return: 7.5 km (4.7 mi) **Allow:** 2.5 hours

Surface: packed gravel, rough

Elevation gain: 150 m (500 ft) **High point:** 165 m (540 ft)

Rating: easy to moderate **Season:** most of the year

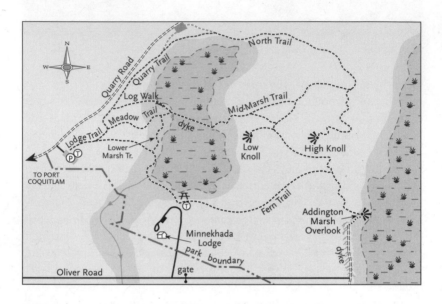

ACCESS

Vehicle: From Coast Meridian Road and Victoria Drive, travel 1.3 km (0.8 mi) east on Victoria then take its left fork, which later becomes Quarry Road. From the fork, continue for 3.5 km (2.2 mi) to the park entrance.

Car GPS entry: Coast Meridian Road & Victoria Drive

Trailhead: 49° 18.002′ N, 122° 42.440′ W

INITIALLY A FARM, then a hunting estate, the 175 ha (430 ac) Minnekhada Regional Park now features a fine trail network, including a broad view from atop a steep hill, and marshland that is home to numerous birds and water creatures.

The trail system starts near the information kiosk at the parking lot, with the choice of routes to either right or left. Going right, you come to a

The view of Minnekhada Lake and beyond from Low Knoll.

marsh that you keep on your left until you arrive at the groomed picnic area, from the top of which a road to the Minnekhada Lodge veers to the right. (The lodge is an elegant 1934 heritage building, open to the public during selected hours.) Take advantage of the viewing platform, then continue into the forest on the aptly named and undulating Fern Trail. At a three-way crossing, the right fork leads to a once-striking view across Pitt-Addington Marsh Provincial Wildlife Management Area that is now, unfortunately, quite reduced by growing trees. Your next stop is the Low Knoll, which is undergoing the same fate. From there, and immediately after rejoining Fern Trail, you reach a major junction: left takes you across the marsh on a dyke, then you may take either Log Walk or Meadow Trail to your starting point; right commits you to the long perimeter trail.

Going right, you soon come to yet another fork, the right-hand branch of which leads you panting to the top of the sharp rise to High Knoll lookout. Below you, close in, lie the marshes; farther out lie cranberry fields and Goose Bar in the Pitt River. On your return to the T-junction, go first right, then left, gaining height and losing it again as you turn west on North Trail. At the next fork, right heads away uphill towards Quarry Road, but you go left and down to marsh level, enjoying the profusion of marsh plants in season until you merge into Quarry Trail, which parallels the road south. This portion of the route is probably the least attractive, so you may decide to detour along Log Walk, which takes you to the dyke that separates the Upper and Lower Marshes. Again, you have a choice: follow the view trail along Lower Marsh or take the Meadow Trail, both of which connect with the Lodge Trail for the final stretch back to your vehicle.

GRANT NARROWS

Katzie Marsh loop: 6.5 km (4 mi)   **Allow:** 2.5 hours

Long loop: 12 km (7.5 mi)   **Allow:** 4.5 hours

Surface: trail, packed   **Rating:** easy

Season: Most of the year. Crane and Homilk'um Dykes are closed during nesting season mid-March to mid-July.

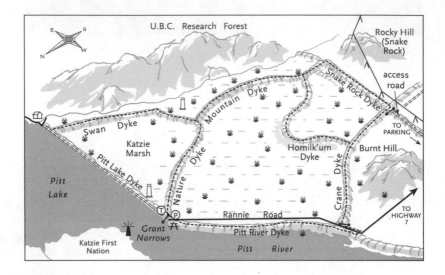

ACCESS

Vehicle: In Pitt Meadows, from Highway 7 (Lougheed Highway) turn north on Harris Road, east on McNeil Road and north on Rannie Road, then travel to a parking lot at Grant Narrows.

Car GPS entry: McNeil Road & Rannie Road

Trailheads: 49° 20.939' N, 122° 36.937' W

THE NETWORK OF dykes at Grant Narrows was built to funnel Pitt Lake, one of the largest tidal lakes in the world, into the Pitt River, thus converting a natural floodplain into fertile agricultural fields. The dykes provide an ideal surface for walking and cycling against a backdrop of spectacular views of Pitt Lake and its surrounding mountains. Cool mountain winds, however, may flow down Pitt Lake, so carry extra clothing. (Since 2011,

Pitt Lake, with Grant Narrows on the left.

this area, formerly known as Grant Narrows Regional Park, is now the Pitt-Addington Recreation Area, managed by the Katzie First Nation.)

The Katzie Marsh Loop begins at the parking area, as does the eastbound Pitt Lake Dyke, but it diverges southeast onto the tree-clad, rooty Nature Dyke. Watch for wildlife or, at least, signs of their presence. After some 30 minutes, you come to a viewing tower with lots of information about the birds and animals that are resident at different times of the year. More than 200 species of birds have been spotted. Ignoring the dyke that heads off to the south, continue north past a screen of trees and on to the open Swan Dyke, with the fine mountain vista ahead and lush pond plants on either side. This route brings you back to the east end of the Pitt River Dyke, along which you march to complete your circuit, observing the lake with pleasure craft on one hand and marsh life on the other.

The Long Loop circuit starts on Pitt Lake Dyke, then turns south on Swan Dyke to meet Nature Dyke, where you might also begin for a walk shorter by 1.9 km (1.2 mi). From this common point, continue south on Mountain Dyke to Homilk'um Dyke, which takes you westwards into the marsh and brings you to a T-junction, where you go right once again. Now on Crane Dyke, make your way to Rannie Road while observing the sandhill crane nesting area on your left. (Note that this area is closed during nesting season and becomes overgrown. Mown grass strews the trails after opening.) Turn left at the road for a short distance to a track leading onto the Pitt River Dyke on the far side of the ditch. Here, you go right on a multipurpose trail with views across Pitt River to Widgeon Slough and surrounding ridges as you make your way back to the narrows and your car.

CHATHAM REACH

Return: 11 km (6.8 mi) or less   **Allow:** 2.5 hours or less

Surface: packed   **Rating:** easy   **Season:** all year

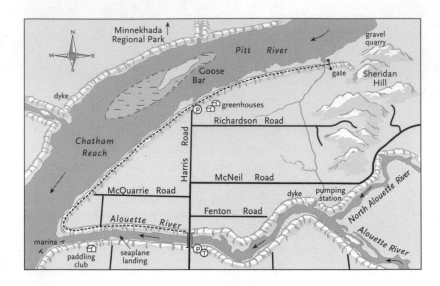

ACCESS

Vehicle: From Highway 7 (Lougheed Highway), turn north onto Harris Road, drive 3.7 km (2.3 mi) to a bridge over the Alouette River and park in the lot on the south bank.

Car GPS entry: Lougheed Highway & Harris Road

Trailhead: 49° 15.837′ N, 122° 41.353′ W

PITT RIVER, WITH its large dyke system, offers many fine outings; this one has particularly superb upriver views. You have a choice of distance as well: the full 11 km (6.8 mi) return along the waterside or a shorter version gained by returning along Harris Road, saving 1.5 km (0.9 mi). (Walk 86 heads east from the same parking lot.)

From Alouette Bridge, your walk begins with crossing to the north bank prior to setting off westwards, downstream. A variety of boathouses and watercraft in various states of repair, and the Pitt River Paddling Club, make use of the Alouette River, while on the opposite side lie expanses of

Tying up at a wharf on the Alouette River.

blueberry fields. Rounding the corner onto the banks of the Pitt River, you note the lines of rotting posts that once served as anchors for log booms and other river activities, and the wide, marshy shoreline, home to many kinds of waterfowl as well as herons, raptors and land-based creatures. Now, on the right, the land is populated with mega-houses on mini-estates with equestrian facilities. But the view straight ahead is the most eye-catching: the Pitt-Addington Marsh (which you can overlook from Minnekhada Regional Park, see Walk 83), occupies the inner elbow as the Pitt bends sharply; beyond that are the ridges and knolls surrounding Widgeon Slough and, forming a beautiful backdrop, are the snow-capped mountains at the head of Pitt Lake. Conveniently placed benches invite you to sit and enjoy.

Once again, the landscape changes a bit where Harris Road, your possible shortcut route, meets the dyke. Expansive greenhouses, and other evidence of industrial activities such as the construction of flood control systems, are screened from the dyke by a narrow band of trees, purposefully left in place as wildlife habitat. Just beyond the gate and your turnabout is an active gravel pit on Sheridan Hill, the source of the dull noise that increases as you approach. If you've been curious about a very large building isolated amongst trees in the distance, it belongs to a golf resort.

Your return views are certainly no match for the outgoing landscape, but you can spot Simon Fraser University atop Burnaby Mountain and the towering pillars of the Port Mann Bridge in the distance. Your only decision on the return will be which route to take at the Harris Road exit.

ALOUETTE RIVER DYKES

Return: 14.8 km (9.2 mi)   **Allow:** 3.5 hours

Surface: packed   **Rating:** easy   **Season:** all year

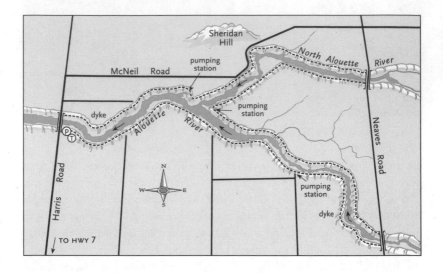

ACCESS

Vehicle: From Highway 7 (Lougheed Highway), turn north onto Harris Road, drive 3.7 km (2.3 mi) to a bridge over the Alouette River and park in the lot on the south bank.

Car GPS entry: Lougheed Highway & Harris Road

Trailhead: 49° 15.837′ N, 122° 41.353′ W

SITUATED IN THE heartland of Pitt Meadows, this walk has much to offer: low-level, easy walking and magnificent mountain scenery (on a clear day) amidst rural peace and serenity. Your route essentially covers three stages of approximately equal length, with bridges marking the divisions along the multi-use paths. (Walk 85 heads west from the same parking lot.)

Head upstream (east) from the parking lot, sharing this busiest portion of the dyke with the Trans Canada Trail for the first hour or so and passing several small sandy beaches loved by dogs who frolic in the water. Within 25 minutes, you arrive at the confluence of the North Alouette River and

Extensive blueberry fields are protected by the dykes.

the Alouette proper; both are wide and slow moving as they traverse the flatlands. Now the dyke turns southeast and even due south on occasion, following the windings of the river until, at a bridge, you meet Neaves Road, which you have been paralleling for the last while.

Cross the bridge, turn left onto the grassy dyke along the north side of the river and embark on the most peaceful part of the trip, the two sides of the triangle that are enclosed between the two branches of the Alouette River. Some of the original marsh remains, but dyking, draining and cultivating, begun in the latter part of the 19th century, continue to reshape the landscape and alter the habitat of creatures dependent on marshlands, such as the great blue herons that nest in the vanishing cottonwood trees. Nowadays, extensive blueberry fields have taken their place. After about 30 minutes, you are back at the meeting of the waters, where one of several pumping stations controls water levels. Here, there is a bench, one of many dotted along the route, where you might rest and survey your surroundings. This point, the crotch of the large, slightly contorted Y shape that is your route, is your halfway point.

Now you head northeast where the dyke runs straight, with a wide margin of marsh between you and the meanderings of the North Alouette and a full view of the peaks and ridges of the Golden Ears. Quite soon, your path bends eastwards, between river and drainage canal, towards Neaves Road and a clear view to Mount Baker. Over the bridge, turn left to resume your walk along the grassy north bank, looking ahead now to Sheridan Hill, whose base you eventually reach before you round a bend. The trail, now gravelled, leads you for the third time to the confluence of the two Alouettes before bending back on the last lap to Harris Road, your vehicle and the end of your excursion.

UBC RESEARCH FOREST

Blue Trail via Knoll: 8 km (5 mi)

Surface: rough

Elevation gain: 300 m (984 ft)

Rating: moderate

Allow: 3.5 hours

High point: 335 m (1100 ft)

Season: most of the year

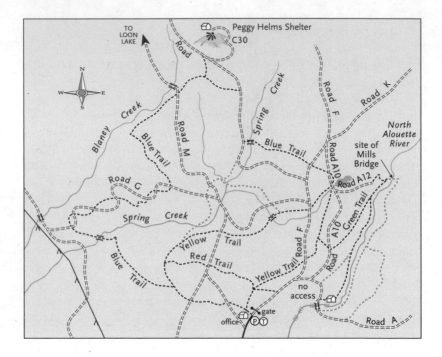

ACCESS

Vehicle: In Maple Ridge, follow the signs for Golden Ears Park north from Highway 7 (Lougheed Highway), staying on 232nd Street when the park road (Fern Crescent) turns right at the roundabout. Turn right onto Silver Valley Road and follow it to a parking area.

Car GPS entry: 14027 Silver Valley Road

Trailhead: 49° 15.856′ N, 122° 34.380′ W

THE UNIVERSITY DEMONSTRATION Forest, with its arboretum and network of trails, lies within the much larger Malcolm Knapp Research Forest, which is maintained by the University of British Columbia's Faculty of Forestry as a research area for its students. Trail and other information is available at the office near the parking lot, as well as online at www.mkrf. forestry.UBC.ca. (Note gate closure hours. Also note that dogs are not permitted in this forest.)

The easy Red Trail takes up to an hour and the Green one a little longer. Yellow provides the most detailed information about various aspects of forestry and requires about 2 hours for its 3.2 km (2 mi). The Blue Trail, described here, adds a side trip to a knoll with a view and ends with a detour along the North Alouette River.

Walk left past the office through the arboretum and across an old road, then enter the forest. The Blue Trail soon diverges left, descends to cross Spring Creek and continues to a forest road (G), which it crosses again and again as it winds through a managed plantation. As you approach Blaney Creek, murmuring from the valley on the left, you turn right, rise and cross yet another road (M). Follow the blue markers northwards to a fork just as you start to veer east. Take the left fork up to meet a wide logging road on which you jog right then left onto a side road (C30), circling a forested knoll whose summit and shelter you finally attain from the north side. Views extend northwards to Golden Ears and westwards over Pitt Meadows and the Fraser Valley.

Returning, retrace your steps to the wide logging road, go left and follow the (infrequent) blue markers along the road for some distance. Re-enter the forest on the left, cross Spring Creek, continue over a rough section of trail, cross two roads and finally meet the Yellow Trail beside a small pond. Now, go left on the road (A12) beside the pond then onto a trail down to the Alouette River. As there is no bridge, walk downstream for a couple of minutes to a fork. You may return on the Green Trail to the right or, in dry weather, to the left, on a narrow track above the riverbank. It leads to a shelter just short of the road bridge, where there are some spectacular rapids. The forest between the bridge and the parking area is closed, so you must plod up Road A to join the main Road F and go left, back to your vehicle.

MIKE LAKE

With lake circuit: 8 km (5 mi)   **Allow:** 2.5 hours

Lake circuit alone: 2 km (1.2 mi)   **Allow:** 45 minutes

Surface: packed, unimproved trail

Elevation gain: 180 m (590 ft)   **High point:** 430 m (1410 ft)

Rating: easy to moderate   **Season:** March to November

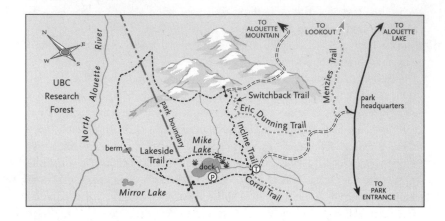

ACCESS

Vehicle: From Maple Ridge, follow the Golden Ears Park signs to the park entrance, then drive 4.5 km (2.8 mi) to the Park Headquarters/Mike Lake turnoff and go left. Immediately branch left again. Continue 2 km (1.2 mi) to park at the Mike Lake road end.

Car GPS entry: 232 Street & 132 Avenue

Trailhead: 49° 16.363′ N, 122° 32.296′ W

MIKE LAKE, WITH its little dock and forested, marshy surroundings, is popular with fisherfolk, whereas the Incline Trail, some 200 m before the parking area, sets hikers on their way into the backcountry towards Alouette Mountain and Blanshard Peak. This excursion is good for a leg stretch on a drizzly day, the most notable attraction being the peaceful surroundings of nature.

You have a choice of two trails or their combination: one, a 2 km (1.2 mi) circuit of the lake, another, a longer loop within the forest, with the option

Mist creeps amongst the trees.

of including the lake circuit at the end. Both begin by passing a gate at the
west end of the parking lot onto a disused road. Within 5 minutes the Lakeside Trail goes off right. (This drops to lake level in a series of switchbacks
and over eroded roots to a boardwalk, beyond which is the best view of the
lake.) Staying on the road, however, takes you into the Malcolm Knapp UBC
Research Forest (Walk 87), where generations of students have conducted
studies. Some 10 minutes later, your easy striding is suddenly halted at a
berm; this marks the beginning of a decommissioned section where a narrow track bounces up and down across a steepish hillside, sounds of the
North Alouette River rising from below. This section lasts for about 30 minutes until the former roadbed resumes at a sharp bend south. Now you see
boundary markers for the research forest, then, at a 4.8 km marker, a gate.
This is a junction for hikers and mountain bikers, and your route on the
Incline Trail heads down here. You will be treading where, almost a century
ago, old-growth logs were hauled down to Mike Lake using a cable system
and railcars. Look for the rotting remains of the foundation of a steam donkey (stationary engine) near the Lakeside Trail junction.

From this junction, you may continue to the road nearby and back to
your vehicle, or you may jog right onto the eastern end of Lakeside Trail to
circuit the lake, exiting on the road described earlier. Finally, take some
time to visit the dock near the parking lot and read a bit of the area's history, trying to imagine a camp of 600 loggers bustling about in this now-
peaceful setting.

ALOUETTE NATURE LOOP

Return: 6 km (3.7 mi)   **Allow:** 2.5 hours

Surface: trail   **Elevation gain:** 170 m (558 ft)   **High point:** 320 m (1050 ft)

Rating: easy   **Season:** March to November

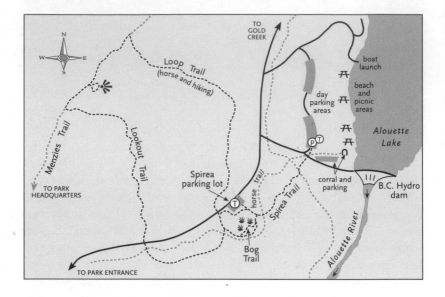

ACCESS

Vehicle: On 232nd Street in Maple Ridge, follow signs to Golden Ears Provincial Park. From the park gate, drive 7.2 km (4.5 mi) then turn right into a day-use area, 1 km (0.6 mi) past the Spirea Trail parking lot. In Lot 2, park near the south end.

Car GPS entry: 232 Street & 132 Avenue

Trailhead: 49° 17.284' N, 122° 29.500' W

WHAT TITLE DO you give a walk that embraces sections of four trails— Spirea, Lookout, Menzies and Loop—in Golden Ears Provincial Park? Our suggestion, as above, takes account of the fact that part of the loop is on the lower slopes of Alouette Mountain, that it provides a circuit and that a portion of it is a self-guided nature trail, the placards increasing your knowledge of forest lore as you walk along. Add interesting stretches of marsh

A boardwalk bridges the bog along the universal access trail.

with sphagnum moss and skunk cabbage, a second-growth forest of hemlock, a lookout over Alouette Lake and even a picnic table by its shore at the end of your outing.

Begin your walk on the Spirea Nature Trail, entering the forest on the opposite side of the access road. Almost immediately, you drop to a creek with a bridge. After crossing the bridge, traverse a gravel access road to Alouette Dam before re-entering the trees and beginning to rise in nice, open forest, the bright green of the moss in the understorey attesting to generous precipitation in the valley and the many large stumps reminding you of the grandeur of the original forest.

Cross the horse trail, then, at a T-junction, go left until you come to a fork where the trail from the Spirea parking lot joins and you are now on the universal access trail that circumnavigates the bog, crossing muddy ground on boardwalks. Shortly thereafter, as the path begins to curve right, go left on the signed Lookout Trail, cross the horse trail yet again, then cross the main park road and start rising in the forest. Eventually, your trail joins the Menzies Trail, where you turn right. Soon after, a clearing to your right provides a view over the lake and towards Mount Crickmer, which you may enjoy from a bench on a rock bluff.

Continuing, seek out a bridle trail on the right, signed Loop Trail, for your descent; it leads to the park road near the Spirea parking lot. Cross the road and go left on the horse trail, then left again on the pedestrian path. This section takes you between road and bog until, within sight of the parking area, you swing away right to rejoin your outward route east of the boardwalk. Now, go left and retrace your steps downhill to your starting point.

Before the drive home, you may descend to the popular beach at Alouette Lake for a final pause, perhaps a picnic or a dip.

GOLD CREEK WEST: ALDER FLATS

Return: 13 km (8 mi)   **Allow:** 4.5 hours

Surface: packed, rough   **Elevation gain:** 300 m (984 ft)   **High point:** 490 m (1608 ft)

Rating: challenging   **Season:** May to October

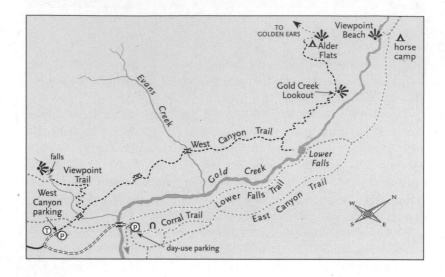

ACCESS

Vehicle: On 232nd Street in Maple Ridge, follow signs to Golden Ears Provincial Park. From the gated park entrance, drive 11.6 km (7.2 mi) to a signed fork. Go left, then left again for the West Canyon parking lot.

Car GPS entry: 232 Street & 132 Avenue

Trailhead: 49° 19.635′ N, 122° 27.800′ W

ALDER FLATS IS a broad, brushy basin below the sheer east face of Edge Peak, one of three mountains in the Golden Ears group that looms over Metro Vancouver. The stunning scene on a sunny day is worth the challenge presented by rocky sections and the clambering over steep roots on the otherwise generally easy trail.

From the parking lot, the West Canyon Trail follows an old railway grade. Within 10 minutes, the signed Viewpoint Trail heads left. (Although this

The northeast face of Edge Peak in the Golden Ears group.

is a pleasant trail on easy grade, the views at the destination are partially obstructed. As of late 2013, improvements are planned for this destination and upgrading has begun on the main trail.) Continuing on the West Canyon Trail, your route rises gently through mixed forest until, after crossing, on sturdy bridges, two major creeks with impressive erosion, you reach the railbed's end at a fork. A red, diamond-shaped marker on a tree denotes 3.1 km. The right fork drops rather steeply over the next 400 m to a brushy view of the Lower Falls, which are better approached and enjoyed from the Lower Falls Trail on the other side of Gold Creek (see Walk 91).

Staying with the left branch, you head up steeply over a creek bed of loose rocks and roots for about 15 minutes, after which the trail levels as it contours above the canyon before arriving at a large trailside stump. All that remains of a former lookout is a tunnel view of upper Gold Creek Valley and, through branches, Mount Nutt across the creek. From the stump, you must clamber steeply down a few paces and pass some upended tree roots before again reaching smooth walking. The trail now swings away from the canyon and crosses several creeks and boggy areas on bridges and boardwalks until it forks at tent sites in the forest. Your route goes left across a rocky creek bed—which may be uncrossable after heavy rains—to end at a heap of large boulders, the perfect place to rest and enjoy the view of Edge Peak and the Golden Ears. (The right fork continues to the mountains above.)

As you ascend the trail, and then descend on your return, you may spot the occasional artifact—a piece of rail, a hauling cable or burned remnants of trees, all that remain of what was one of the largest railway logging operations in the province in the 1920s, operated by the Abernathy and Lougheed Logging Company. In 1931, a spark from logging operations across the valley caused an extensive forest fire (a common hazard), ending logging in the area.

GOLD CREEK EAST: VIEWPOINT BEACH

Return: 8 km (5 mi)   **Allow:** 3.5 hours
Surface: rough   **Elevation gain:** 180 m (590 ft)
High point: 350 m (1150 ft)
Rating: moderate   **Season:** most of the year

Lower Falls return: 5.4 km (3.4 mi)   **Allow:** 2 hours
Surface: packed   **Elevation gain:** minimal
Rating: easy   **Season:** most of the year

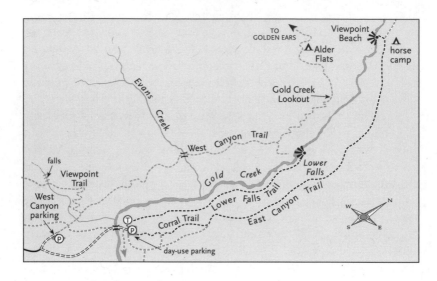

ACCESS

Vehicle: On 232nd Street in Maple Ridge, follow signs to Golden Ears Provincial Park. From the gated park entrance, drive 11.6 km (7.2 mi) to a fork. Go left, then right for the Gold Creek day-use area parking lot.

Car GPS entry: 232 Street & 132 Avenue

Trailhead for both: 49° 20.073' N, 122° 27.399' W

TRAILS ON THE east side of Gold Creek are gentler and more popular than those on the west side (see Walk 90); they feature access to beaches, close-up views of a seasonally changeable waterfall and backside views of the inspiring Golden Ears mountains.

For a family-friendly walk, you may follow the well-maintained Lower Falls Trail that runs more or less parallel to Gold Creek. A beach halfway to the falls provides access to the creek. After nearly an hour on this trail, you arrive at the well-fenced viewpoint for the spray-enshrouded Lower Falls. Awe-inspiring in its power, the creek cascades 10 m (33 ft) over a ramp of rock into a deep, seasonally placid pool surrounded by massive boulders, before flowing onward to its ultimate destination, Pitt River.

Although the Lower Falls Trail is undoubtedly the most popular Gold Creek walk, you may want to try the longer, more challenging East Canyon Trail to Viewpoint Beach, also known as Hikers Beach. For the East Canyon Trail, begin on the unmarked Corral Trail that is located by an overgrown corral just north of the parking lot. Very soon, this path rises to meet the main East Canyon Trail and you go left on a wide gravel path, rising gently but continuously through dense forest and, in spring, fording innumerable streamlets and crossing the rubble from runaway creek beds, which are prone to flooding during heavy storms.

After some 30 minutes, you come to an old metal gate, a reminder that your route was once a logging road. Next, you may note on your left a rudimentary trail that provides an alternative return route by descending dramatically over rough terrain and rooty sections to emerge at the Lower Falls viewpoint. The East Canyon Trail crests at a spot with a glimpse through the trees of Blanshard Peak before it trends downwards to return to creek level. The trail continues through the forest over flatter ground for some distance, until, at a fork, left takes you to Viewpoint Beach, a truly spectacular destination. Here, you may pause to picnic on the sand and pebble beach while you contemplate the quiet strength that is Gold Creek and gaze upwards at the towering ramparts of Edge Peak and the mountains that gave the park its name.

KANAKA CREEK TRAILS

Riverfront Trail return: 3 km (1.9 mi)   **Allow:** 1 hour

Canyon loop: 3.3 km (2 mi)   **Allow:** 1.5 hours

Surface: packed, trail   **Rating:** easy   **Season:** all year

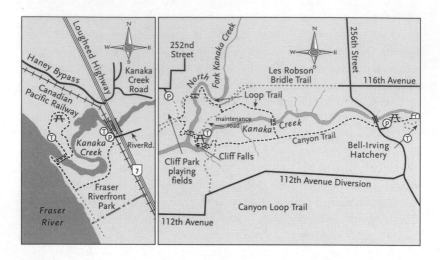

ACCESS

Transit: Riverfront Trail—various routes to Tamarack Lane at Lougheed

Vehicle: From Highway 7 (Lougheed Highway), just east of the Haney Bypass/Kanaka Way junction, turn west onto River Road then immediately into the parking lot.

Car GPS entry: 23272 River Road, Maple Ridge

Trailhead: 49° 12.001′ N, 122° 34.782′ W

Access: Canyon Loop—From Dewdney Trunk Road in Maple Ridge, travel south on 256th Street to the fish hatchery and parking lot.

Car GPS entry: 11450 256 Street, Maple Ridge

Trailhead: 49° 12.673′ N, 122° 30.561′ W

TWO PEARLS WITHIN the 12 km- (7.5 mi)-long Kanaka Creek Regional Park are the Riverfront Trail, where Kanaka Creek meets the Fraser River (described first), and the Canyon Loop—Cliff Falls trail farther inland. Other park attractions include a fish fence that operates in late fall and a fish hatchery.

The Kanaka Creek overlook on Riverfront Trail.

Within 5 minutes of setting out on the Riverfront Trail, you come to a tower that overlooks marshland caught within the last slow meander of Kanaka Creek before it joins the Fraser River. Farther along, turning right at the Fraser, you have occasional access to the sandy shore, or you may rest on a deck and read of historical activities, and, on the arching bridge, of the Hawaiian origin of Kanaka Creek's name. Next, a narrow nature path leads through woodlands back to the trailhead. If you want more walking, continue along the dyke for 1 km (0.6 mi) to the trail's end near a sawmill and other light industrial activity.

Canyon Loop Trail, where Kanaka Creek's north fork meets the main watercourse, has quite a different character. From the parking lot at the fish hatchery, which is certainly worth a visit, cross 256th Street to a yellow gate and begin your walk on Canyon Trail. This path gradually rises above creek level, mainly amidst cottonwoods and moss-covered maples. Quite soon, you come to a fork; straight ahead leads to Cliff Falls, where you can watch the splashing rapids and falls in their ceaseless sandstone-eroding work. You next cross a bridge over the north fork and ascend to a junction, where you turn right towards 116th Street, only soon to recross the creek on a metal bridge. A quick right then left at a junction to stay with the Loop Trail takes you back to meet the Canyon Trail and, minutes later, your vehicle.

Kanaka Creek has yet more to offer if you drive west onto Kanaka Creek Road immediately north of the bridge on 240th Street. During October and November, a one-way fish fence is erected below the bridge; some of the trapped fish are taken for hatchery use, and the rest are released to spawn upstream. Drive farther west to a roadgate, park, then walk less than 10 minutes to the Trans Canada Trail and along it to the Rainbow Bridge for views of the creek and surrounding wetlands.

HAYWARD LAKE: RAILWAY TRAIL

Return: 12 km (7.5 mi)   **Allow:** 3.5 hours

Surface: good   **Rating:** moderate   **Season:** most of the year

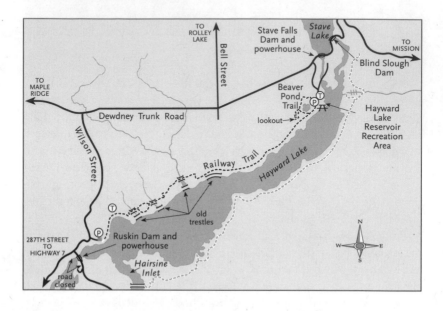

ACCESS

Vehicle: From the east, drive west from Mission on Highway 7 (Lougheed Highway), turn right on 287th Street, then continue north on Wilson Street until it meets Dewdney Trunk Road, where you turn right. Drive east on Dewdney Trunk Road and turn right just west of Stave Falls Dam at the Hayward Lake Reservoir Recreation Area. From the west, drive east from Maple Ridge on Dewdney Trunk Road, then proceed as above.

Car GPS entry: Wilson Street & Dewdney Trunk Road

Trailhead: 49° 13.338' N, 122° 21.578' W

HAYWARD LAKE RESERVOIR was created in 1930, when the Ruskin Dam was built across a narrow granite gorge of the Stave River, approximately 6 km (3.7 mi) downstream from Stave Falls Dam. A railway along the lake's west side carried supplies from Ruskin to the dam and the company town at Stave Falls, and returned loaded with cedar logs, shakes and shingles.

Ghostly trestles stand through the mists of time.

That was long ago. All that remains today is the former railway right-of-way and support pilings where once trestle bridges carried the railway line across the mouth of inlets.

The Railway Trail walk starts from the Hayward Lake Recreation Area, where you should begin by orienting yourself at the information board that describes the trail closure at Ruskin Dam. Additional to the longer Railway Trail walk, there is a short nature loop, Beaver Pond Trail, which gives you a chance to see the work of beavers, their skill in dam-building rivalling that of their human counterparts.

After walking south for some time on the level, gravelled Railway Trail, you encounter the first inlet and trestle; here, the trail makes the first of several detours over creeks and ravines once traversed by railway trestle bridges. It leaves the right-of-way, enters the forest and rounds the bay before rejoining the railbed trail. These detours, such as at Elbow Creek, take you up and over, with staircases, footbridges and walkways supplying the crossings in lieu of the derelict bridges. At one inlet detour, an alternative track, signed "Tall Tree Loop," which takes you past a solitary majestic Douglas-fir, enlivens your walk before you arrive at a beach and viewpoint for the Ruskin Dam intake. This must be your turnaround; continuing farther and crossing over the Ruskin Dam to join the Reservoir Trail (Walk 94) is not possible because of the closure created by maintenance and upgrading being done by B.C. Hydro and projected to last until 2018. For more information about Ruskin Dam and B.C. Hydro recreation sites, see www.bchydro.com/community/recreation_areas.html.

HAYWARD LAKE: RESERVOIR TRAIL

Return: 8 km (5 mi)   **Allow:** 3 hours

Surface: good   **Rating:** moderate   **Season:** most of the year

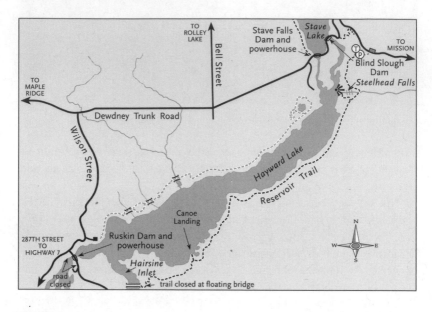

ACCESS

Vehicle: From the east, drive west from Mission on Highway 7 (Lougheed Highway) and turn right on 287th Street, then continue north on Wilson Street until it meets Dewdney Trunk Road, where you turn right and drive east. Continue over the Stave Falls and Blind Slough Dams, staying on Dewdney Trunk Road until you reach the trailhead parking lot. From the west, drive east from Maple Ridge on Dewdney Trunk Road, then proceed as above.

Car GPS entry: Wilson Street & Dewdney Trunk Road

Trailhead: 49° 13.773′ N, 122° 20.838′ W

THE ONE-TIME RAILWAY track between Stave Falls and Ruskin gives us the Railway Trail walk along the west side of Hayward Lake (Walk 93). Its sibling Reservoir Trail, more recently completed in 1999 with the joint efforts of Forest Renewal B.C., B.C. Hydro and the District of Mission, takes you along the east side of Hayward Lake through the second-growth cedar

Reservoir Trail. *Photo: Stephen Mullock*

and Douglas-fir of the Mission Municipal Forest. Over the years, Reservoir Trail has aged gracefully into a welcoming woodland trail as the construction scars left by its builders, and handrails fashioned from naturally curved branches, have become carpeted with moss.

Begin by orienting yourself at the information boards that describe the trail closure at Hairsine Inlet. Descend from the parking lot and stay left at two T-junctions. Soon, your trail traverses a long walkway over Brown Creek and crosses Steelhead Creek before it arrives at a junction. The track dropping right takes you to a well-built platform and vantage point for the beautiful Steelhead Falls.

Continue your undulating forested route, noticing as you go the benches and chairs carved out of stumps and logs by the original trailbuilders. After a lengthy interlude, and after crossing many bridged creeks, you arrive at a junction where you may go right to descend to the lakeshore at Canoe Landing. From here the trail climbs above the lake before descending from the forest to Hairsine Inlet, where you find a unique floating walkway built to avoid the steep and rocky terrain that surrounds the inlet. Alas, this must be your turnaround as, until 2018, the walkway is closed during the upgrading of Ruskin Dam. For more information about Ruskin Dam and B.C. Hydro recreation sites, see www.bchydro.com/community/recreation_areas.html.

MISSION TRAIL

Return: 6.4 km (4 mi)

Surface: paved, packed, rough

High point: 200 m (655 ft)

Rating: easy to moderate

Allow: 2.5 hours

Elevation gain: 150 m (500 ft)

Season: all year

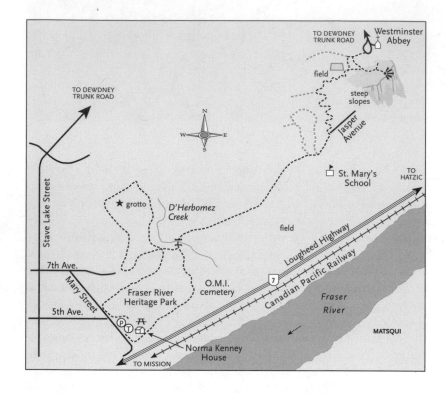

ACCESS

Vehicle: On Highway 7 (Lougheed Highway), at the east end of Mission, turn north on Stave Lake Street, then east on 5th Avenue. Park near the park buildings.

Car GPS entry: 7494 Mary Street, Mission

Trailhead: 49° 8.269′ N, 122° 17.259′ W

THE MISSION TRAIL begins at the Fraser River Heritage Park, where you gain a peek into the history of First Nations peoples, pioneer settlers and missionaries of not so long ago. The Heritage Park preserves the remains and expansive grounds of the former St. Mary's Mission and Residential School, which operated from 1862 to 1961. (New facilities were built thereafter, a short distance away.) A steep trail east of the park climbs to Westminster Abbey and the Benedictine monks' seminary, which has occupied the hilltop 150 m above since 1954.

From your vehicle, head towards Norma Kenney House, where a flat, groomed walkway leads east. Your route passes cement foundations that supported mission buildings for a century, offers an optional side loop to the Oblates of Mary Immaculate cemetery, crosses a bridge spanning D'Herbomez Creek, stretches through open fields and woods to (the new) St. Mary's School grounds, then ends at a cul-de-sac on Jasper Avenue. Here, there is a Heritage Park information board. Just before the main trail ends, watch for a footpath heading uphill and prepare for an invigorating ascent to the ridge and the abbey above.

Generally, ignore forks on the left as you head up and, for interest, note the religiously themed names such as Jacob's Ladder and Hail Mary attached to junctions. Be alert for mountain bikers and, in the fall, enjoy the bright colours of bigleaf maples that populate the hillside. Eventually, as you approach the ridge, your route levels out at a small open junction of trails. From here, the path rolls up and down along the ridge for perhaps 15 minutes until it emerges into the open at the end of a wide field. Make your way to a gravel road going right, the abbey tower visible to the left over rolling, grassy slopes. Soon, you are rewarded with an expansive, bluff-top view over the Fraser River to gentle Sumas Mountain in the middle; mighty, snow-clad Mount Baker dominating the horizon to the right; and the jagged Cheam Range to the left. When you're ready to move on, stay right on the surfaced path to visit the abbey and seminary, then continue around to find your trail by the field.

Your best return is by the same route, though once descending (south, or left) from the ridge, you may opt to choose an alternative trail for variety. These exit at the groomed walkway on which you began your outing.

GREEN TIMBERS URBAN FOREST

North and Centre sections: 3 km each (1.9 mi)   **Allow:** 1 hour each

South section: 5 km (3.1 mi)   **Allow:** 1.5 hours

Surface: unimproved trail, packed, paved   **Rating:** easy   **Season:** all year

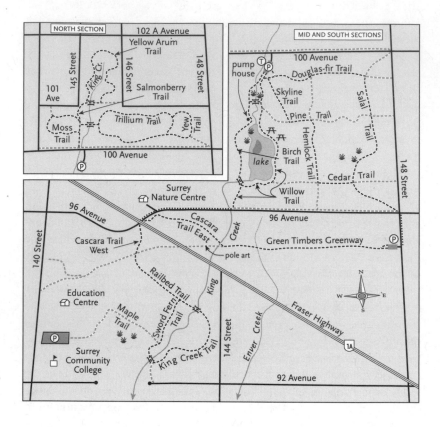

ACCESS

Transit: Route #341 to 148 Street at 100 Avenue

Vehicle: In North Surrey, make your way to 100 Avenue. The parking lot is on the south side of 100 Avenue, between 144 and 148 Streets.

Car GPS entry: 100 Avenue & 144 Street

Parking: 49° 11.037′ N, 122° 49.210′ W

SURROUNDED BY URBAN development, this forested oasis owes its existence to the efforts of the Green Timbers Heritage Society. After being logged against protest in 1930, reforestation, then a pioneering concept, began immediately. Today this forest is a mix of logging survivors and natural regeneration but, unfortunately, is divided into three sections by 100 and 96 Avenues.

To walk the north section, carefully cross busy 100 Avenue from the parking lot and look for the trailhead a few paces left. Salmonberry Trail, a one-time logging railway, connects three loops: Moss Loop was an experimental Scotch pine plantation, Yellow Arum Loop edges the marsh that forms the headwaters of King Creek and the Trillium-Yew Loop leads you through a fine stand of Douglas-fir that survived the logging of the 1920s as young trees.

Back at the parking lot, you can now do a horseshoe-shaped loop of the mid-section. Go left on the Douglas-fir Trail to Salal Trail, where you turn south (right) and continue to Cedar Trail, where you turn right again. This large wet area supports alder, maple and cottonwood trees, and ferns, salal and huckleberry bushes, amongst others. Turn right yet again onto Hemlock Trail, where there is a mix of mature coniferous forest with young red alder and cottonwood. Go left on Pine Trail to the picnic sites at Green Timbers Lake, where again you go left to circle the lake, enjoying the waterfowl and scenery until you are back at your vehicle.

For the south section walk, you may extend your mid-section walk by exiting onto 96 Avenue at 148 Street from the Salal Trail south of Cedar Trail then crossing to the Green Timbers Greenway a few paces south on 148 Street. Alternatively, you may park in the B.C. Hydro lot south of 96 Avenue on the west side of 148 Street. From 148, follow the multi-use, paved Green Timbers Greenway west to Cascara Trail East, where there are some rare yew trees, cross Fraser Highway at the lights and re-enter the forest on Cascara Trail West. The aptly named Railbed Trail crosses King Creek, the first tricklings of which you saw on the north section's Yellow Arum Trail, then becomes King Creek Trail, where the reforestation was most successful. Next, keep right on Sword Fern Trail, where there are lots of overarching vine maple trees and ferns, until you meet Railbed Trail, from where you retrace your path. A brief diversion off Sword Fern Trail onto Maple Trail passes through wetlands with a variety of deciduous trees and some nice Douglas-firs. From your turnaround point, retrace your steps to return to your vehicle.

TYNEHEAD REGIONAL PARK

Return: 5.5 km (3.4 mi)   **Allow:** 2 hours

Surface: improved trail   **Rating:** easy   **Season:** all year

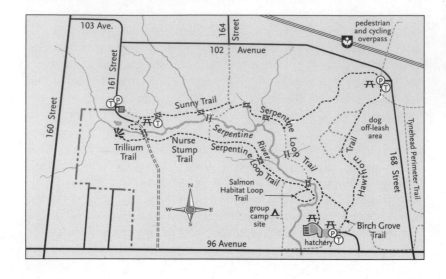

ACCESS

Transit: Route #388 to 96 Avenue at 168 Street

Vehicle: Make your way to 168 Street and 96 Avenue in Surrey. The Tynehead Hatchery parking lot entrance is 100 m west of 168 on the north side of 96.

Car GPS entry: 96 Avenue & 168 Street

Trailhead (hatchery parking): 49° 10.675′ N, 122° 45.687′ W

THE PROXIMITY OF this trail to the Serpentine River and its many feeder streams, and the impressive number of enormous nurse stumps that nourish large second-growth trees in this area, are two of the highlights along this pleasant, winding walk.

At the hatchery entrance, pick up a brochure at the information kiosk then head north on the Birch Grove Trail, which very soon divides. The right fork, the aptly named Hawthorn Trail for the many hawthorn trees, takes you through dog heaven, an unfenced off-leash area that traverses one-time

This tree began life on a nurse log that has now rotted away.

farmland to the northeast entrance on 168 Street, an alternate access to this walk. Nearby, a footbridge arches over Highway 1. Next, bearing west through a tunnel of hawthorn trees and then bearing southwest, you meet the northern loop of the Serpentine Loop Trail, where you go right, passing some intriguing nurse stumps en route. Successive crossings of headwater tributaries are particularly attractive in spring. At another fork, left leads to a bridge over the main waterway, so keep right, ignoring the trail out to 102 Avenue. Make your way along the southern edge of a meadow via Sunny Trail, beyond which you come to a picnic area with tracks going off in various directions; cross the bridge at the bottom of the meadow then go right on Trillium Trail. This route takes you past more fascinating nurse stumps and up a 5-minute ascent ending at a viewing platform that overlooks rearing habitat for coho and steelhead fry.

After descending, you follow the Nurse Stump Trail downstream to rejoin the Serpentine Loop Trail. Signage along the way reminds you that these trails wind through sensitive habitat for the fish that live here throughout the year, in all their life's stages. Both humans and dogs, therefore, need to avoid temptations to play in the water. The Serpentine Loop Trail ends in a 10-minute interpretive loop just before an arching bridge. Cross this and keep right for the final lap back to your vehicle and a possible visit to the hatchery.

Tynehead Park also features the Perimeter Trail, a multi-use interpretive trail on the Tynehead Greenway. The 4.8 km (3 mi) rolling circuit, which includes some long uphill sections, requires about 90 minutes to complete. This trail lies to the east of 168 Street and may be accessed from both the hatchery and Serpentine parking lots, the latter off the north end of 168 Street.

REDWOOD PARK

Return: 4.5 km (2.8 mi) or less **Allow:** 1.5 hours

Surface: trail, paved **Rating:** easy **Season:** all year

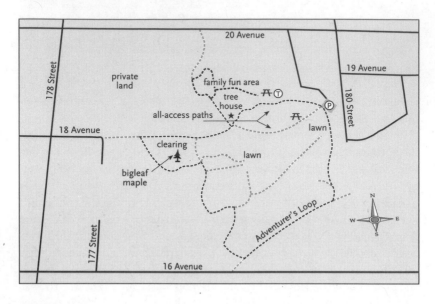

ACCESS

Vehicle: Make your way to Highway 15 (176 Street) and 20 Avenue, where you turn east. Continue to the Redwood Park sign on the south side of 20 Avenue, 250 m past 178 Street, then drive 300 m through the woods to the parking lot.

Car GPS entry: 20 Avenue & 180 Street

Trailhead: 49° 2.144′ N, 122° 43.505′ W

ALTHOUGH SMALL AT only 26 ha (64 ac), Redwood Park has something of interest for the whole family. At the parking lot, check the information board and pick up a pamphlet to help with your planning. You have a choice of three main trails: the 1.5 km (0.9 mi) Adventurer's Loop footpath, which winds amongst groves of exotic trees; the paved, 650 m universal-access path; and the 1.3 km (0.8 mi) Family Fun footpath.

Exotic trees? How did these come to be here? They are the result of a passion by twin (and deaf) brothers, David and Peter Brown. Their father, who

The wee door to a troll house at the base of a tree.

homesteaded and logged this sloping, wooded hill in the late 19th century, gave each brother 16 ha (40 ac) on their 21st birthday. The brothers then began to plant the area with seeds of 32 species of exotic trees collected from around the world, including Europe, Asia and North Africa. Amongst these are California redwoods, giant sequoia, European beech and Chinese chestnut, and the brothers included native conifers and maples as well. (*The Redwood Park Tree Guide* is available on the City of Surrey website.)

The Family Fun footpath takes you past the treehouse where the Brown brothers lived for several decades until the 1950s, though this is a contemporary model built to replace previous structures. A signboard gives a short account of its history. Elsewhere on this trail, to the north of the treehouse, look for wee troll-house doors at the base of trees, a fun project by the Girl Guides many years ago.

Although you may wander the network of trails at random—and not all are marked on the map—the Adventurer's Loop covers most of the features. As you pass through clearings, try to catch a view out to the San Juan Islands. The trail takes you west from the treehouse to a fence marking private property, south on a downhill slope to a swampy area and an old railroad grade by a small canal, then left and northeastwards up a gentle slope to a lawn and the parking lot.

The City of Surrey has been making improvements to the trail and picnic facilities to meet universal access standards. The many covered tables near the parking lot are ideal for large groups, and there is a good playground and grassy area nearby.

BARNSTON ISLAND

Return: 10 km (6.2 mi)　　**Allow:** 2.5 hours

Surface: paved　　**Rating:** easy　　**Season:** all year

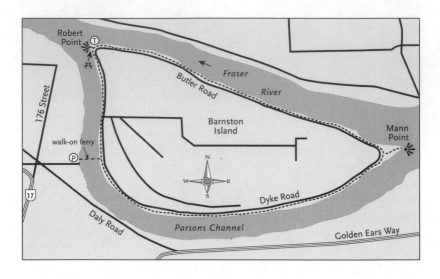

ACCESS

Vehicle: From Highway 1, take Exit 53 (176 Street) north onto Highway 15, drive to its end then go right on 104 Avenue to the parking lot at the end of the road.

Car GPS entry: 104 Avenue & 176 Street

Trailhead (parking lot): 49° 11.514′ N, 122° 43.620′ W

YOUR FIRST STEPS on this little adventure are onto a tugboat/barge-combo ferry for a free 5-minute ride to Barnston Island, which sits in the middle of the Fraser River between Surrey and Pitt Meadows. Your remaining steps follow a paved country road that circuits the island between operations of two of B.C.'s economic foundations—agriculture and forestry—and passes through part of Katzie First Nation Reserve, though the entire island is within Katzie traditional territory. There are no stores on the island.

Once off the ferry, turn right to make the circuit counter-clockwise. Then, when you reach the picnic site at the northwest corner of the island,

Barges and booms on the Fraser River off Robert Point.

you will be ready for a rest; there are no other resting spots en route. Initial impressions of prosperity are followed by mixed impressions at the sight of abandoned homes, now being reclaimed by nature's brambly arms. However, on the rest of your walk, you see cattle, sheep, even a couple of llamas, and other farming activities. Across the river in Port Kells are the busy lumber mills and their resulting mountains of woodchips. Watch for eagles overhead and listen for the prehistoric squawk of the heron.

About 4 km (2.5 mi) from the start, as the road begins to curve around the east end of the island, look for a signpost off the road beside a narrow trail leading to Mann Point. If, however, it appears too brambly, walk another 100 m along the road to a rough off-road vehicle track through the woods to the point. Here, on a sandy beach, you see river and birdlife, and a close-up view of the Golden Ears Bridge and the mountains beyond. Beavers have been active along the shoreline; look for the "beavers' workyard."

Back on the pavement, you next see Pitt Meadows on the opposite shore with its little airport, busy with the comings and goings of small aircraft. The sight of log booms at anchor, barges in tow and fishboats continues in this stretch of the river. On land, you pass colourful acres of cranberries. Other products of this small island are hay, herbs, beef and organic dairy products. Finally, Robert Point lies ahead, 4 km (2.5 mi) from Mann Point. The secluded picnic setting is an attractive place to rest and watch the river scene.

The last leg of your stroll, about 2 km (1.2 mi), takes you back to the ferry and a peaceful return to your vehicle across the water.

DERBY REACH REGIONAL PARK

Heritage site return: 5 km (3.1 mi)   **Allow:** 1.5 hours

Including Houston Trail loop: 8 km (5 mi)   **Allow:** 2.5 hours

Surface: improved   **Rating:** easy   **Season:** all year

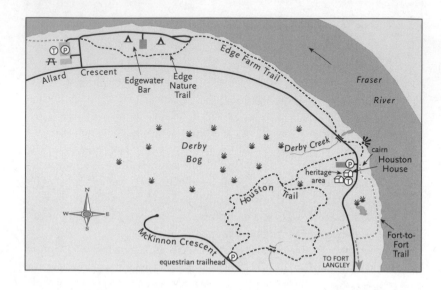

ACCESS

Vehicle: From Highway 1, take Exit 58 (200 Street) north, go along the 201 Street diversion to 96 Avenue, turn east, continue to 208 Street, go left (north) and stay with 208 as it curves east onto Allard Crescent. Continue about 2 km (1.2 mi) to the entrance to Edgewater Bar on your left.

Car GPS entry: 208 Street & Allard Crescent (Langley Township)

Trailhead: 49° 12.485′ N, 122° 37.040′ W

POPULAR WITH WALKERS, family cyclists and dog walkers, this well-groomed trail follows the inner bend of the Fraser River from Edgewater Bar to a cairn marking the location of the original Fort Langley. En route, you may be treated to magnificent views of the Golden Ears mountains, log-sorting activities across the water, hungry birds looking for lunch and perhaps a curious seal.

Begin your walk by approaching the river and going right at the campground onto the Edge Nature Trail. (It is named for the Edge family, who once farmed here. A member of the family was killed nearby, in January 1880, when a massive landslide into the Fraser on the Haney side inundated the river's south shore and caused severe destruction.) The Edge Trail winds through woodlands with imposing cottonwood trees and old stumps for 1 km (0.6 mi) until it nears the river again at the end of the campground. A few steps along it then becomes Edge Farm Trail. The path stays close to the water's edge. Repeat visitors will notice the Fraser's changing moods: high water attacks and erodes the riverbanks; low water exposes muddy "beaches" to explore. After a short diversion beside the road, you reach the heritage area, where you can learn about and imagine life at the time of European settlement.

From here, you have three options: you may return the way you came; you may continue another 5.2 km (3.2 mi) to Fort Langley Historic Site on the similarly graded Fort-to-Fort Trail, though this is best done with two cars; or you may take the Houston Trail. This latter is a 4 km (2.5 mi) loop with many steepish ups and downs. It starts across the grass from the parking area, goes left and meets the trail proper in about 10 minutes. If you then take the left fork, you will pass through a mixed forest with some fine cedars and bigleaf maples, the path rising and falling. (At a large junction, left (east) leads to Allard Crescent, where you must walk 200 m east along the road to join the Fort-to-Fort Trail, an optional return.) Continue straight ahead and eventually arrive at the horse-unloading lot off McKinnon Crescent.

The final lap of the Houston Trail begins across the parking area, winds up and down towards Derby Bog, skirts right of the swampy ground and finishes at your original fork and the path back to the heritage area. Your return now lies downstream once more on the Edge Farm Trail.

BRAE ISLAND TRAILS

Return: 4.2 km (2.6 mi)   **Allow:** 1.5 hours

Surface: gravel   **Rating:** easy   **Season:** most of the year

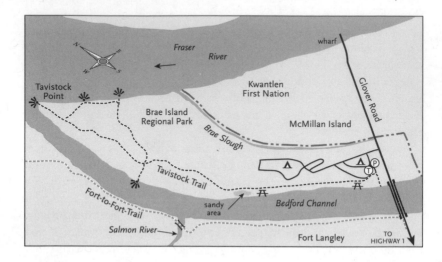

ACCESS

Transit: Route #C62 to Fort Langley

Vehicle: From Highway 1, take Exit 66 (232 Street) north to Glover Road. Turn north and continue on Glover Road through the village of Fort Langley, cross the bridge then turn left into the parking lot for Brae Island Regional Park.

Car GPS entry: Billy Brown Road & Glover Road

Trailhead: 49° 10.390' N, 122° 34.530' W

BRAE ISLAND, AS the western end of McMillan Island is known, was once a separate body of land, but the channel between them has filled in over time. McMillan Island, which lies across the 70 m (230 ft) wide Bedford Channel opposite Fort Langley, is composed primarily of settled silt and debris from the Fraser River and has been shaped and reshaped by the Fraser's forces. When the river's waters are high in the spring, they may flood parts of the trails, making them impassable. The Kwantlen First Nation occupies much of McMillan Island, which is its administrative centre. And

The three summits of the Golden Ears group, left to right: Golden Ears, Edge Peak and Blanshard Peak.

McMillan? In 1824, he was chief trader for the Hudson's Bay Company and led the preliminary survey party for the establishment of Fort Langley.

Begin your walk on the Tavistock Trail at the map board near the parking lot. The gravel path runs between the campsite and water until, at the end of the campsite, you come to an open picnic area that overlooks Bedford Channel. Continue along the wooded trail until you arrive at a four-way junction. Go left for a short walk to the first viewpoint of Bedford Channel on the west side of the island; the Fort Langley Golf Course lies opposite. Return to the trail and go left towards Tavistock Point. After about 500 m, you encounter another junction with a short trail on your left to the second viewpoint. After returning to the main trail, turn left and walk a short distance through a corridor of cottonwoods to Tavistock Point, noting as you do the Tavistock Loop Trail junction on your right. Tavistock Point marks the northern tip of Brae Island and on a clear day provides scenic views of the Fraser River and both shorelines.

Once you've absorbed the view and the variety of activities on the river, walk back to the Tavistock Loop Trail junction. Go left for an alternative return route. Not far along, you come to a viewpoint from which you look north across the Fraser River to the distant Coast Mountains, including the Golden Ears group. Continue along the loop as it weaves through the forest and across small wooden bridges over freshwater marshes before re-joining the main trail. Go left at the junction to return to your starting point, passing the picnic tables and campsite en route.

NICOMEKL FLOODPLAIN TRAIL

Return: 6 km (3.7 mi)   **Allow:** 1.5 hours

Surface: paved, gravel   **Rating:** easy   **Season:** all year

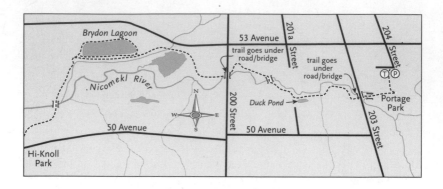

ACCESS

Transit: Route #502 or #C64 on 53 Avenue to 204 Street, and walk 250 m south to Portage Park

Vehicle: From Highway 1, take Exit 58 (200 Street) and go south 5.8 km (3.6 mi) to Highway 1A (Fraser Highway). Turn left and go east to 204 Street. Turn south on 204 to Portage Park.

Car GPS entry: 53 Avenue & 204 Street

Trailhead: 49° 5.800' N, 122° 39.450' W

YOUR OUTING BEGINS at Portage Park, where in 1824, Hudson's Bay Company chief trader James McMillan, having travelled up the Nicomekl River from Mud Bay, began a 7 km (4.3 mi) portage overland to the Salmon River on his way to the Fraser River to choose a site for Fort Langley. John Work, a clerk with the party, described the river as thick with willows and with low banks "well wooded with pine, cedar, alder and some other trees." Compare his description with what you find on your walk today.

From your vehicle, walk through the playground and turn right on the paved floodplain walkway. Soon, you encounter the first of several bridge crossings over the Nicomekl River, after which you walk towards and then under 203 Street. Emerging from under the street and after a slight uphill

The Nicomekl River on a lazy August day.

section, you come to the Duck Pond, a favourite stopping place for people of all ages and ducks alike. Next, take the right turn at the T-junction, then soon thereafter turn right again to cross the bridge over the Nicomekl River to its north side. Once across the bridge, you leave the pavement and continue on a gravel trail towards, and then under, 200 Street. Here, you may want to leave the trail momentarily and wander over the grassy meadow to the riverbank. The trail swings right as the floodplain widens, and soon the entrance to Brydon Lagoon nature trail appears on your right. The lagoon, a settling pond for sewage treatment until 1973, now provides an opportunity for a quiet walk with glimpses of wildlife, such as songbirds, bullfrogs, turtles, rabbits and waterfowl.

After your loop around Brydon Lagoon, turn south as the trail heads onto the floodplain. Soon, you come to your third and final bridge on this walk, where you may decide to pause, contemplate the steady flow of the Nicomekl and compare your view with that described by John Work. During Work's time, this area lay within an extensive intertidal zone, which farmers began to reclaim for agricultural purposes half a century later. Sea dams were built on the Nicomekl and Serpentine Rivers and the City of Surrey began an ambitious program of flood control in 1997, but seasonal flooding persists in some areas.

The bridge makes a good turnaround spot, or, for a longer walk, you may continue 250 m to Hi-Knoll Park and explore its woodland trails.

CAMPBELL VALLEY
REGIONAL PARK

Shaggy Mane Trail return: 11 km (6.8 mi)   **Allow:** 4 hours   **Surface:** packed, rough

Little River Loop Trail: 2.3 km (1.4 mi)   **Allow:** 1 hour   **Surface:** packed, smooth

Rating: easy   **Season:** all year

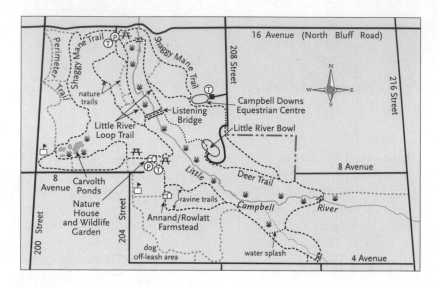

ACCESS

Vehicle: From Highway 1, take Exit 58 (200 Street) and drive 15 km (9.3 mi) south to 16 Avenue (North Bluff Road). Turn east and go 600 m to a parking lot on your right.

Car GPS entry: 16 Avenue & 200 Street

Trailhead: 49° 1.766′ N, 122° 39.640′ W

THIS NATURE PARK, bisected as it is by the Little Campbell River, takes full advantage of the surrounding countryside. The 28 km (17.4 mi) of trails range from a valley floor walk near the river's banks on Little River Loop Trail to a half-day circuit of the whole park on the multi-use (watch for horses!) Shaggy Mane Trail.

The Little River Loop Trail begins near the southeast corner of the parking area and passes through trees to a boardwalk over wet meadows

Little Campbell River at the Listening Bridge.

bordering the river. On the far side, it turns south, parallels the verge of the marsh to the Listening Bridge, which it crosses, then meets a T-junction on the west side. Here, you turn north, heading back on the loop trail and crossing a wide meadow. For variety, consider taking one of several detours through woodland routes on its west side.

If you opt for the Shaggy Mane Trail, walk towards the parking lot entrance then, just before 16 Avenue, turn east and cross the river before rising to level ground. More attractive, however, is to follow Little River Loop Trail across the boardwalk and south to a fork where a minor trail rises to the left out of the valley and joins Shaggy Mane Trail, passing south of an equestrian centre. Alternatively, stay with the loop trail to the Listening Bridge junction where you join the Deer Trail. This goes straight ahead across a meadow and enters the trees beyond. This route takes you southeast by the Little River Bowl and finally joins Shaggy Mane as it descends to the valley floor.

Next comes a turn to the right at a major fork where you cross the watercourse. A stretch of open country follows as you wind circuitously until, just past the off-leash area, you turn onto Ravine Trail on your right. This descends stairs into a picturesque little valley where, just across a small creek, you come to a fork. Right takes you past a lookout over the marsh; left emerges in a meadow near a heritage farmstead, with the one-time schoolhouse a little beyond. Leaving the farm, the trail heads north across an open field to a picnic area and the park's 8th Avenue Nature House and Wildlife Garden.

To return to your vehicle, you may drop into the valley and take the Little River Loop Trail's west leg, its scenic meadow particularly attractive in fall. Or you may stay above, on the rim of the valley, using Shaggy Mane Trail to round the western perimeter before dropping to your starting point.

ALDERGROVE REGIONAL PARK

Pepin Brook Loop: 4 km (2.5 mi)   **Allow:** 1 hour

Rock'n Horse Trail: 7 km (4.3 mi)   **Allow:** 2 hours

Surface: improved trail   **Rating:** easy   **Season:** all year

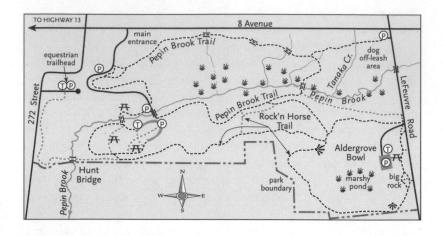

ACCESS

Vehicle: From Highway 1 in Langley, take Exit 73 (Highway 13) and follow 264 Street south to 8 Avenue. Turn left (east) onto 8 Avenue. Continue across 272 Street to the park entrance 200 m beyond. Turn right into the park, descend into the valley, perhaps taking a few minutes to look at the information board at a pullout, then park on the far side of the brook.

Car GPS entry: 8 Avenue & 272 Street

Trailhead near brook: 49° 0.709′ N, 122° 27.940′ W

FEATURES OF THIS park include expansive views, an enormous glacial erratic, heritage homes and farms, and habitat for the endangered Nooksack dace and Salish sucker fish—rare minnow-sized survivors of the ice age.

Pepin Brook Trail begins as a pleasantly winding trail beside the watercourse before climbing to stay above the marsh. After 700 m, you pass two trails to the right that connect with the Rock'n Horse bridle trail. Ignore these and descend gently into the peaceful Pepin Brook valley. As you cross

A bridge over Pepin Brook and marsh.

the long arching bridge over the brook, pause to view the adjacent marsh, an area often flooded thanks to the activity of beavers. Soon after leaving the bridge, a side trail leads to a fenced off-leash area. Take this trail for an interesting diversion to view the fish habitat improvements at Tanaka Creek. Back at the junction, the Pepin Brook Trail ascends steadily up the valley wall to treetop level, where you traverse a short ridge section with the ground dropping away on either side. Finally, you pass through a meadow then descend through forest until you reach the road, which you follow back to your start.

For a longer circuit, walk west from your parking spot and circle the sand and grass play area to join the Rock'n Horse Trail. This multi-use route heads east then south, where it leaves the comfort of the trees to emerge on the edge of the Aldergrove Bowl, a one-time gravel pit now green with grass, trees and a picnic site. Keep right, skirting the hollow, and gradually work your way around to the east, into a treed valley and out again, eventually arriving at a viewpoint. Here, broad berry fields stretch south and east with Mount Baker and other great peaks of the Cascade Range providing the backdrop.

Resuming your walk, you turn north into the trees on an undulating trail, pass an enormous boulder deposited by a long-ago receding glacier and emerge onto a park road. Cross the road and continue west on the Rock'n Horse Trail above the marshy valley before finally descending to join Pepin Brook Trail. Go left for a quick return to your vehicle, or right, as described previously, for the short circuit.

MATSQUI DUO

Each section return: 14 km (8.7 mi) or less   **Allow:** 4 hours or less each

Surface: dyke, trail   **Rating:** easy

Season: all year; possible closures during spring runoff

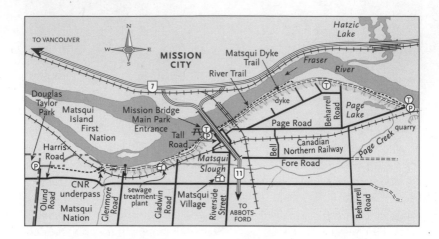

ACCESS

Vehicle: From north or south of the Fraser River, make your way to Highway 11 (Abbotsford-Mission Highway) and the south end of the Mission Bridge. Travelling from the north, immediately south of the bridge, take the Riverside Street exit northbound. From the south, take the Matsqui Village exit and travel north on Riverside Street. Watch for park entrance signs and park in the lot.

Car GPS entry: Tall Road & Riverside Road

Mission Bridge parking: 49° 7.270′ N, 122° 18.167′ W

MOUNTAIN VIEWS, RIVER watching, woodlands and farmers' fields—these are attractions along this trail between Page Road in the east and Douglas Taylor Park (Olund Trailhead) in the west. Travelling end to end makes a long return trip, though you could arrange a car shuttle for a one-way walk. However, by starting at the Mission Bridge, you may go in either direction. Begin by orienting yourself at the information boards near the Mission Bridge parking and picnic facilities for historical and trail information.

The impressive Mount Judge Howay. *Photo: Paul Adam*

Heading east, the more picturesque of the two walks, you may either stay on the dyke or drop to water's edge on the River Trail, which threads through tall cottonwoods that gradually mute the sounds of traffic. Just shy of your midpoint, the Fraser River makes a dogleg bend, the River Trail rejoins the dyke and you find a conveniently located bench and outhouse. Look to the hilltop across the river to see the tower of Westminster Abbey (see Walk 95) above the town of Mission. Soon, an intervening ridge to the north gradually recedes to reveal the stunning peaks of Mounts Judge Howay and Robie Reid in Golden Ears Park; the Cheam Range dominates the eastern view and Mount Baker the southern. At one point, a trail drops to the water's edge to provide you with an alternative path to your turnabout at Page Road Trailhead.

As you stroll the trails, you might reflect on how different your surroundings are today from a century ago, before the dykes were built, when the Fraser River was a major transportation artery, and when footpaths provided peaceful inland routes.

Heading west from Mission Bridge towards the Olund Trailhead at Douglas Taylor Park, you have an immediate choice of staying on the dyke or taking a path along the river's edge. These trails unite at Gladwin Road to skirt the J.A.M.E.S. sewage treatment plant. From Gladwin Road, where you enter the Matsqui First Nation Reserve, the trail begins with a loose gravel surface as it passes through marshland. It then becomes earthen and climbs steeply to the bench above the river, where it passes through forest and field, until it arrives at the Olund Trailhead at Douglas Taylor Park, your turnabout.

DISCOVERY TRAIL/FISHTRAP CREEK

Fishtrap Creek Nature Park Loop: 3.5 km (2.2 mi) **Allow:** 1.5 hours
Discovery Trail Section 1, return: 7.2 km (4.5 mi) **Allow:** 3 hours
Surface: paved **Rating:** easy **Season:** all year

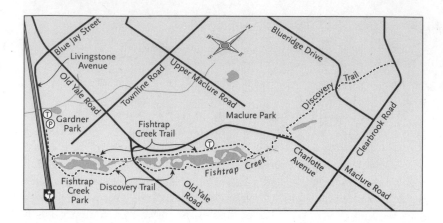

ACCESS

Vehicle: From Highway 1, take Exit 83 (Fraser Highway/Highway 1A) north and then east to Livingstone Avenue, then turn right and continue to Gardner Park. Park in the lot on the north side of Livingstone.

Car GPS entry: Livingstone Avenue & Maclure Road

Trailhead: 49° 3.059' N, 122° 21.799' W

DISCOVERY TRAIL, WHEN complete, will be a 30+ km (18+ mi) all-season recreational corridor through Abbotsford. This walk includes part of Section 1, which passes through Fishtrap Creek Nature Park on land that was used by First Nations, logged by pioneers and housed the Abbotsford Lumber Company. Most recently, a stormwater management facility was built here, which includes a paved loop that wanders around the constructed wetlands that provide habitat for wildlife and green space for human recreation.

From the east end of the parking lot, follow Discovery Trail east and over a wooden bridge to a junction at the southern tip of Fishtrap Creek Nature Park. From the junction, go right to stay on Discovery Trail, noting that

A pair of mallards at rest.

you will return to this junction on the other trail, the Fishtrap Creek Trail, which traverses the west side of the creek.

You will catch glimpses of the southern basin of the Fishtrap Creek wetlands on your left as you walk north on the gently undulating trail. Eventually, the trail leaves the forest temporarily at Dehavilland Drive. Turn right and walk to Mitchell Street, where you turn left to Old Yale Road. Cross Old Yale Road at the pedestrian crossing and turn right to the entrance for Discovery Trail, where you re-enter Fishtrap Creek Nature Park at its northern basin. Along the trail, notice the gnawed stumps of fallen trees, sure signs of beavers at work. On the water, look for aquatic birds such as mergansers, mallards, Canada geese and great blue herons. Amongst the variety of trees, see if you can spot Sitka spruce and redwood. Allow time to pause at a bench or on a bridge to absorb the details of this natural but human-built landscape.

Eventually, you leave the wetlands and encounter the T-junction with Fishtrap Creek Trail. For a short loop walk, go left to return to your vehicle on the west side of the creek. To stretch your legs with a longer walk, stay on Discovery Trail, cross Charlotte Avenue and continue to Maclure Road. Cross Maclure at the pedestrian-controlled light, then turn right to rejoin Discovery Trail as it enters the forested Fishtrap Creek area of Maclure Park.

A curving boardwalk takes you over a widening of the creek before the trail begins a gradual ascent towards Blueridge Drive. Cross at the pedestrian-controlled light and continue on Discovery Trail until you reach Clearbrook Road, your turnaround point.

HERON RESERVE/ROTARY TRAIL

Nature Reserve loops: 3.6 km (2.2 mi) or less   **Allow:** 1.5 hours or less

Surface: gravel dyke, improved trail   **Rating:** easy   **Season:** all year

Rotary Trail: 14 km (8.7 mi) or less   **Allow:** 4 hours or less

Surface: gravel dyke, packed   **Rating:** easy   **Season:** all year

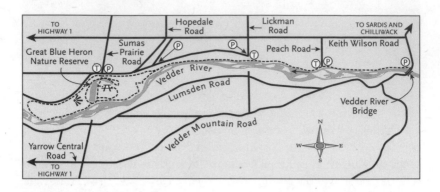

ACCESS

Nature Reserve Loops

Vehicle: From the west on Highway 1, take Exit 104 (Dixon Road) and go east on No. 3 Road. Turn left on Boundary Road then right over the bridge to Keith Wilson Road. Drive east to Sumas Prairie Road, turn right (south) and follow signs to the Great Blue Heron Nature Reserve.

Vehicle: From the east on Highway 1, take Exit 116 (Lickman Road) south, turn west onto Keith Wilson Road, then turn south onto Sumas Prairie Road to the Nature Reserve.

Car GPS entry: 5200 Sumas Prairie Road, Chilliwack

Interpretive Centre: 49° 5.757′ N, 122° 2.662′ W

Rotary Trail

Vehicle: From Highway 1, take Exit 119 (Vedder Road) south and continue through Sardis and Vedder Crossing. Turn right into the trailhead parking lot just before the Vedder Bridge.

Car GPS entry: Vedder Road & Chilliwack Lake Road

Vedder River Bridge parking: 49° 5.874′ N; 121° 57.815′ W

Adults herons nesting at the reserve in March.

THE GREAT BLUE Heron Nature Reserve is a 130 ha (325 ac) site located on the undyked floodplain of the Vedder River. It protects wetland habitat required for the survival of the at-risk, non-migratory great blue herons that live here. Between March and July, the most interesting season to visit, the colony broods in more than 150 nests. During this time, the Heron Colony Loop Trail is closed and the best viewpoint is on the dyke, west of the parking area. Trail brochures, available at the interpretive centre, provide descriptions of the various loops in and around the lagoons and describe highlights along the way to enrich your experience. (See chilliwackblue-heron.com for more information and www.trailtalker.ca for a downloadable audio tour.)

Should you wish to have a longer outing, you could walk all or a portion of the 7 km (4.3 mi) distance upstream along the Vedder River to the Vedder Bridge. (For this, you might consider arranging a car shuttle.) Walk south from the interpretive centre past the iron truss structure left by military engineers from the 1940s and '50s, cross the bridge between the north and south lagoons and continue to a T-junction where you turn left onto Rotary Trail East. The trail meanders through forest before emerging at the banks of the river atop a gravelled dyke. The many benches along the trail invite you to stop from time to time to absorb the sights and sounds of the river.

The Vedder Bridge marks a name change in the river: above, where it collects water from the North Cascades watershed and fills Chilliwack Lake before running through the valley, it is called the Chilliwack River; below, where it crosses the floodplain and is harnessed into the Vedder Canal, it is known as the Vedder River. If you have organized two cars, this is the end of your outing; if not, this is your turnaround point for the walk back to the nature reserve and to your vehicle.

SEVEN SISTERS

Low level return: 4.8 km (3 mi)

High level return: 10 km (6.2 mi)

Surface: trail, road

High point: 325 m (1065 ft)

Rating: moderate

Allow: 1.5 hours

Allow: 4 hours

Elevation gain: 290 m (950 ft)

Season: most of the year

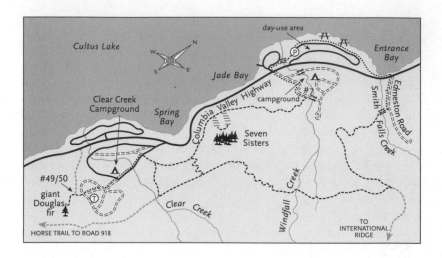

ACCESS

Vehicle: From Highway 1, make your way south to the Columbia Valley Road via Exit 119 (Vedder Road) south or Exit 104 (No. 3 Road) for Yarrow. Drive past Cultus Lake village to Cultus Lake Provincial Park and park at the Entrance Bay day-use area.

Car GPS entry: Cultus Lake Road & Vedder Mountain Road

Trailhead: 49° 3.379' N, 121° 58.238' W

THE SEVEN SISTERS is the puzzling name of a grove of 500-year-old Douglas-firs that survived the logging of the original forest a century ago and whose seeds have undoubtedly contributed to the regeneration of the surrounding forest. This walk highlights an up-close encounter with many of these old-growth giants as it wanders over the slopes above Cultus Lake.

From your vehicle, walk west through trees, cross Windfall Creek, cross the highway near the boat launch and proceed through the Entrance Bay

A giant Douglas-fir in the Seven Sisters grove.

campground to the corner past campsite #7. Now your trail ascends out of the valley, rising and falling gently through mixed second-growth forest, until a large Douglas-fir and a flight of steps signals the Seven Sisters grove.

For a short stroll, you may return from this spot, but continuing to Clear Creek campground gives you a chance to see a solitary giant. En route, for future reference, note the ends of two trails on your left, descending from the bench above. Once in the campground, turn left and ascend the access road, cross Clear Creek, stay left at a fork and finally reach a five-way junction with washrooms. Take the road just below the washrooms until you reach the trail between campsites #49 and 50, which is joined by another from the right that meets the Columbia Valley Highway. The giant Douglas-fir is nearby. Visiting this monolith is truly worth the effort, if only because of the silent record it provides of its 800-year history. If you retrace your route from here, you will have had a walk of 4.8 km (3 mi).

For the longer route, return through the Clear Creek campground onto the Seven Sisters Trail, turn uphill at the first fork (noted earlier), go left at the T-junction onto the high-level horse trail and, after about 15 minutes of steady ascent, note a track joining from the left. This is the other trail you passed on your outward trip; it provides a possible return and a walk of 6 km (3.7 mi).

Your onward route eventually levels off just before you reach the upper waters of the appropriately named Windfall Creek. After this, it is virtually downhill all the way to a former logging road now reverting to nature. Here, you turn left and descend to Edmeston Road, a short distance above the highway at Lakeside Lodge. A brief walk back left along the highway returns you to the beach and, eventually, your car.

TEAPOT HILL

Short circuit: 5 km (3.1 mi)

Long circuit: 7 km (4.3 mi)

Surface: trail and service road

Elevation gain: 280 m (920 ft)

Rating: moderate

Allow: 2 hours

Allow: 3 hours

High point: 360 m (1180 ft)

Season: most of the year

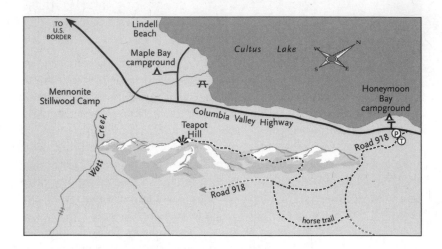

ACCESS

Vehicle: From Highway 1, make your way south to the Columbia Valley Highway Road south of Highway 1 via Exit 119 (Vedder Road) south, or Exit 104 (No. 3 Road) for Yarrow. Drive past Cultus Lake village to Cultus Lake Provincial Park and drive 2.3 km (1.4 mi) to the Teapot Hill parking lot on your left.

Car GPS entry: Cultus Lake Road & Vedder Mountain Road

Trailhead: 49° 2.553′ N, 121° 59.034′ W

YOUR REWARD FOR ascending this sporty little bump? Wide views of Cultus Lake and its surroundings and, on the longer return, a delightful walk through mossy second-growth forest.

From the parking lot, the trail rises steeply at first to join, within minutes, the service road where you soon pass a map of the trail system. The trail then settles in to a steady uphill grade on Road 918. After some

The undulating Teapot Trail.

800 m, a trail joins from the left, with a sign to the Horse Trail Loop, a possible return route. Shortly thereafter, you arrive at your next intersection, where the trail to Teapot Hill goes right, then, not long afterwards, a signboard describes some of the local flowers.

Your trail eventually reaches the ridge at an open area where a sign tells the story of a large Douglas-fir that was struck by lightning, then, a few steps onward, is the view you've been waiting for. It stretches over Cultus Lake to the distant Fraser Valley and across to Vedder Mountain. Thereafter, the trail to the main summit proceeds uninterrupted.

At the top, a chainlink fence guards against inadvertently approaching too close to the sheer drop. Immediately below is the Maple Bay picnic area and campground close to the south end of Cultus Lake, and farther off is the residential settlement of Lindell Beach. Farther south still lies the international boundary, and, as before, the ridges of Vedder Mountain fill the view to the north. And the reason for the name of the hill? A brass teapot was found here when the trail was first built.

Your return is by the same route as far as the intersection with Road 918. Here, you may choose a somewhat longer return than by the main trail. For this alternative, go right on Road 918 and then almost immediately go left on the horse trail. On this, you meander through the mature second-growth forest of Western red cedar, Douglas-fir and bigleaf maple, festooned with moss, rising high above a floor of ferns, Devil's club and stinging nettles. After 30 minutes and many undulations, you descend steeply and arrive at a fork. Leave the horse trail here and go left, descending once more to Road 918, where a right turn brings you back eventually to your parking spot.

WEBSITES

Bus and SkyTrain information
www.translink.ca

Natural history
www.bcnature.ca
www.natureguidesbc.com

Regional Parks
www.env.gov.bc.ca/bcparks
www.fvrd.bc.ca (tabs: Services;
Parks & Trails)
www.metrovancouver.org
(tabs: Services; Regional Parks
& Lower Seymour Conservation
Reserve)

Walking groups
www.meetup.com
www.wanderung.ca
Search also online for groups in your
area, including through community
centres.

Trail information
www.clubtread.com
www.vancouvertrails.com
www.tctrail.ca
Search also for "greenways" in
your area

REGIONAL LINKS

Squamish
www.squamish.ca (tabs: Recreation;
Nature & Outdoors; Trails)

West Vancouver
www.westvancouver.ca (tabs: Transportation & Roads; Cycling and Walking; Walking; Walking and Hiking)

City of North Vancouver
www.cnv.org (tabs: Parks, Recreation & Culture; Parks & Greenways;
Greenways)

District of North Vancouver
www.dnv.org (tabs: Play; Parks)

**Lower Seymour Conservation
Reserve trails map**
www.metrovancouver.org/about/
maps/Maps/lscrTrailMap.pdf

Richmond
www.richmond.ca (tabs: Parks, Trails
& Cycling; Trails)

Delta
www.delta.ca (tabs: Visitors; Parks;
Trail and Bike Routes)

Surrey
www.surrey.ca (tabs: Culture &
Recreation; Parks; Nature Trails)

Burnaby
www.burnaby.ca (tabs: Things To Do;
Explore Outdoors; Nature Trails)

New Westminster
www.newwestpcr.ca (tabs: Parks; Trails)

Abbotsford
www.abbotsford.ca (tabs: Visitors; Parks, Recreation & Culture)

Coquitlam
www.coquitlam.ca (tabs: Recreation, Parks & Culture; Parks & Trails; Trail System)

Chilliwack
www.chilliwack.com (tabs: Parks, Recreation & Culture; Parks & Trails)

Port Coquitlam
www.portcoquitlam.ca (tabs: Recreation & Culture; Parks, Sportfields and Trails; Traboulay PoCo Trail)

Port Moody
www.portmoody.ca (tabs: Parks & Recreation; Parks; Trails & Paths)

Pitt Meadows
www.pittmeadows.bc.ca (tabs: Visitors; Parks & Facilities; Parks, Recreation & Culture)

Maple Ridge
www.mapleridge.ca (tabs: Parks & Leisure; Parks & Trails)

District of Mission
www.mission.ca (tabs: Community; Municipal Forest; Trails)

City of Langley
www.city.langley.bc.ca (tabs: Recreation & Community; Parks & Trails)

Township of Langley
www.tol.ca (tabs: Parks & Recreation; Trails)

INDEX OF WALKING TIMES

* one-way time, + or longer, - or shorter

Time (hrs)	#	Walk Name
1.5	60	Confederation Park/Capitol Hill (Capitol Hill circuit)
1.5	63	Barnet Trails (Barnet and Cougar Cr)
1.5	64	Burnaby Mountain South, short circuit
1.5	66	Burnaby Lake (short loop)
1.5	69	Byrne Creek Ravine Park
1.5	92	Kanaka Creek Canyon loop
1.5	96	Green Timbers Urban Forest (south section)
1.5	98	Redwood Park
1.5	100	Derby Reach Regional Park (heritage site)
1.5	101	Brae Island Trails
1.5	102	Nicomekl Floodplain Trail
1.5	106	Discovery Trail/Fishtrap Creek (Nature Park loop)
1.5-	107	Heron Reserve/Rotary Trail (nature reserve loops)
1.5	108	Seven Sisters (low level return)
2	5	DeBeck Hill
2	16	Lighthouse Park
2	24	Baden-Powell Trail (Grouse Mtn)
2	28	Rice Lake (Lynn Cr circuit)
2	36	Dog Mountain and Dinkey Peak (Dog Mountain direct)
2	37	Mystery Lake and Peak
2	41	Chancellor Woods (long circuit)
2	42	UBC Gardens Tour
2	43	UBC Botanical Garden
2	45	Hastings Mill to Spanish Banks
2	46	Kitsilano/False Creek
2	58	Elgin Heritage Trail (long circuit)
2	61	Burnaby Mountain/SFU (short circuit)
2	67	Brunette River
2	72	Belcarra Regional Park (Jug Island Beach)
2	72	Belcarra Regional Park (Burns Point)
2	75	Shoreline Trail
2	76	Coquitlam Crunch Plus
2	77	Ridge Park Loop

2	91	Gold Creek East: Viewpoint Beach (Lower Falls)
2	97	Tynehead Regional Park
2	104	Aldergrove Regional Park (Rock'n Horse Trail)
2	109	Teapot Hill (short circuit)
2.5	4	Four Lakes Trail
2.5	9	Killarney Lake
2.5	11	Seaview/Larsen Bay
2.5	25	Mosquito Creek
2.5	33	Historic Mushroom loop
2.5	34	Three Chop/Old Buck loop
2.5	36	Dog Mountain and Dinkey Peak (via Dinky Peak)
2.5	38	Baden-Powell Trail (Deep Cove)
2.5	44	Musqueam/Fraser River
2.5	47	False Creek
2.5	50	Vancouver Fraser Foreshore
2.5*	52	Lulu Island Dykes (Middle Arm and West Dyke)
2.5	55	Brunswick Point
2.5	60	Confederation Park/Capitol Hill (combo circuit)
2.5	64	Burnaby Mountain South (long circuit)
2.5*	65	Stoney Creek/SFU
2.5	66	Burnaby Lake (long loop)
2.5	68	Deer Lake Park
2.5	70	Burnaby Fraser Foreshore Park
2.5*	71	Edmonds/New Westminster Quay
2.5	80	Colony Farm Regional Park
2.5	83	Minnekhada Regional Park
2.5	84	Grant Narrows (Katzie Marsh loop)
2.5-	85	Chatham Reach
2.5	88	Mike Lake trail (and lake circuit)
2.5	89	Alouette Nature Loop
2.5	95	Mission Trail
2.5	99	Barnston Island
2.5	100	Derby Reach Regional Park (Houston Trail loop)
3	1	Brohm Lake and Powerline Trails

Time (hrs)	#	Walk Name
3	2	Brohm Lake Interpretive Forest
3	12	Whyte Lake loop
3	15	Caulfeild Trail/Klootchman Pk
3	23	Bowser Trail Plus
3	27	Lynn Headwaters loop (Debris Chute)
3	29	Two-Canyon loop (long circuit)
3	39	Indian Arm Parks (Cates Park)
3	48	Canada Place to Brockton Point
3	51	Sea Island
3	56	Boundary Bay Duo (north section)
3	61	Burnaby Mountain/SFU (long circuit)
3	62	Burnaby Mountain summit loop
3	73	Sasamat Lake/Woodhaven Swamp (Sasamat Lk circuit/connector tr)
3	78	Coquitlam River/Town Centre Pk
3	79	Traboulay PoCo Trail: Coquitlam River
3	94	Hayward Lake: Reservoir Trail
3	106	Discovery Trail/Fishtrap Creek (Section 1)
3	109	Teapot Hill (long circuit)
3.5	13	TCT/Nelson Creek loop
3.5	19	Hollyburn Heritage Trails
3.5	63	Barnet Trails (Burnaby Mountain)
3.5	74	Buntzen Lake (footbridge loop)
3.5	82	DeBoville Slough/North Pitt River
3.5	86	Alouette River Dykes
3.5	87	UBC Research Forest
3.5	91	Gold Creek East: Viewpoint Beach
3.5	93	Hayward Lake: Railway Trail
4	3	Levette Lake Loop (Copperbush-Skyline loop)
4	8	Keats Island
4	17	Hollyburn Mountain
4	30	Fisherman's Trail
4	53	Steveston Greenways

4	57	Watershed Park to Mud Bay
4	81	Woodland Wanders
4	103	Campbell Valley Regional Park (Shaggy Mane Trail)
4-	105	Matsqui Duo (west from Mission Bridge)
4-	105	Matsqui Duo (east from Mission Bridge)
4-	107	Heron Reserve/Rotary Trail (Rotary Trail)
4	108	Seven Sisters (high level return)
4.5	6	Shannon Falls (High Bluff)
4.5	18	Lower Hollyburn
4.5-	20	Brothers Creek Trails
4.5	32	Bridle Path
4.5	74	Buntzen Lake (Penstock loop)
4.5	84	Grant Narrows (long loop)
4.5	90	Gold Creek West: Alder Flats
5	3	Levette Lake and Levette Lake diversion
5	7	Langdale Falls/Sidewinder loop
5	22	Capilano Canyon (Ambleside Park to dam)

INDEX OF RETURN DISTANCES
* one-way distance, + or longer, - or shorter

Distance (km)	#	Walk Name
2	88	Mike Lake (lake circuit)
2.3	103	Campbell Valley Regional Park (Little River loop)
2.5	6	Shannon Falls (to Olesen Creek)
2.7	21	Ballantree
2.7	60	Confederation Park/Capitol Hill (Nature loop)
3+	14	Cypress Falls Park
3	28	Rice Lake (LSCR lake circuit)
3	52	Lulu Island Dykes (Terra Nova loop)
3	59	South Surrey Urban Forests (Sunnyside Acres)
3-	59	South Surrey Urban Forests (Crescent Pk)
3	73	Sasamat Lake/Woodhaven Swamp (Sasamat Lake circuit)
3	92	Kanaka Creek Riverfront Trail
3	96	Green Timbers Urban Forest (north section)
3	96	Green Timbers Urban Forest (centre section)
3.3	31	Maplewood Flats
3.3	58	Elgin Heritage Trail (short circuit)
3.3	92	Kanaka Creek Canyon loop
3.5	69	Byrne Creek Ravine Park
3.5	106	Discovery Trail/Fishtrap Creek (nature park loop)
3.6	22	Capilano Canyon loop (dam to dam)
3.6-	107	Heron Reserve/Rotary Trail (nature reserve loops)
3.9	41	Chancellor Woods (short circuit)
4	1	Brohm Lake Circuit
4	5	DeBeck Hill
4	10	Whytecliff
4	35	Goldie and Flower Lakes (Two-lakes loop)
4	43	UBC Botanical Garden
4	63	Barnet Trails (Barnet and Cougar Cr)
4	64	Burnaby Mountain South (short circuit)
4	104	Aldergrove Regional Park (Pepin Brook loop)

Distance(km)	#	Walk Name
4.2	37	Mystery Lake and Peak
4.2	101	Brae Island Trails
4.4	54	Deas Island Regional Park
4.5	39	Indian Arm Parks (five-park circuit)
4.5*	40	Point Grey/Wreck Beach (Trail 7 to Acadia Beach)
4.5	56	Boundary Bay Duo (south section)
4.5-	98	Redwood Park
4.7	24	Baden-Powell Trail (Grouse Mtn)
4.8	29	Two-Canyon loop (short circuit)
4.8	108	Seven Sisters (low level return)
5	26	Mahon Park
5	36	Dog Mountain and Dinkey Peak (Dog Mountain direct)
5	42	UBC Gardens Tour
5	60	Confederation Park/Capitol Hill (Capitol Hill circuit)
5	61	Burnaby Mountain/SFU (short circuit)
5	66	Burnaby Lake (short loop)
5	77	Ridge Park Loop
5	96	Green Timbers Urban Forest (south section)
5	100	Derby Reach Regional Park (heritage site)
5	109	Teapot Hill (short circuit)
5.2	27	Lynn Headwaters loop (Lynn loop)
5.2	72	Belcarra Regional Park (Burns Point)
5.3	38	Baden-Powell Trail (Deep Cove)
5.4	91	Gold Creek East: Lower Falls
5.5	49	The 3-C Circuit
5.5	72	Belcarra Regional Park (Jug Island Beach)
5.5	97	Tynehead Regional Park
5.7	76	Coquitlam Crunch Plus
6	12	Whyte Lake loop
6	16	Lighthouse Park
6	28	Rice Lake (Lynn Cr circuit)
6	36	Dog Mountain and Dinkey Peak (via Dinky Peak)

Distance (km)	#	Walk Name
6	41	Chancellor Woods (long circuit)
6	45	Hastings Mill to Spanish Banks
6	67	Brunette River
6	75	Shoreline Trail
6	89	Alouette Nature Loop
6	102	Nicomekl Floodplain Trail
6.2	60	Confederation Park/Capitol Hill (combo circuit)
6.4	33	Historic Mushroom loop
6.4	95	Mission Trail
6.5	84	Grant Narrows (Katzie Marsh loop)
6.7	11	Seaview/Larsen Bay
6.7	19	Hollyburn Heritage Trails
7	4	Four Lakes Trail
7	46	Kitsilano/False Creek
7	58	Elgin Heritage Trail (long circuit)
7	68	Deer Lake Park
7*	71	Edmonds/New Westminster Quay
7	104	Aldergrove Regional Park (Rock'n Horse Trail)
7	109	Teapot Hill (long circuit)
7.2	1	Brohm Lake and Powerline Trails
7.2	3	Levette Lake Loop (Copperbush-Skyline loop)
7.2	15	Caulfeild Trail/Klootchman Pk
7.2	106	Discovery Trail/Fishtrap Creek (Section 1)
7.5	83	Minnekhada Regional Park
7.6	2	Brohm Lake Interpretive Forest
7.7	34	Three Chop/Old Buck loop
7.7	64	Burnaby Mountain South (long circuit)
7.7*	65	Stoney Creek/SFU
7.9	23	Bowser Trail Plus
8	9	Killarney Lake
8	25	Mosquito Creek
8	29	Two-Canyon loop (long circuit)
8	44	Musqueam/Fraser River

Distance (km)	#	Walk Name
8	47	False Creek
8	50	Vancouver Fraser Foreshore
8	62	Burnaby Mountain summit loop
8	70	Burnaby Fraser Foreshore Park
8	73	Sasamat Lake/Woodhaven Swamp (Sasamat Lk circuit/connector tr)
8	80	Colony Farm Regional Park
8	87	UBC Research Forest
8	88	Mike Lake and trail (lake circuit)
8	91	Gold Creek East: Viewpoint Beach
8	94	Hayward Lake: Reservoir Trail
8	100	Derby Reach Regional Park (Houston loop)
8.2	6	Shannon Falls (High Bluff)
8.5	13	TCT Nelson Creek loop
8.5	56	Boundary Bay Duo (north section)
8.5	61	Burnaby Mountain/SFU (long circuit)
9	27	Lynn Headwaters loop (Debris Chute)
9*	52	Lulu Island Dykes (Middle Arm and West Dyke)
9	78	Coquitlam River/Town Centre Park
9.3	63	Barnet Trails (Burnaby Mountain)
9.5	51	Sea Island
9.6-	81	Woodland Wanders
9.8	55	Brunswick Point
10	8	Keats Island
10	17	Hollyburn Mountain
10	66	Burnaby Lake (long loop)
10	99	Barnston Island
10	108	Seven Sisters (high level return)
10.2	74	Buntzen Lake (footbridge loop)
10.5	3	Levette Lake and Levette Lake diversion
10.5	39	Indian Arm Parks (Cates Park)
10.5	79	Traboulay PoCo Trail: Coquitlam River
11-	20	Brothers Creek Trails

Distance (km)	#	Walk Name
11-	85	Chatham Reach
11	103	Campbell Valley Regional Park (Shaggy Mane Trail)
11.5	32	Bridle Path
12	18	Lower Hollyburn
12	48	Canada Place to Brockton Point
12	82	DeBoville Slough/North Pitt River
12	84	Grant Narrows (long loop)
12	93	Hayward Lake: Railway Trail
12.4	7	Langdale Falls/Sidewinder loop
12.7	74	Buntzen Lake (Penstock loop)
13	30	Fisherman's Trail
13	90	Gold Creek West: Alder Flats
14	57	Watershed Park to Mud Bay
14-	105	Matsqui Duo (west from Mission Bridge)
14-	105	Matsqui Duo (east from Mission Bridge)
14-	107	Heron Reserve/Rotary Trail (Rotary Trail)
14.3	22	Capilano Canyon (Ambleside Park to dam)
14.8	86	Alouette River Dykes
15	53	Steveston Greenways

ACKNOWLEDGEMENTS

WE ARE INDEBTED to the late David and Mary Macaree for the enormous amount of enthusiasm and work that they put into the exploration of Lower Mainland trails for the first six editions of this guide. Their legacy continues to inspire others who have assisted with the revision of the current edition, for which we are most grateful. Most notably, Paul Adam, rather like a ghost author, assisted with finding new trails, with proofreading and with many other tasks. Fred Douglas accompanied Alice on the trails, tracking them on GPS, and he unfailingly provided encouragement and support throughout the whole project. Finally, the British Columbia Mountaineering Club (BCMC), whose involvement began with the first edition of this book, has continued its valued support.

INDEX

ABOUT THE BCMC

THE BRITISH COLUMBIA Mountaineering Club is a group of like-minded individuals who participate in outdoor activities. The club was established in 1907 and currently has more than 600 members. The club organizes mountaineering, rock climbing and backcountry skiing trips throughout the year. The BCMC holds monthly socials, offers courses to members and represents the interests of mountaineers and backcountry skiers in British Columbia. The club dedicates royalties received from sales of this book to conservation efforts. See BCMC.ca for more information.